READING THE
LANDSCAPE OF AMERICA

READING THE

May Theilgaard Watts

LANDSCAPE OF AMERICA

REVISED AND

EXPANDED EDITION

Collier Books

A Division of Macmillan Publishing Co., Inc.

New York

Collier Macmillan Publishers

London

Macmillan Publishing Co., Inc.
866 Third Avenue, New York, N. Y. 10022
Collier Macmillan Canada, Ltd.

Library of Congress Cataloging in Publication Data

Watts, May Theilgaard.
  Reading the landscape of America.

  Includes bibliographical references and index.
  1. Botany—United States—Ecology.   I. Title.
QK115.W37   1975   581.5'26   74–22152
ISBN 0–02–063810–8

Reading the Landscape in America is also published in a hardcover
edition by Macmillan Publishing Co., Inc.

For permission to quote from published material, thanks are due to
the editors of Ecological Monographs and The American Midland
Naturalist; also to Dr. William Albrecht, author of an article in The
Land, and to the Chronica Botanica Company, publisher of Francis
Ernest Lloyd's The Carnivorous Plants.

First Collier Books Edition 1975
Printed in the United States of America

Preface

The land offers us good reading, outdoors, from a lively, unfinished manuscript.

Records, prophesies, mysteries are inscribed there, and changes—always changes. Even as we read from some selected page, whether mountaintop, forest, furrow, schoolyard, dune, bog, we see changes: in stirrings and silences, flavors and textures, spacing, tolerances, and confrontations and tensions at the edges.

Some hidden records have taken long to find, and longer still to decipher; like the story of pollen grains at the bottom of a bog, or the record of invasion preserved in an adobe brick from an old California mission.

The original edition of this book presented areas of the Midwest. My first experiences at working in soil came there, in gardening with my Danish father; and my first experiences in reading the landscape came from Dr. Henry C. Cowles, pioneer American ecologist, who led field trips from the University of Chicago, in the then-new subject called ecology.

For this present volume I have revisited each of the areas considered twenty or more years ago, to see what changes had come in the intervening years. And I have ventured further afield across the land, from New England salt marshes to southwestern deserts.

My good companions in the original book were my husband, Raymond Watts, and our children, Erica, Nancy, and Tom Watts. On the revisiting trips, invaluable help was given by people living in the various areas (their names appear with discussion of their homesites); and always by my friend Helen Turner. On the new areas, farther afield, some part of my family was always available. From the Morton Arboretum, special help came from the library staff, and Floyd Swink, Charles Lewis, and Richard Watson; and from former students: Sidney Tarbox, Jane Sindt, and Glidden Baldwin. Two editors at Macmillan have given valued help: Carol Woodward with the first edition; Constance Schrader with the second.

My hope is that you who read this book will close it, and go outdoors to read from the original.

Contents

READING THE
LANDSCAPE OF AMERICA

1

In Search of Antiques

OR

THE FORESTS OF THE GREAT

SMOKY MOUNTAINS

WE FOUND, in the Great Smoky Mountains, the several antiques that were our goal.

For one of us the find was a woven bedspread.

For one the find was a song.

For another the find was a word.

For me the find was a forest.

The bedspread, the song, the word, the forest, had one quality in common. Each of them was not only an antique but also a disjunct. That is to say, each of them had been, long ago, cut off, isolated, or disjoined, from others of its kind.

The presence of disjuncts was to be expected there in the Smokies, the region that had so long been a sort of sanctuary, or refugium, for cut-off groups of plants and men and customs.

It was twilight when we entered the Smokies and we were eager to reach our cabin before dark; but we, who had been stopped all the

way across Indiana, Kentucky, and Tennessee by hanging lamps and
melodeons, by Bennington ware and patchwork, could not fail to pull
to the side of the road when an authentic floral antique shone white
out of the dusk of the roadside woods.

A magnolia flower it was.

As I stood at the side of the hard modern road by the shiny modern automobile, and cupped the moonlight of the magnolia flower in
my two modern prehensile hands, the warm June dusk around me
seemed to brighten to a warm dawn—the dawn or flowering on the
young earth. I could imagine the plash of broad reptilian feet behind
me, and could pretend that I was seeing what no man ever saw, one of
Nature's first experiments in producing a showy flower.

First things, beginnings, have fascination, and to anyone familiar
with botanical literature, here was a first—the flower at the base of the
"family tree" of flowers; the first tree in the book of Sargent's fourteen-
volume "North American Silva"; the first family described in Pool's
"Flowers and Flowering Plants"; the first family discussed in Arnold's
"Paleobotany" in the chapter Ancient Flowering Plants; the flower
named for Pierre Magnol (1638–1715), professor of botany at Mont-
pelier, who was the first to indicate the natural families of plants.

I looked long at the great white flower, and at the umbrella of
broad leaves behind it, checking off the features that bespoke its antiquity among the flowering plants of the world today.

The petals, each one separated to its base, suggested that this was
one of the world's earliest flower patterns. Petals of more modern
flowers tend to be united along their sides.

The very way in which the flower fitted into my cupped hands
was primitive. Such a wide open bowl does not tend to direct the path
of an incoming insect visitor in any way. He may land, gather food,
and take off, without depositing pollen on the sticky receptive surface
that must receive it if the flower is to fulfill its destiny as a seed pro-
ducer. In a later model the joined petals would form some sort of tube
or jug, narrowed to a constricted entry-way that would route the incoming insect into contact with the sexual parts of the flower.

The large number of the pollen-laden stamens confirmed the evidence of the petals. In flowers that have developed united petals and
constricted entry-ways, the production of pollen has been reduced and
stamens have become so few that they can be counted on the fingers.

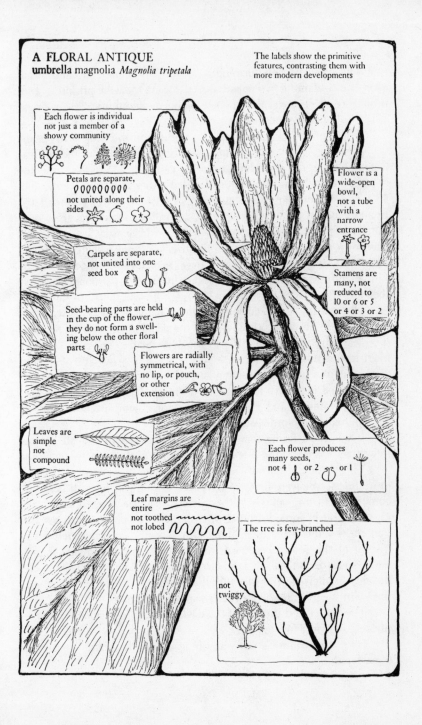

A FLORAL ANTIQUE
umbrella magnolia *Magnolia tripetala*

The labels show the primitive features, contrasting them with more modern developments

Each flower is individual not just a member of a showy community

Petals are separate, not united along their sides

Flower is a wide-open bowl, not a tube with a narrow entrance

Carpels are separate, not united into one seed box

Stamens are many, not reduced to 10 or 6 or 5 or 4 or 3 or 2

Seed-bearing parts are held in the cup of the flower, they do not form a swelling below the other floral parts

Flowers are radially symmetrical, with no lip, or pouch, or other extension

Leaves are simple not compound

Each flower produces many seeds, not 4 or 2 or 1

Leaf margins are entire not toothed not lobed

The tree is few-branched

not twiggy

The many carpels forming a cone in the center of the flower, each one containing two potential seeds, these too were primitive. In a more recently evolved flower these would be combined into a single vessel to hold the seeds.

The loneliness of that great flower there in the dusk—that again was primitive. How different from the aggregate communities of minute flowers in the dandelion, or in the center of a daisy—as different as a mountain hermit from an assembled group of factory hands.

The leaves, large and plain, spoke of an outmoded pattern. Leaves even on oaks and sycamores, according to fossil records, were not so deeply lobed in the youth of the world as they are now. The very form of the little tree was primitive—if those paleobotanists are right who contend that primitive trees were few-branched. It stood, simple and uncomplicated, against the intricacy of its more twiggy associates.

One feature it lacked, an evergreen habit of the leaf, which is considered to be more primitive than the deciduous habit. Its relative, the great hard-leaved magnolia of the Gulf States, however, has this older feature added to the rest.

Magnolia relatives are abundant in Asia, living, and in Europe, dead, turned to stone. There are fossil magnolias in Greenland, too, and in Wyoming, and Portugal, but living, blooming ones only in Asia and parts of North America.

It was most fitting that we should be greeted first of all by this flower as we entered the Great Smokies, haven of disjuncts.

This particular magnolia, *Magnolia tripetala*, was past its heyday of freshness. We were lucky to have seen it at all, in June. It began to come apart in my hands, and I completed its disrobing, carefully taking off, one by one, first the sepals, then the petals, and last the stamens. I wanted to see the floral formation that is considered reminiscent of the inflorescence of the ancient family of cycads, represented today by only a few fernlike or palmlike plants. In fact, the entire floral pattern of the magnolia has much similarity to the pattern shown in fossils of the now wholly extinct cycadeoids.

The flower and the last of the daylight were both gone. Antique-hunting was over for that day.

Early next morning we were off again, on the search for an antique forest.

It was as if we were hunting through an "old curiosity shop" that had stood firm through the years, quietly carrying on business at the old stand while civilizations of plants and animals shifted or swept by entirely.

In the attic of this forest "antique shop" was a unique exhibit, living quarters of a bygone age, preserved intact.

We stepped into that exhibit so suddenly that it seemed unreal. A few yards away from a teeming parking area at Newfound Gap, we had simply walked a short piece along the Appalachian Trail, and found ourselves plunged into antiquity.

Massive boles of hemlock and red spruce uplifted their durable canopy into a blue mist. Their dark boughs dripped with mist and moss. Broken raindrops, shattered by layer after layer of needles, and enmeshed in webs of moss draperies, sank soundlessly into the deep receptive green of club moss, lichens, liverworts, and oxalis leaves.

This forest told a story of cold and ice pushing down over the northern hemisphere, driving vegetation southward. Here, it was the vegetation of New England and eastern Canada that was forced down into the Smokies.

When the cold retreated, these evergreens were crowded out of the lower places, crowded out (as evergreens seem ever destined to be from the more modern situations by the more modern flora), until only the mountaintops were left to them. Probably this forest climbed up from the lower parts of the Smokies, to take over the ridges only after the cold had ameliorated enough so that there was no longer a timber line this far south. "Relicts," these left-behind plants are called. There they stand, thriving massively, in the daily dripping mists, and associating with plants that were native to the region long before this northern infiltration took place.

We had found an antique forest, and we spent the day richly within it; but we were not content, any more than one who was looking for a tomb of the Pharaohs would be satisfied with a Victorian parlor. We were looking for greater antiquity than that of the glacial period.

The story of the mountains is long, starting with deposition under water, then continuing through upheavals and uplifts, and slow ages of erosion. The vegetation of the Smokies offers records, not only of this local heaving, but also of changes and separations in other parts of the world, changes that have resulted in leaving many stranded or dis-possessed plants in the sheltering arms of these mountains.

The breaking of the old land bridge to Eurasia is one such an-cient event that is recorded here in the Smokies. That record is found in so-called "paired species" of plants. No two are exactly alike, but many differ only slightly, as might be expected when connections are broken off and close relatives are permanently segregated. Among such paired species are our ironwood, *Ostrya virginiana*, and the European hornbeam, *Ostrya carpinifolia*; our wood anemone, *Anemone quin-quefolia*, and the European wood anemone, *Anemone nemorosa*; our wild lily of the valley, *Maianthemum canadense*, and the European *Maianthemum bifolium*; and many others. The American member of each pair is growing today in association with plants such as the tulip tree, sassafras, magnolia, witch-hazel—plants whose ancestors were eliminated from Europe when the glacial cold drove them south, and the mountaintop cold of east-west mountains stopped their retreat.

The breaking of the old land bridges to Asia, and to Greenland, is recorded in the presence of plants growing here and in eastern Asia today, and occurring as fossils in Greenland. The tulip tree is such a plant.

The list of plants in eastern America and eastern Asia, but not in Europe, is long. It includes the genera of our sweet gum, *Liquidam-bar*, and of our mayapple, *Podophyllum*; of *Trillium*, *Catalpa*, *Phlox*, *Jeffersonia*, and many others.

Famous botanists have long focused their thoughts on this prob-lem of distribution. The naturalist, Louis Agassiz, linked the distribu-tion to parallel development under similar conditions. Asa Gray con-nected the present distribution with ancient migrations under climatic changes. He said, "I cannot imagine a state of circumstances under which the Siberian elephant could migrate, and temperate plants could not." It was Sir Joseph Hooker who realized that of all plants that migrated southward before the glacier, those in eastern America and eastern Asia were the only ones that did not meet adversity in the form of mountain barriers.

The previous existence of a warmer climate is suggested by the presence of a few plants whose relatives are largely in the tropics. Sil-verbell, *Halesia*; pawpaw, *Asimina*; and fringe tree, *Chionanthus*, are examples of this group.

The story of the uplift of the western mountains, and their drying effects on the prevailing westerlies is recorded in the presence here of plants that are found as fossils in Wyoming and elsewhere along the shores of the western sea that once cut America in two; beech, walnut, hackberry, elm, and persimmon were a few of the members of the widespread forest that were driven out by drought.

Certainly individual antiques such as these were abundant enough to satisfy almost any antique hunter. But we were far from satisfied. We wanted to step into a forest of the Tertiary period, a forest intact. It might have seemed like an unachievable goal (as if some antique hunter in a shop had looked up from old crayon portraits and flower prints and demanded to see a cave man in the act of painting bison on the walls of his cave) if we had not read about the actual existence of such a forest here in the Smokies.

It was along the Alum Creek Cave trail that we stepped back over the intervening ages, into that ancient forest.

Suddenly we were in a forest of the opera backdrop, of storied tapestries, of blue-green, fairy-tale illustration.

Unchanged, it had survived while mountains bulged and crumbled; unchanged, while mammals grew and reptiles shrank; unchanged, while prairies spread, and teeth and hooves grew hard; unchanged, while man learned to make fire, and pots and cloth, and war.

Unchanged? Not entirely. There was a great change in the extent of this forest. Once it spread around the world. But after the land bridges were broken, the western mountains uplifted, and the glacial cold had pushed down, this forest in the southern Appalachians was all that was left in America. Stretches of it remained in the Cumberland Mountains, and small, rich remnants of it survived in the sheltered coves of the Smokies.

One other major change had come to the forest. Some of the trees of antiquity, when the forest was widespread, have persisted in distant parts of the world, but are not found here. Others have remained the same throughout the centuries.

We walked gratefully where dignified boles lifted the canopy high to make a timeless green shade that urged the saplings below into a similar dignity. The understory plants held their foliage flat and broad, like begging hands that caught each green-gold strand of sunshine.

By the time the understory of small trees and the third story of shrubs had entangled each thread of light, it was only an occasional frayed wisp that dangled down to touch the forest floor. But out of those frayed wisps the forest floor had woven itself a garment that enfolded everything in richness.

The most beautiful single aspect of the entire forest was, surely, the insteps of the trees. A more suitable union of tree and earth could hardly exist. Those arched and clutching roots wore lichens and mosses, liverworts, ferns, and fungi, tucked into crannies, enshrouding curves, and lushly molded to muscular bulges.

This richness of growth covered any bark characteristics at the base of the trees until you might think that the trees were all of one kind. But all of one kind they decidedly were not—nor of two kinds, nor of a few kinds. Nowhere in America could one see so many different kinds assembled in one natural forest.

What should this forest be called?

We, who were accustomed to forests named for their dominant trees, such as oak-hickory, beech-maple, or spruce-fir, could not find here any two trees dominant enough to give their names to this formation.

We went that day, and on succeeding days, to several cove forests. Always we found this rich assortment of many kinds of trees. The ones that seemed to be most abundant in the canopy were basswood (the white basswood, *Tilia heterophylla*, not the basswood of our northern deciduous forest), sugar maple, sweet buckeye, tulip tree, yellow birch, beech, and hemlock. Somewhat less abundant were red oak, bitternut hickory, white ash, and cucumber magnolia.

The most surprising member of the association was *Halesia*, the silverbell. We had met it often, but only as a shrub. Here it attained the stature of a tree.

In some areas of the cove forests, certain trees appeared to be dominant; but we would no sooner decide on the name "silverbell" forest for example, than the character of the forest would change and weave its elements into a new pattern of "beech-hemlock" or "tulip-hemlock-dead chestnut."

It soon became easy to understand why certain ecologists have coined a new sort of name for this rich mixture, calling it the "Cove Hardwood Complex," or the "Mixed Mesophytic Association." The latter phrase is taken directly from E. Lucy Braun's "Deciduous Forests." Her concept of the forests of the southern Appalachians is the chief basis for the ideas of the Smokies as set forth here.

We dallied in the coves, sitting on mossy bulges to inspect the markings in the throats of flowers with our hand lenses, and to trace plants unknown to us, through botanical keys to identification.

Insects came to rest, now and then, on the moss, the leaves, the pages of our books. They seemed to move as lazily as we did in the green shade. Identify them we could not, except as further additions to our antique finds. A recent "Study of Summer Foliage Insect Communities in the Great Smoky Mountains" shows that the insects of the coves tend to be primitive ones.

"So to the moist, productive, ancient environment of the cove forests is matched a nematoceran-dominated, productive, primitive, and moderately diverse foliage insect community.

"It is suggested that the primary correlation of modernity is with drying power of the atmosphere. It is suggested that primitive insects with relatively delicate body coverings and unspecialized respiratory apparatus are less able to withstand a dry-hot environment than more advanced and more specialized insects."

Perhaps it was not an illusion that these insects around us did not buzz so busily as do our northern Illinois insects. Another study concludes that more modern, more active insects tend to appear in environments of high energy intensity—midday, midsummer, and the tropics—and more primitive insects in environments of low energy intensity.

I was knee-deep in mosses, hunched over a hand lens, when a voice behind me asked, "Well, found *Shortia* yet?"

A smiling stranger had paused on the path behind us to ask that question, the famous question that had been passed from botanist to botanist in these mountains in the 1840s, when many had joined in the search for this lost plant.

The story of *Shortia* starts in 1781, when André Michaux, outstanding French botanist, landed in America to collect plants for His Majesty Louis XVI, to add to the already fabulous gardens at Versailles. Incidentally, one can hardly enter the Smokies without being conscious of Michaux. Stretches of the highway are lined with the delicately foliaged tree *Albizzia*, one of his spectacular gifts from Asia by way of Europe. Certainly one cannot use a botanical key without being well aware of Michaux, because so many of the plants have the abbreviation "Michx." following the scientific name, indicating that he was the first to describe the plant in question.

A herbarium of pressed specimens went back to France with Michaux. At the end of the collection were plants labeled *"plantae ignotae."* And among those unknowns, unidentified for half a century, was a small specimen without flowers, bearing only leaves and fruit.

In 1839 Asa Gray, later a natural history professor at Harvard, came to France to look at Michaux's herbarium. That sheet, without a name, without a flower, caught his attention. He realized that this was a real find, a new plant—not only a new species, but a new genus. Having been first to recognize the plant as a new genus, he was entitled to name it. He decided to call it *"Shortia"* for his botanical friend, Dr. Charles Wilkins Short.

In 1840 when Gray returned to America, botanists began a long-continued hunt for this plant.

Gray described the flower as he thought it should be, on the basis of the fruit. One day, looking through an old Japanese herbal, his attention was suddenly caught by a familiar form in one of the woodcuts. Then he realized that he was looking at leaves that were scalloped and shaped and veined like the leaves of Michaux's pressed specimen. And the flowers depicted with them were much as he had predicted they would look.

Botanists pursued their hunt, now with better knowledge of what to look for, but the plant was not found until ninety-eight years after Michaux had first seen it. So ended the historical quest for the lost antique.

The extreme and apparently increasing rarity of shortia may be a mark of an old species, probably on the verge of extinction; or it may be due to the fact that its seeds have no arrangement for dispersal.

No, we did not find the antique named *Shortia galacifolia*, or Oconee bells. But we found plenty of plants with "Michx." appended to their scientific names; and one plant with "Michx.f." appended. The "f." records the fact that Michaux's son, designated "Michaux *fils*," had come to this country to botanize in the footsteps of his father.

As we hunted out the lush coves, we crossed intervening slopes and hollows that held other types of forest, each forest made up of parts of the Mixed Mesophytic Association. It was as if we saw individual facets of the jewel that was a rich cove forest. In another sense, it was as if, from the richly and intricately woven fabric of the coves, a few strands had been drawn off into a heavy tassel here, or a coarsely woven net there, or a fringe on another side, or a few tattered threads where the wear was great.

In still another sense, it was as if the Mixed Mesophytic Association of the coves was an imposing organization, having within it several committees on specialized activities. One such committee might have been called "Committee in Charge of North-facing Slopes." It was dominated by beech and sugar maple, and reminded us of Warren's Woods near Three Oaks, Michigan.

Another forested area might have been called "The Committee in Charge of Sheltered North-facing Slopes along a Deep Valley." This situation was dominated by beech; in fact, most of the trees were beeches. We were reminded of a forest at Turkey Run State Park, in Indiana.

On southerly slopes of lower altitudes, dead chestnuts, hemlocks, and tulip trees were prominent. One slope, thick with sugar maple, was reminiscent of the north-facing side of a ravine in the Morton Arboretum.

A low knob with oaks and blueberries might have been part of the older dune area in Indiana, or a part of the Ozarks.

Again, a ridge with oak and hickory might have been back home at the edge of the prairie.

Altitude, or exposure, or soil, has selected the strands of the cove forests that are woven into each of the outlying forests.

These selected strands of the cove fabric, or facets of the cove jewels, or committees of the cove forest organization—whatever we choose to call them—have been given the name "Mixed Mesophytic Association segregates."

Each segregate we saw seemed to be a sample of a forest somewhere outside of this southern Appalachian area.

Here no vacationer need be homesick long. If he comes from eastern Asia he can sit on a heath bald under great rhododendrons; if he comes from the Great Lakes area, he can find his forest of beech-maple-hemlock; if he comes from the prairie's edge, he can seek out a dry southerly slope and hobnob with oaks and hickories; if he longs for Canada, he can climb up among the spruces and firs.

We started home, even more full of antique-talk than when we arrived. The one of us who had bought a bedspread told that it was the "Whig Rose pattern," a disjunct pattern, brought to the Smokies long ago by pioneers for whom the word "Whig" had a meaning, and handed down through generations long after the meaning was forgotten.

Another one of us said she had heard an antique word. She had not succeeded in hearing any of the Shakespearian words said to have been brought to the mountains long ago, and to have suffered little change. But as she was talking with a woman on a porch between an old hand loom and a new washing-machine, the fox terrier had barked; and the woman had said to it, "Feeling feisty, aren't you?" Alberta Hannum had written: "Out of Chaucer comes their word 'feisty,' meaning impertinent."

The antique-song collecting had come close to being a failure. Certainly no one had heard the one song that we most desired to hear since reading that John Jacob Niles had heard a Holiness preacher singing it, the song that had been "recorded only once before in modern times, by Ralph Vaughan Williams in England." That song was "Down in yon forest hall, Sing May, Queen May, Sing Mary." But we did hear a boy and girl in an old Ford on a mud road singing "Barbara Allen"; and, in spite of the fact that very possibly it may have been taught to them by a music teacher from New England, we were satisfied. That durable ballad, woven of threads from English and Scottish ballads, "Bonny Barbara Allen," and threads of North Carolina mountain life, might perhaps have entered these mountains along with the pattern for the Whig Rose coverlet.

Talking of antiques and disjunct weaving, and words, and songs, and plants, and forests, we left the mountains, starting northward toward home.

We were traveling northward as the deciduous forest had traveled from the refugium of the southern Appalachians when the glacier retreated.

We stopped to look at forests. It was plain to us now that a new element was shaping their assemblage. Plants continued to be eliminated by soil, and by exposure, but altitude was of little importance. Latitude was becoming increasingly important. The cold finger of frost was laid on species after species.

By the time we reached the famous Cox Woods near Paoli, Indiana, the linden of the southeast had been eliminated, and the sweet buckeye, *Aesculus octandra,* was gone. So was *Halesia,* and fringe tree, magnolia, and sourwood, and many others. Beech and sugar maple had become more prominent.

We walked long among those well-born trees of proud stature, remembering that this type of forest had once extended across Indiana and Ohio, and had worn out many an axe, many a saw, many a pioneer, before it had been wiped out in favor of corn and wheat.

Then we moved northward again, watching latitude do its work, not only on plants, but also on the number of porches and rocking chairs, and chewing-tobacco signs; and Baptist churches.

As we swerved toward the west, the effect of the Rocky Mountains began to enter the picture. Added now to the influence of soil, exposure, and latitude, was the high-evaporation ratio. Beech and flowering dogwood dropped out of the picture; oaks, oaks, oaks, took their places, with a little hickory. We had seen this forest on a dry slope in the Smokies.

Presently, fingers of prairie began to pry into the oak woods—and we were back home, unloading our antiques and our memories of antiques.

Great Smoky Mountains—Revisited

Early in March, 1974, we came again to the Smokies, to see whether the antiques were surviving the invaders. News stories had reported the numbers advancing, on foot, on horseback, on wheels.

The antiques were holding their own against the invaders—the human ones. True, the Appalachian Trail (68 miles of it lie within the boundaries of a national park) seemed wider than the narrow brown path that I remembered, and was crossed by more conspicuous roots sculpted into higher relief by the feet of horses and hikers. And camp sites and overnight shelters showed specially heavy use. But the park staff has been alert and has taken some necessary measures, including the banning of horses from most vulnerable points, such as 35 percent of the Appalachian Trail, as well as other well-used trails. They have limited the number of permits issued to hikers to an agreed-upon and listed number for each shelter, ranging from four to fourteen hikers. They have changed the Chimneys Campground into a picnic area, and are planning new campgrounds in outlying areas.

Yes, the forests have come to terms with humans. Not so with other invaders, especially those from across the sea.

The inroads of one of these was conspicuous in the view from Newfound Gap. Among the massed green spires of Fraser firs rose some spires that were whitish gray, dead, or dying. The juices of the living layer that lies just beneath the bark had been sucked out by the balsam woolly aphids (the "balsam" in the name is there because the aphid first affected the balsam firs of the north woods, and has spread gradually down to the closely related Fraser fir that is restricted to a limited area on the mountaintops of the southeast).

Because a single adult balsam woolly aphid can increase to more than a million in a single year, its sucking and injection of a saliva poisonous to firs make it a powerful killer. A feeding adult, only $1/25$ of an inch long, fastened for life to one place on the bark, its feeding apparatus sunk between the cells of the bark, is part of an invasion that kills fast. Mount Mitchell was the first place in the southeast mountains where the onslaught was observed, in 1957. By 1973 aphids had killed 275,000 trees.

Researchers are seeking a biological control; but the pest came from Europe accidentally, to New England, and evidently its natural controls did not come along.

While the search goes on, firs are being cut in some places, in an effort to gain a little time by preventing the aphid population from spreading too fast. Some chemical sprays are being used, cautiously, watchfully, lest they have side effects on other living things. And seedlings are being raised in a protected place, to ensure the future of the Fraser fir.

While the aphids suck on the mountaintops, two other foreign invaders, Asiatic vines, are strangling and smothering some natives that live lower down. Both of these were brought over from Asia, and planted intentionally. One of them, the Japanese honeysuckle, is even now being planted, for its fragrance, on fences and roadsides by people who must not realize how its viny sprawl overwhelms the native growth. The other one, the kudzu vine, introduced as a possible source of starch from its roots, but chiefly to secure roadsides and banks from erosion, has converted those roadsides, when its leaves turn brown, into a disaster area of rotten-looking sodden draperies.

Another invader from across the sea (England and Scotland) had left records in the coves and on the slopes—records that the forest is erasing. We sought out places where pioneer farmers had wrenched their farmsteads from the wilderness.

Certainly such a farmer would have considered the tulip tree an invader on the stony land that he cleared of forest to gain space for a stony sloping cornpatch, and a small meadow for his cow, and space for an apple tree or two. The farmer's wife, homesick perhaps for some English garden, would have yanked out any seedling tulip tree that might appear among her daffodils, or daylilies, or might be threatening to shade her black-green boxwood, or her Japanese quince, and other treasures of the dooryard, brought like her from across the sea.

The time came when the pioneer farmers had to leave their farms which had become a part of a national park. By 1932 the last one had left. Then the pioneer of the forest, the tulip tree, advanced in solid erect ranks—the return of a native.

We were shown many old farmsteads by Ranger Ronnie Click, and that connoisseur of big trees, Dr. Glidden Baldwin. Many of the farmsteads had their old stout farmhouses still standing, and a spring, and a stone wall, and an old apple tree; but the most inevitable marker was the bright yellow of a clump of daffodils (the pioneer farmers must have shared bulbs with each other), and the new green of a spreading mass of daylilies. Those two will continue to keep alive the memories of the pioneer farmers until the shade of the advancing forest deepens, and ferns and trilliums and hepaticas take their place.

In one of the farmsteads the daffodil bulbs were lying uprooted on top of newly disturbed soil. Other plump storage-roots, of Solomon's Seal, spring beauty, daylily, and more, were lying about, some with a bite taken out of them.

The hard nose of a European boar had rooted them out. In several farmsteads, and in the forest, we saw large traps baited with corn, ready for this, the most destructive of the invaders from across the sea.

ABANDONED PIONEER FARMSTEADS
ARE INVADED BY PIONEER TULIP TREES—

in cornpatches

in orchards

in stone walls

Suddenly our forest ranger pointed ahead, "Look! We got one."

And there one stood, glaring at us with his tiny eyes on a bulky head, with ears erect in their sunlit ragged fringe. His head looked exactly like the one I had seen mounted on the wall of a hunting lodge above the Rhine. Such a head was the mark of Richard III of England.

A more-recent Englishman brought boars across the ocean to stock his hunting lodge in North Carolina, where deer and elk could be hunted as well (for a fee). He built a stout fence. But after a time the venture was given up, and the introduced animals were on their own. The elk and deer did not long survive freedom and hunters. But the boar, able to root under fences, as temporarily captured ones have rooted out of their cages in the park, found plenty of bulbs and storage roots. In 1959 they had advanced into the national park, and advanced and advanced. The abundant spring flora of the Smokies is at their mercy, and they are merciless.

What a triumph in biological controls it would be if the boars were to find the farinaceous roots of the kudzu vine tasty!

While the foreign boars were rooting out the spring flora of the Smokies, native bulldozers were rooting out a particularly famous spring flower, fifty miles away. They were adding another chapter—perhaps the final chapter—to the often-told saga of the rare antique called *Shortia galacifolia*, or Oconee-bells, the plant that so many botanists had searched for after Asa Gray saw parts of it in the herbarium sheets of Michaux, in Paris.

One botanist who joined in the hunt was Charles Sprague Sargent, later to be head of the Arnold Arboretum. In the diary that Michaux had kept of his plant-hunting in America, Sargent read,

The roads became more difficult as we approached the headwaters of the Keowee on the 8th of December, 1788. . . . There was in this place a

daylily

spring beauty

daffodil

Solomon's seal

A TRAPPED BOAR
some of plants he had rooted out

little cabin inhabited by a family of Cherokee Indians. We stopped there to camp and I ran off to make some investigations. I gathered a new low woody plant with saw-toothed leaves creeping on the mountain at a short distance from the river. . . .

December 11. . . . I came back to camp with my guide at the head of the Keowee and gathered a large quantity of the low woody plant with the saw-toothed leaves that I found the day I arrived. I did not see it on any other mountain. The Indians told me that the leaves had a good taste when chewed and the odor was agreeable when they were crushed, which I found to be the case.

Directions for finding this plant:
The head of the Keowee is the junction of the two torrents which flow from cascades in the high mountains. This junction is made in a little plain which was formerly a city or village of the Cherokees. In descending to the junction of the two torrents, having the river on the left and the high mountains which look to the north on the right, one finds at about thirty paces from the confluence a little path formed by the Indian hunters. Continuing in this direction one arrives at last at the mountains where one finds the little shrub which covers the soil along with *Epigaea repens* (trailing arbutus).

There, at the juncture of the Toxaway River and Horsepasture Creek, ninety-eight years later, Sargent found the lost plant and sent home a specimen to Asa Gray, which helped him forge another link between the similar floras of southeastern North America and Asia.

And now the bulldozers have found that place. They have scraped the mountain clean of shortia, and its companions, trailing arbutus, galax, partridgeberry, rhododendron, and anything else that might get in the way of constructing a dam 385 feet high to hold back the waters of the new Lake Jocasee.

To prepare for this lake of 7,500 acres, and the larger Lake Keowee of 18,372 acres, it took several hundred men four years to remove the timber from the area to be flooded. They harvested 17.5 million board-feet of pine sawtimber, 15 million feet of hardwood sawtimber, and 51,800 cords of pulpwood. Tulip trees, as wide as seven feet in diameter and more than 200 years old, were cut.

But, according to the brochure of the "Keowee-Toxaway Project": "One section of this ancient forest, above the water line of Lake

Jocasee, will be preserved in its wilderness state for naturalists and lovers of the untouched out-doors. This tract, which has been named the Coon Branch Natural Area, consists of fifteen acres. . . ." Fifteen acres?

But the project will bring power, and recreational facilities, and there is a visitors' center, landscaped in part with trees, shrubs, and flowering plants taken from ground now under water. Colorful exhibits and brochures offer explanations of why the new nuclear power plant, one of the world's largest, will not cause thermal pollution in the water of the lakes; why a nuclear explosion cannot happen here; how the nuclear fuel will, when it becomes less effective, be shipped away to a reprocessing plant which will recover the reusable uranium and plutonium for "use in medicine and other peaceful purposes"; and how the entire project will yield over $20 million annually in local and state taxes, and $24 million in federal taxes.

Shortia is reported to be growing wild in scattered locations in North Carolina, South Carolina, and Georgia. And it is growing in many gardens.

Perhaps this antique, as well as the ones we considered in the nearby Smokies, will survive the various invaders.

BIBLIOGRAPHICAL NOTES

Deciduous Forests of Eastern North America by E. Lucy Braun. Blakiston, Philadelphia, 1950.

"Certain Floristic Affinities of the Trees and Shrubs of the Great Smoky Mountains and Vicinity" by Stanley A. Cain. *Butler University Botanical Studies* 1 (September, 1930), 129–156.

"A Biological Spectrum of the Flora of the Great Smoky Mountains National Park" by Stanley A. Cain. *Butler University Botanical Studies* 7 (April, 1945), 11–24.

"The Undifferentiated Forest Climax and the Association Segregate" by E. Lucy Braun. *Ecology* 16 (July, 1935), 514–519.

"A Study of Summer Foliage Insect Communities in the Great Smoky Mountains" by R. H. Whittaker. *Ecological Monographs* 22 (January, 1952), 1–44.

"The Great Smoky Mountains—Their Geology and History" by Philip B. King and Arthur Stupka. *Scientific Monthly* 71 (July, 1950), 31–49.

An Introduction to Paleobotany by Chester A. Arnold. McGraw-Hill, New York, 1947.

Flowers and Flowering Plants by Raymond Pool. McGraw-Hill, New York, 1941.

The Silva of North America; A Description of the Trees Which Grow Naturally in North America Exclusive of Mexico by Charles Sprague Sargent. Houghton Mifflin, Boston, 1947.

"Asa Gray and His Quest for *Shortia galacifolia*" by Charles F. Jenkins. *Arnoldia* 2 (April 10, 1942), 13–36.

"Evolutionary Level in Relation to Geographic, Seasonal, and Diurnal Distribution of Insects" by Clarence Hamilton Kennedy. *Ecology* 9 (October, 1928), 367–379.

"The Tertiary Character of the Cove Hardwood Forests of the Great Smoky Mountains National Park" by Stanley A. Cain. *Torrey Botanical Club Bulletin* 70, 213–235.

"Vegetation in the Great Smoky Mountains" by R. H. Whittaker. *Ecological Monographs* 26 (January, 1956), 1–80.

The Appalachians by Maurice Brooks. Houghton Mifflin, Boston, 1965.

"Forests of the Smokies" by Millard C. Davis. *The Living Wilderness Quarterly*, (Spring, 1966).

"Ominous Problem: What to Do with Radioactive Waste" by Dennis Farney. *Smithsonian*, 5, (April, 1974).

2

In Pursuit of Tolerance

OR

WIND, SHADE, AND SALT

IN MASSACHUSETTS

FOR LOOKING at the New England coast, Thanksgiving time is best. Then it endures openly, and its tolerances show.

We started out with a pre-Thanksgiving service at the Old South Church in Boston, where costumed "Pilgrims" filed in to fill the front rows. Elder William Brewster, Governor William Bradford, Myles Standish, Oceanus Hopkins, Humility Cooper, Resolved White, and many others were there. We heard of the hardships they endured in their pursuit of religious tolerance, and as we left we were each given a small envelope containing five grains of corn in memory of a Pilgrim's daily ration during the worst of the hungry years. We came out onto a street patched with snow and curbed with granite (granite!—we mid-westerners were used to nothing nobler than concrete) and decided we were all set to face the kind of landscape that the Pilgrims faced at the same time of year, in 1620.

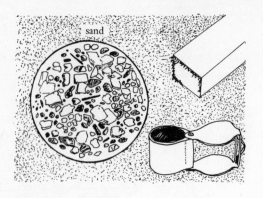

For a starter we would go to Plum Island, it was decided.

There we made for the ocean's edge, kicking loose sand and crunching snow patches through a landscape stripped of grace, and fragrance, and birdsong, and wearing such a poker face as the coast of New England must have presented to those homesick Pilgrims. We hurried in the urgent way that humans show when approaching the sea, according to the observations of Ishmael, in *Moby Dick:*

> But look here comes more crowds, pacing straight for the water and seemingly posed for a dive. Strange! Nothing will content them but the extremest limit of the land; loitering under the lee of yonder warehouse will not suffice. No. They must get just as nigh the water as they can without falling in.

The tide was almost out. What it was leaving behind, we, and the sanderlings bobbing on twinkling stilts, picked up. They could only eat their finds. We were luckier. We could take off a mitten and feel the smoothness of the indigo lining of the quahog, and the whorls of the moon shell. We could pick up a bit of gneiss or schist probably broken off from the rocky shore of Maine and still paved with colonies of crowded acorn barnacles, but dead barnacles, no longer waiting between tides for the next chance to open their plates and wave their plumy appendages to draw in food from the water. And we could take out our hand lenses and look at a handful of sand.

A handful can contain a jumbled history of New England. In my handful I thought (perhaps I wanted to think) that a large milky-white grain might be marble. If it was, that would have been a very early event in the geological story, the laying down of limestone by the sea. Later, that limestone was to be buckled and heated and cooled into crystals, and thus metamorphosed into Vermont marble, for the carving into tombstones with fingers pointed heavenward, and lambs, and weeping willows. (My bit of marble may have been a fragment of one of those fingers—broken off in a nearby churchyard, and almost worn away by the sea.)

Some jagged, light-gray bits were evidently slate, metamorphosed from shale by folding, straining, pressing, to become a substance easily scratched into skeleton faces above angels' wings, for rows of dark headstones in Lexington and Boston and elsewhere.

But my handful was composed, almost entirely, of the ingredients of the volcanic rocks that make up most of New England. Part of them might represent older granite, metamorphosed into the twisted, layered, tortured-looking gneisses and schists that are so conspicuous along recent road-cuts. Part of them might represent a more recent granite that, whether it reached the surface before cooling, or was exposed later as the older covering wore away, made the White Mountains and furnished the curbstones of Boston and many other towns, and the Bunker Hill Monument and many others.

The great ice sheet had a part in making my handful, as it gouged its way southward, breaking off ledges of rock and dragging the broken pieces frozen into its creeping mass, shaping Cape Cod to mark its last stand, and strewing the land with the boulders that were to form many miles of stone walls as the farmers cleared their plowland.

Glacial meltwater, and the wind, and the sea, freezing and thawing, and the rain, each had a hand in shaping, jumbling, transporting, selecting, the grains that composed my handful of sand.

The hand lens showed round grains, angular grains, long narrow grains—no flaky grains, because the sea had kept the flakes of mica and floated them away. Most abundant were the angular, glassy, larger flakes of quartz. There were plenty of the smaller, rounded, pinkish or light-gray grains of feldspar—the stuff of the clay that the glacier shaped into the boat-shaped drumlins of Boston, one of them to become the setting for the battle of Bunker Hill. There were dark-gray to blackish grains. Some of them must have been hornblende. (Later, at home, we got out a magnet and drew it through the sand to select out the dark grains of hematite or ilmenite that were there. Such bits of iron were oxidized by the acid waters of bogs on Martha's Vineyard to form bog-iron to make the cannon balls fired by Old Ironsides.)

On the beach, after my handful of history had been put away in an envelope, we turned again to the line of wrack left by the tide. The biggest object was a long strand of kelp. Its rubbery brown length lay cast ashore, no longer able to lean on the sea, responding to its support and buffeting. The reason why it had lost its place in a forest of kelp on the ocean floor was easy to see, because the mussel to which the kelp had been anchored was still clutched by the kelp's holdfasts. These are not roots. The kelp, bathed in nourishment, does not need roots. Holdfasts are rubbery discs that spread and flow over the support and gradually harden into rigid firmness. The mussel in the kelp's clutch had furnished a firm foothold because it, too, had been secured to something by a tangle of threads that it exuded as a milky substance hardening in the sea water.

That something might have been the knobby pavement formed by a bed of oysters. Those oysters may have laid down that pavement on a mudflat cleared by a storm. The mussels needed such a support as the oyster pavement provided. But the mussels may, in time, have smothered the oysters. Or the oysters may have died off because of wastes settling around them and clogging their gills. Or they may have died because of certain pollutants that made their shells remain closed when they needed to be opened for feeding. However it happened, the kelp was dead.

Everything we could see in that long line of wrack was dead. If there was anything living we were walking on the roof over its lairs. But life down within such an exposed and unsheltered beach would be sparse, and probably would have retreated deeper down at this season, after the freezes, no longer stretching long tubes up into tide-wet sand. Even if the beach flies, called sandhoppers, were still inclined to leave their burrows above the tide line and to follow the tide out, scavenging for what it might have brought, they would not come out till after dark.

But life beckoned to us from the edge of the cliff that high tides had bitten into the face of a dune. There the marram grass, *Ammophila breviligulata*, dominated the scene that few plants could tolerate. A close relative of this grass must have been present on the last bit of land the Pilgrims saw when they left Holland, and when they left England, and on the first bit they saw when they landed on Cape Cod. Here is tolerance: of wind, of drought, of moving sand. Two other hardy plants had succeeded in the slight shelter and tenuous stability of the marram grass. They were the seaside goldenrod, and the beach pea, both of them browned by freezing nights.

As soon as we had climbed up through the sag between two cliffs of grass-held sand, the rhythm of the dunes became apparent, as it was shaped by landward trips of moving sand: mount—pause—tumble; mount gradually, pause in marram grass shelter, tumble in a steep slope; and then do it again, and again.

On the next dune there appeared the first woody plant, stunted, bent. It was bayberry. We were still in the area reached by salt spray. One after another appeared the plants that tolerate that most trying of conditions: more bayberry; then a subdued and beaten beach plum; then multiple stubby ends of poison ivy twigs protruding from the side of a dune; then huckleberry; then staghorn sumac; then a hollow lined with Hudsonia; then the first few pitch pines; then rugosa roses still full of fat rose hips shriveled with frost.

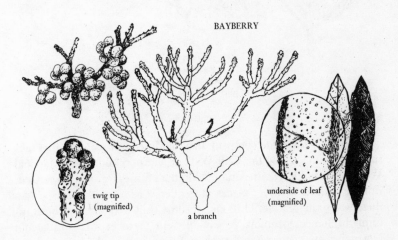

BAYBERRY

twig tip
(magnified)

a branch

underside of leaf
(magnified)

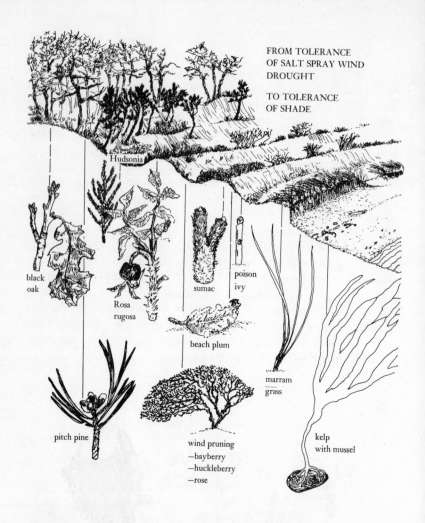

FROM TOLERANCE
OF SALT SPRAY WIND
DROUGHT

TO TOLERANCE
OF SHADE

Hudsonia

black
oak

Rosa
rugosa

sumac

poison
ivy

beach plum

marram
grass

pitch pine

wind pruning
—bayberry
—huckleberry
—rose

kelp
with mussel

This was the same company that had lined our path in other salt-spray exposures: along the Cliff Walk at Newport; along the Marginal Way at Ogunquit, Maine; and on Martha's Vineyard, and Cape Cod. But we walked in those places at gentler seasons of the year, when there was some grace of blossom, or some fruit to nibble, or some autumn brilliance to enjoy. It was different to meet them on a cold November day, stripped and ready to face winter, and winter nights.

The bayberry still held some leaves, but the berries were gone. I rubbed a leaf between my fingers for the smell of Christmas Eve, and then inspected the underside of a leaf, with the hand lens. It gleamed with globules of oil that looked like tiny beads of amber.

The winter buds of pitch pine wore globs of resin; and there was dense hairiness on the winter buds of sumac and beach plum; and all growth was short, dwarfed-looking, compact. The shrubs looked pruned, not just pruned once, but pruned often from their early youth on, until they conformed to the stature of the group. Not pruned by men with pruning shears. They were shaped like the wind-pruned trees of the Rockies timberline, and like the drought-pruned shrubs of the Pacific Coast chaparral. Any twig that put out a spurt of excessive growth that lifted it above the protective huddle of its fellows would be a target for strong winds, or severe cold, or intense prolonged heat. We could see twigs that had failed to conform. They were shriveled and dead.

Further inland, beach plum stood taller, unpruned, as did pitch pine. And the sand was being stabilized by plants. Bayberry, sumac, rugosa roses, and Hudsonia were being "phased out," as the need for salt-tolerance dwindled, and the need for a new tolerance crept in.

Shade was the new feature. Black oaks were coming in. (Such dry sandy or gravelly ridges across the eastern part of the country belong to them.) As the black oaks closed their ranks, the bracken fern came in. The pitch pine had the sunnier places; the beach plum had the edges.

Such an association of pitch pine and black oak dominates many sandy reaches of the Atlantic Coast. In addition to great native expanses, there are the plantings made by men in an effort to stabilize stretches of sand from which the cover had been removed.

Both members of this pitch pine–black oak fraternity have an added propensity for survival. They tolerate, or at least recover from, fire.

That pitch pine could survive fire seems impossible when we remember the wild performance, in a fireplace, of a pitch-pine knot. Such knots, full of pitch, earned the common-name of "candlewood," and another name, "flambeau," dating back to nights when a hunter would use a flaming torch for "shining the deer," holding it so that it would reflect from a deer's eyes. (I remember a night when our car came up over a rise on Ridge Road in the Rockies, and for an instant we saw, reflected in the headlights, three pairs of eyes of startled deer that had been feeding in that alpine meadow.) Both pitch pine and black oak, when a tree is burned, can produce sprouts from the roots; and some pitch pines have those closed cones that are opened by the heat of the fire, and then reseed the area.

But even these enduring trees have their limit of tolerance. There comes a time when the layers of pine needles, oak leaves, and huckleberry leaves, of ferns, mosses, and lichens, receive a white oak acorn, for example, that grows into a tree that overtops them. Shade deepens and deepens. The time for pioneers is past.

Because Plum Island is specially suited to pioneers, we left its wind and salt spray and instability, and headed inland in pursuit of shade tolerance.

When the Pilgrims came, forest had long ago woven its closed canopy over much of New England. The forest was composed of sugar maple, beech, yellow birch, and hemlock—it was often referred to as the Northern Hardwoods-Hemlock Forest. Its high tight canopy was woven of the crowns of mature, long-trunked trees; and there were similar trees of various ages and statures down below. Always one was ready to mend a rip in the canopy left when an old tree died.

Already, before the Pilgrims came, there were breaks in the continuity of the forest. Some breaks were the work of Indians who had set fires to clear places for cornfields. Some breaks had been made by hurricanes which laid wide stretches of forest low. In breaks, whatever their cause, the seedlings and saplings of the Northern Hardwoods-Hemlock Forest were rising through the downed trees, and the less shade-tolerant white pines and gray birches were finding temporary homes in the sunny niches.

On pages 30 through 32, these events and other probable ones are listed, and diagramed, in the order in which they may have happened. (To avoid complication, variations in contour and exposure are not included.)

Tolerance of salt spray, instability, drought, fire, cold and shade—these do not cover the whole story of the new scenes that the Pilgrims saw. At least one more must be considered—tolerance of inundation by tides.

We explored several salt marshes of several inlets on the Massachusetts coast. The story recorded in one of them seemed like the story recorded in the next one, going like this:

An inlet began to change, imperceptibly. The sea was drawing a sandbar across its entrance. Over the accumulating sand, the tides flowed in and out freely twice a day, for a time. But gradually the sandbar built up until it slowed the ebbing tide, causing it to drop more and more silt. One day the retreating tide revealed a long wet ridge of sand. A flock of sanderlings along the beach extended their run onto this new-made stretch, and marked its creation with a lacery of footprints, which the next tide erased.

An empty ecological niche now awaited the coming of a pioneer plant. A pioneer of special tolerance it would have to be—greater than that of pitch pines, or bayberries, or marram grass, or Pilgrims, per· haps.

Many seeds came, by one method or another, to that sandy neck, only to be washed away by the next tide. Finally, somehow, a few spindly grass seedlings survived, gripped the wet sand while the incoming tide combed them landward and the ebbing tide combed them seaward, and their stems strained the sea and gained a few grains of silt and sand toward a firmer footing.

The colony spread and grew in sturdiness and stature. The new place belonged to a single species, saltwater cordgrass, or salt thatch, *Spartina alternifolia*. It can survive having its roots always in contact with salt water, and being totally submerged, sometimes twice a day.

As I stood on a beach that November day, waiting for the tide to withdraw, I thought about salt water, and about the pitch pine up there on the dunes, holding its niche partly by being able to survive salt spray, and about the sugar maple at the road's edge dying as a result of road salting.

Seedlings of *Spartina alternifolia* on sandbar

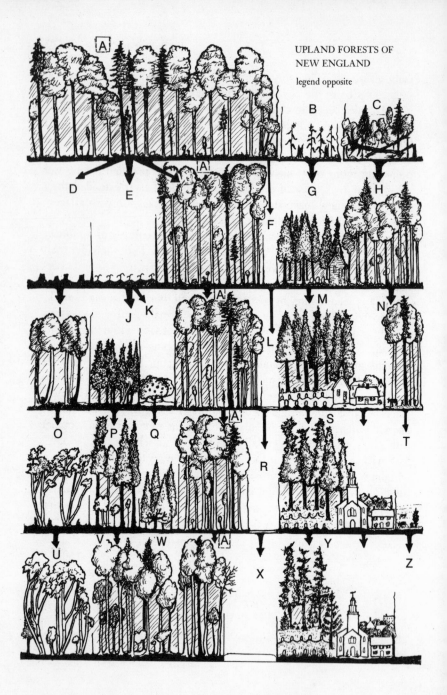

UPLAND FORESTS OF
NEW ENGLAND

legend opposite

Legend for Diagram of the Hardwoods-Hemlock Forests of New England from the Pilgrims' Time to Ours

TOP ROW

    A - represents closed-canopy forest of various-aged trees of sugar maple, beech, yellow birch, and hemlock.

    B - shows Indian corn planted around charred stumps of a clearing. An Indian trail is on the left of the clearing.

    C - shows the trees downed by a hurricane, and original forest renewing itself, with some white pine and birch in sunny spots.

SECOND ROW

    D - shows the stumps left where the original forest has been cut for lumber.

    E - shows a plot cleared of stones and roots and used for plowland.

    A - represents the remaining Northern Hardwoods-Hemlock Forest.

    F - indicates a dirt road replacing the Indian trail.

    G - shows where a good seed year filled the now-abandoned Indian corn plot with pine seedlings, able to thrive in the sun and produce an even-aged stand, which invited a pioneer church with its burial plot.

THIRD ROW

    I - shows the stumps producing root sprouts.

    J - shows the abandoned plowland taken over by "old-field white pine" and a few birch.

    K - shows a part of the abandoned plowland and a section of the original forest planted with apple trees.

    A - represents the remaining piece of the original forest.

    L - shows the dirt road widened and paved.

    M - shows how the town and graveyard have grown.

    N - shows the reduced piece of forest has cows grazing in it, and can no longer be self-replacing.

FOURTH ROW

O - shows that when the sprout forest had burned repeatedly, birches seeded it, and a birch grove grew.

P - shows the pine stand being taken over by red oak, white oak, ash, and black cherry. (In past times the chestnut would have been important, but that was before the chestnut blight came to this continent.)

Q - shows white pines closed in around the apple trees, and shading them to death, after the farmer had moved away.

A - represents the remaining original forest, after it has again been reduced by—

R - the widening of the road.

S - shows the enlarged cemetery, church, and town.

T - shows that the last of the old trees in the grove at the edge of town has been cut, and the cows are grazing on a pasture of bluegrass from Europe. An occasional red cedar dots the pasture.

FIFTH ROW

U - shows the birch grove being invaded by oaks and ash, and by white pines in the sunny spots.

V - shows that the oak forest has taken over, with red oak dominating. Down underneath, sugar maple seedlings appear, perhaps prophetically.

W - shows how the site of the apple orchard has filled with oaks, succeeding in the shade of the pines, and replacing them.

A - represents the remaining bit of the original forest. The sugar maples along its edge cannot tolerate the salt used in winter on—

X - the new wide highway.

Y - shows the town filled with new kinds of trees: a Norway spruce by the church, and many Norway maples, Colorado spruces, and a few weeping willows from the Orient.

Z - shows that the pasture has been paved for parking.

As soon as the tide had finished its turn, I had mine, squishing in among the stiffened brown stems. There, as I stooped a lot and imagined a bit, the sight resembled a forest of straight tall trunks, muddy at the base, rising from a floor without underbrush.

I thought of the old specter of reverse osmosis that a gardener is warned against, lest he put a plant into a hole with too generous an amount of fertilizer and too stingy an amount of water, and come back the next day to a dying plant, "burned by fertilizer," he usually says. Down in its hole his plant was unable to take in water through the wet membranes of its root tips, because water moves from the less concentrated solution to the more concentrated solution, tending to make the concentrations equal. The gardener's valuable plant would simply contribute its water to the hole. What about this saltwater cordgrass, then, why does it not contribute its water to a thinning-down of the seawater around its roots? How did it ever succeed in getting any water in the first place?

The answer is not apparent on a cordgrass sandbar. It is necessary to turn for an explanation to the accounts of observers who have looked long and hard with eyes and microscopes at cross sections and test tubes, and who have had long experience of salt marshes.

One of the chief qualities of *Spartina alternifolia* which selected it out for survival in this habitat was evidently the ability of its cells to increase the concentration of salt in their internal water so that it is above the concentration of the surrounding seawater. Spartina does not increase the concentration of all salts contained in seawater: it selects those that have little importance in cell functions. Common table salt, sodium chloride, is the one that is concentrated.

That is not all of the salt problem. The sap of the plant would become too salty for it to tolerate, unless some system of disposal existed. It does. Small glands are scattered over the surface of spartina, special glands that can pick out salt from the sap and secrete it through special pores on the leaf surface. The water secreted with the salt evaporates and the salt crystals remain, sparkling until the next tide washes them off.

A set of hollow tubes runs from the spartina's leaves down to its roots. Oxygen enters the stomatal openings on the leaves and travels by diffusion to the hollow roots. The air passages might be flooded by a high tide, and oxygen would then travel too slowly. This is prevented by the firm closing of the stomata in the face of the tide. Oxygen, put out by the roots, oxidizes the iron in the mud, rendering it soluble and fit to fill spartina's iron needs.

With such aids to survival, the salt-marsh cordgrass spread as the sandbar grew wider and longer. No other plant grew there, except for a delicate tracery of algae filaments. As the sandbar and its grasses slowed down the carrying power of the tides more and more, deposits of silt collected on the landward side and began to spread toward the shore.

Turning away from the tall grasses, I found that I was looking down at a much shorter grass, two feet tall or less. Its slender leaves and stems were swirled into a cowlick formation. This was the other one of the two spartinas that dominate the salt marshes. This one, *Spartina patens*, salt meadow grass or salt marsh hay, comes in and practically takes over as soon as the pioneer, *Spartina alternifolia*, has prepared the way for it by causing the accumulation of more and more silt. In that mud, the *Spartina patens* thrives and tolerates, in a mild sort of way. It cannot tolerate as frequent and deep inundation by the tides as can the other spartina, but it thrives where it is flooded only by the high tides. A stiffer grass, *Distichlis spicata*, makes a minor ingredient of this salt meadow.

Knowing that I was standing on some of the most productive acreage in the world, I peered below the swirled marsh hay. Empty shells of many shapes and sizes, claws of fiddler crabs, the footprint of a raccoon, were there in the dark muck, with its thick deposit of decaying grasses making fertile pasture for plankton, which in turn would nourish oysters, mussels, scallops, and clams. Along the margin of the tidal stream, where the taller spartina grew, was last summer's nest of the long-billed marsh wren, still showing where the female had woven spartina leaves around the side entrance. Down under my feet, deep in the mud into which they had retreated from the first threats of winter, there may have been fiddler crabs, long worms, blood worms, and others.

Toward the limits of the brackish water, the black-green of rushes became part of the scene. Then, at the drier edges, where only a storm would bring saltwater, the seaside goldenrod, the seaside aster, and the sea lavender (all brown on that November day) completed the sequence of the salt marsh.

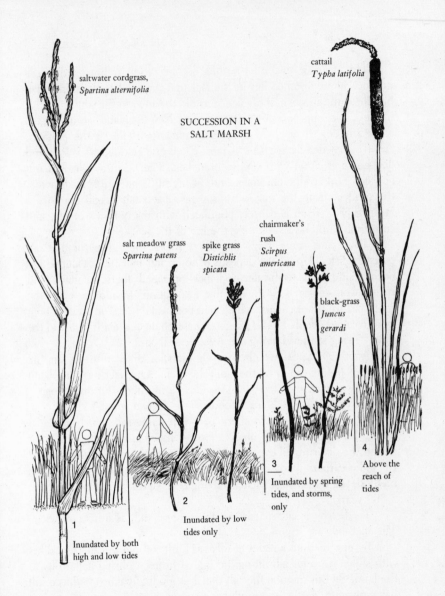

saltwater cordgrass,
Spartina alternifolia

cattail
Typha latifolia

SUCCESSION IN A
SALT MARSH

salt meadow grass
Spartina patens

spike grass
*Distichlis
spicata*

chairmaker's
rush
*Scirpus
americana*

black-grass
*Juncus
gerardi*

1
Inundated by both
high and low tides

2
Inundated by low
tides only

3
Inundated by spring
tides, and storms,
only

4
Above the
reach of
tides

Where the cattails stood tall in tight formation, the marsh was no longer salt.

Beyond, on the dunes, the bayberry and beach plums stood firm and high and dry.

The story of this inlet would not be worth telling, if it were unique. Its importance lies in the fact that the inlet to the north of it had the same succession of events, as did the inlet to the south, as did, in fact, inlets up and down the coast of New England, some larger, some smaller. In each of them *Spartina alternifolia* is the pioneer, and is succeeded by *Spartina patens*. Each one gradually develops and deepens a channel with several branches. The tide flows in and out between ranks of the tall grass, and, at high tide only, it spreads across the mud beneath the low swirling grass. Each salt marsh develops a layer of peat. Each is densely populated with many forms of life, and contributes much to sustaining the life of the sea.

There are some ways in which the stories of particular salt marshes differ. Under the deposits of some salt marshes, evidence has been found that freshwater marshes preceded them. Cattails and rushes were replaced by the spartina association. In another place the roots and trunks of cedars, which had been established in a cedar bog, were covered deeply by salt marsh. These changes are attributed to the slowly rising sea level along the Atlantic seaboard.

Another way in which the salt marshes differ must be in the length of time covered by their development. One fact has long been realized—that it must have taken a long, long time. But how long?

Alfred C. Redfield of Woods Hole Oceanographic Institution decided to date the development of a very large salt marsh at Barnstable, Massachusetts. By observations of the marsh during a 12-year period, he determined the rate of development during the early stages. By radio-carbon analyses, he measured the later stages. By these methods the marsh was dated as having been developing for more than 3,300 years.

To destroy a salt marsh, on the other hand, is quick and easy. The methods are legion.

By one method a series of dikes is built to hold out the sea, dikes with sluice gates for admitting the tide at times, to bring its fertility to the land. By this method the salt marsh is gradually converted into salt hay pasture for cattle, and produces crops of salt hay, some of which is used in gardens as a mulch.

A grid of ditches, too deep for the *Spartina alternifolia* to stabilize, sometimes gradually destroys the marsh. The ditching is done because of the vicious salt marsh mosquitoes whose females require a meal of blood before they can deposit their eggs. The ditches are dug to allow the tides to bring in fish that will eat the mosquito larvae. Other ditches, shallower, are dug to connect pools where the predator fish can stay and eat the larvae.

A marsh can be wiped out by using it as a dump for garbage, sewage, and oily wastes.

Or it can be filled with gravel and quickly converted into a new housing development, or a marina, a shopping center, or parking lot. Or it can become the site for a new factory, or an airport.

Whatever destruction attacks it, or whatever use is made of it, one thing is certain. There will not come again the time, or the opportunity, or the right set of conditions, for that place to produce another salt marsh.

BIBLIOGRAPHICAL NOTES

The Changing Face of New England by Betty Flanders Thomson. Macmillan, 1958.

The Deciduous Forests by E. Lucy Braun. Blakiston, Philadelphia, 1950.

The Atlantic Shore by John Hay and Peter Farb. Harper and Row, 1966.

A Geologist's View of Cape Cod by Arthur N. Strahler. The Natural History Press, Garden City, New York, 1966.

These Fragile Outposts—A Geological Look at Cape Cod, Martha's Vineyard, and Nantucket by Barbara Blau Chamberlain. The Natural History Press, Garden City, New York, 1964.

The Edge of the Sea by Rachel Carson. Houghton Mifflin, Boston, 1955.

The Life and Death of the Salt Marsh by John and Mildred Teal. Little, Brown, Boston, 1969.

The Life of the Marsh by William A. Niering. McGraw-Hill, New York, 1966.

"Can We Save Our Salt Marshes?" by Stephen W. Hitchcock. *National Geographic Magazine*, **141** (June, 1972), 729–765.

"Development of a New England Salt Marsh" by Alfred C. Redfield. *Ecological Monographs*, **42** (Spring, 1972).

"Marshes, Developers and Taxes, a New Ethic for Our Estuaries" by Robert C. Clement. *Audubon Magazine*, **71** (November, 1969).

"The Winter Marsh," a portfolio by Bill Ratcliffe, and an essay by Frank Russell, *Audubon Magazine*, **71** (November, 1969), 36–45.

3

Canyon Story

OR

FOLLOWING A STREAM
IN SOUTHERN INDIANA

THE upland forest where we walked gave no hint of a canyon in its future.

"This is undissected topography," said our geologist.

We were looking for the birthplace of a stream. We had learned that the streams there at Turkey Run, Indiana, have it in their destiny to shape a ravine in their mud-pie childhood, and then knife out a canyon in their whittling youth, before their waters find middle-age spread in Sugar Creek, and old-age resignation in the Wabash.

We wanted to see the whole story—indeed we hoped to find the upland forest pregnant with a canyon not yet born.

But we dallied there, basking in the sunset of summer that emanated from that forest in four bands of brilliance. Highest was the layered canopy of beeches and sugar maples. Beneath them were spread the red-fruited shelves of flowering dogwood. Farther down came the wine color of maple-leaved viburnum. And then there was the forest floor with its herbs and ferns among the fallen leaves.

We walked for a long time in that rich beech-maple forest. Then,

A four-layered forest

sugar maple

beech

flowering dogwood

maple-leaved viburnum

maidenhair fern

abruptly, we found that we were under white oaks. There was only a narrow belt dominated by them, but the trees were of imposing age and size.

No sooner had we commented on this change in the aspect of the canopy than we found ourselves in a belt of still more marked change. Our footsteps made a drier sound. The four-layered aspect was gone. There was only one layer, the canopy of hemlock branches.

A beech and maple forest, then a white oak forest, and then a hemlock forest. It was as if, with a few mighty strides, we had stepped home to the woods of northern Illinois; and then had stepped further north, into a summer camp site in northern Wisconsin.

We continued no further in that direction because, beyond the narrow band of hemlocks, the canyon gaped. Most of the hemlocks were astride its very rim.

We walked among the clutching hemlocks, and suddenly, where there was a break in their dark canopy, we noticed that our feet were treading the green tooled-leather forest floor of northern Wisconsin, or northern Michigan, or Maine.

Crimson partridgeberries shone among those polished leaves, and wintergreen berries, and even the coral-red translucent fruits of yew. We had not needed to travel north to find these plants, because the cold north had delivered them down here long, long ago, driving them south before the icy cold threat of the advancing glacier.

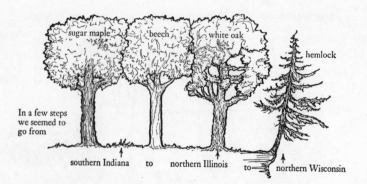

In a few steps we seemed to go from

sugar maple   beech   white oak   hemlock

southern Indiana   to   northern Illinois   to   northern Wisconsin

But the retreat of the glacier had everywhere allowed plants to creep slowly back to their old homes.

How, then, did it happen that this little band of northerners, acquainted with the song of the hermit thrush, the drum of the mighty pileated woodpecker, and the big feet of the snowshoe rabbit, should be isolated here, left behind to hobnob with wood thrushes, and red-bellied woodpeckers, and cottontail rabbits? And why must the northerners cling to the cliff's edge, as though the white oaks were pushing from behind, while the beeches and maples in turn pushed the white oaks?

The time was when they did not need to cling to the cliff's edge. That was when the glacier retreated. During this period probably the upland was dominated by a forest of hemlock and other conifers, with a forest floor covered with trailing arbutus, wintergreen, partridgeberry, and yew. As it grew warmer, the oaks and hickories began to come in, wherever a squirrel had buried a nut and had forgotten

A little band of northerners

partridgeberry   wintergreen   yew   hemlock

where he put it. Some hemlocks survived this invasion—those that happened to grow near the canyon's edge. It is drier there because some ground water escapes through the canyon wall.

The forest of oak and hickory covered the upland, but did not invade the dry edge of the canyon. But presently the oak-hickory forest, in turn, found itself nursing upstarts, changelings, that were not its own offspring. The wind had brought seeds of sugar maples, and squirrels had brought beech nuts. The maple and beech seedlings throve in the accumulated leaf mold, and tolerated the heavy shade.

Then the beeches and maples began to weave a denser shade, denser than white oak seedlings can tolerate. In time the forest of beech and maple took over all of the upland except the drier belt just behind the hemlock edge.

The white oaks cannot move back in among the beeches and maples, no matter if squirrels do carry their acorns back and bury them and forget them. The shade is too dense for their survival. Nor can the hemlocks reinvade that upland territory, no matter if the wind does carry thousands of their seeds back there. It has been found that hemlock seeds do not succeed in rooting in the thick ground cover of rotting leaves.

We turned back toward the beech-maple forest. We had not intended to see the canyon full grown before seeing its birth and its youth. As we walked away from the canyon's brink, we passed, in addition to the change in tree dominants, five other changes.

The soil water in the deeper layers increased markedly.

The tree roots changed from shallow to deep.

The soil acidity decreased.

The herbs of the forest floor changed from those that are typically acid-tolerant (cushion moss, reindeer lichen, pine-tree moss, partridgeberry) to those that are not typically acid-tolerant (downy yellow violet, ginseng, jewelweed, wild phlox).

The number of species on the forest floor changed from few to many.

The last two of these five changes we could easily observe for ourselves. The first three we had read about, in the careful reports of research students from Butler University.

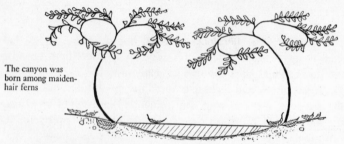
The canyon was born among maidenhair ferns

We walked for a long time, deep into the beech-maple forest.

"Here is a boulder," said the geologist. "Granite. Brought down from Canada probably, by the glacier. We are on glacial till, here."

Beside the boulder grew two plants especially characteristic of the beech-maple forest. One was the northern beech fern; the other was the strange pinkish-tan growth of beechdrops, the saprophyte that has earned its name from its habit of growing on the roots of beech trees.

We found ourselves treading carefully among ferns—silvery spleenwort, rattlesnake fern, fragile fern, narrow-leaved spleenwort, and Christmas fern. Aristocrat among them was the maidenhair, with its mahogany stem upholding a horizontal green swirl.

"Here, I believe, is the place we have been looking for," said the geologist, pointing to a shallow, temporary sort of pool that held last night's rain.

"Want to see the small beginning of what may some day become a canyon?" The geologist walked around to the soggy side of the dish, to the debris that held the rain back, and kicked it out.

The barrier, without our help, would have broken soon. We merely speeded events up by a week, or a month or so, depending on the force of the rains.

"If we could wait here long enough," said the geologist, "we might see that scratch in the upland deepen and extend, until these woods became dissected, first by a ravine, cutting down through the glacial drift, and then by a canyon cutting down through the bedrock beneath. Since we haven't time to wait for the canyon, or even for the ravine, we will follow this water and see the succession of events."

The released water had disappeared at once, down an obscure little draw. We followed. There was only a formless, indefinite depression among the thin-leaved spleenworts and the jewelweed; slight at first, but deepening quickly to a furrow, cutting down into the glacial clay.

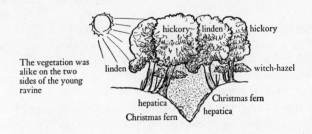

The vegetation was alike on the two sides of the young ravine

hickory · linden · hickory · linden · witch-hazel · hepatica · Christmas fern · Christmas fern · hepatica

"The V-shaped stage of a youthful stream," said the geologist.

Both sides of the young ravine were rich in growth, with shagbark hickory, linden, witch-hazel, bedstraw, and abundant Christmas fern. There seemed to be no difference between the vegetation of the two sides, not even where one of them had a direct south exposure.

The ravine broadened gradually, and deepened, too. It was cutting down through the soft layers of shale that underlay the glacial till.

"Pennsylvanian coal measures," labeled the geologist, crumbling a bit of the shale in her hands.

For a while the ravine ran directly east and west. We could now see distinct differences between the north-facing and the south-facing slopes. On the north-facing slope were wild ginger, maidenhair ferns, thin-leaved spleenwort, hepaticas, blue beech. On the south-facing slope were sassafras, agrimony, catbrier, wild aster, wild currant, goldenrod.

The ravine deepened and widened still more.

"The U-shaped stage," said the geologist.

Differences between the north- and the south-facing sides became still more pronounced. There were more oaks on the south-facing, and more sugar maples on the north-facing side.

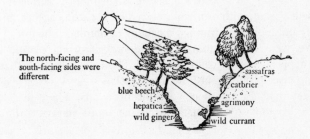

The north-facing and south-facing sides were different

blue beech · hepatica · wild ginger · sassafras · catbrier · agrimony · wild currant

Presently the stream began to wander on the floor of its ravine, depositing a small flood plain on the slow inner side of each curve, and cutting into a shaly bluff on the outer side.

"The meandering stream stage," said the geologist. "The speed of the stream and its downcutting power have slowed considerably."

At this point there were three different types of vegetation: the north-facing slopes were clothed in beech, and an abundance of Christmas fern; the south-facing slope wore white oak, and considerable hepatica; and on the bottom were nettle (*Laportea*), moonseed (*Menispermum*), and hog-peanut (*Amphicarpa*).

The stream had reached a sort of middle age. Its waters were held in a quiet pool. Had this stream continued to cut down through soft materials, its next stage would have been placid old age.

But that was not to happen in this case, we found, when we looked over the barrier that held back the pool.

Suddenly, delightfully, the stream, plunging over the barrier, renewed its youth. The waters that had been so sluggish, now took to whittling again. The stream had cut down through the soft shale, and reached the underlying sandstone.

"Mansfield sandstone," remarked the geologist, "a durable building stone."

As the stream plunged over the hard ledge of sandstone into the bowl that it had gouged for itself below, leaving the middle-aged ravine behind, and beginning life anew in a very young canyon, we too went over the ledge, but more slowly, taking our middle age along with us.

"The V-shaped stage of a young stream again," said the geologist, "but now it is cutting through rock instead of glacial till."

It was cool and shady and windless down there. The term "vapor pocket" was easy to understand, as we stood moistly astride the narrow, swift stream, with our hands braced on each side against dripping mosses, and looked up through a canopy of hemlock boughs.

We were in the domain of the rock-carpeting plants, called "belly-floppers" by one young observer. These are the plants that plaster themselves prone against the moist rock.

Dominant among them were the liverworts. There was an unusual representation of their kind on the moist vertical walls: Mar-

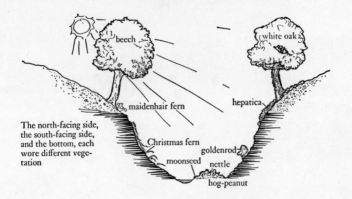

The north-facing side, the south-facing side, and the bottom, each wore different vegetation

beech

white oak

maidenhair fern

hepatica

Christmas fern

goldenrod

moonseed

nettle

hog-peanut

chantia, Conocephalum, Reboulia, Anthoceros, Porella. (The smaller a plant is, the longer its name seems to be. Aren't plants that get short names mostly those that are eaten, or taken for ailments, or grown in cottage gardens?)

The fern-leaved moss, *Thuidium delicatulum,* held close to the rock wall, and so did *Mnium cuspidatum,* and *Umbilicaria,* or rock tripe, which incidentally can be eaten. From every ledge the bulblet bladder fern dripped down.

It was moist and new and young there in the steep-sided narrow canyon. Moist and new, like the conditions on the young earth when the first primitive plants came ashore. And there beside us, right at eye level, were the plants that resemble, probably better than do any other living plants, those first land plants.

"Apparently the Christopher Columbus of the plant kingdom was a liverwort," says Coulter, in his "Story of the Plant Kingdom."

And although the ages since that first successful landing have carried living green to the tops of the driest hills and to the tips of the highest trees, the liverwort form still persists, providing us with a picture of the probable architecture of the first plant that managed to survive on land. Perhaps it was stranded in a tidal basin; and perhaps many others, stranded at the same time, perished, while the one rugged individual somehow survived, desperately suckling the spray-drenched sand.

We lifted one of the liver-shaped ribbons from the moist rock surface to look at its underside, and saw the tentative prophecy of roots

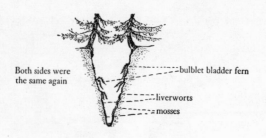

Both sides were
the same again

bulblet bladder fern

liverworts

mosses

scattered there. Not real roots, any more than the green ribbons were real leaves; but we felt that to hold a liverwort in our hands was to hold both a record of the past, because of its resemblance to the plate-like alga that must have been its ancestor in the sea, and a promise of the future, because of this suggestion of roots, and of leaves.

We looked for a long time, in spite of our soggy feet, at the assemblage of liverworts, as we reconstructed the coming of green to the barren, stony earth. We saw that where liverworts had prepared the way and made a foothold on the canyon wall, the mosses had come in. Some of the mosses were prone like the liverworts, but others held their bit of green free from contact with the rock. We were reading the second chapter in the invasion of the land.

It was not far that the mosses lifted themselves from the rock surface. It could not be far, because they had not yet acquired tubes for carrying water up through their structures; and because their sperms must still swim in order to fertilize the ovum, as the sperms swam in the liverworts before them, and in the algae before the liverworts.

As we inspected the canyon wall, we saw how often, where mosses had prepared the way by laying down their plush carpet, the ferns had come in. No need for these to be prostrate, no need for these

Liverworts prepare
the way for mosses

Mosses prepare the way for ferns

to cling so close to the water supply, for the ferns have tubes, a vascular system, for carrying water.

We were reading the third chapter in the invasion of the land.

We looked at the delicate bulblet bladder fern, realizing that it was but a pygmy representative of that great widespread group of ferns and fern allies that helped lay down the coal measures.

It seemed to us as if we were looking at plants that had graduated from the rock-carpeting class, until we remembered that the first stage in the life history of a fern is a tiny heart-shaped prothallium, resembling a liverwort, plastered close against the moist rock, and having sperms that still must swim.

Up above our heads, the hemlock branches represented the fourth chapter in the invasion of the land, the naked-seed plants. Crowding the hemlocks from behind, we knew, were the white oaks, representing the fifth chapter in the invasion, the enclosed-seed plants.

"Not only," ventured the geologist, "do the plants in this narrow canyon take us through the pages of a botany textbook, but they take us through several geological periods as well.

"The first invasion of the land by plants probably took place in the Silurian period, about 400 million years ago. Turkey Run was under the Niagaran Sea then, and trilobites were shucking off their hard three-lobed skins around here, and cephalopods were waving their tentacles from the open ends of their ice-cream-cone-shaped shells.

"The first seed-bearing plants appeared in the Devonian period, but did not amount to much. Turkey Run had primitive fish swimming over it then.

"The fern ancestors dominated the land in the Carboniferous period, while this sandstone that forms our canyon wall was being laid down along the margin of a shallow sea.

"The conifers appeared in the Triassic period, about 200 million years ago. Turkey Run was land then. Probably there were dinosaurs lumbering around here.

"The enclosed-seed plants appeared in the Cretaceous period, about 120 million years ago. Turkey Run could have been making acquaintance of marsupials with their pouches full of offspring at that time."

A dark little newt slithered across the bed of liverwort and moss.

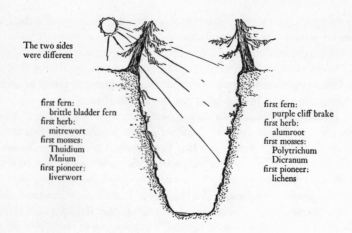

The two sides were different

first fern:
  brittle bladder fern
first herb:
  mitrewort
first mosses:
  Thuidium
  Mnium
first pioneer:
  liverwort

first fern:
  purple cliff brake
first herb:
  alumroot
first mosses:
  Polytrichum
  Dicranum
first pioneer:
  lichens

"How fitting," said the geologist, "a representative of the first animal group to come ashore, scampering across the first land plants—amphibians both of them."

Our shoes were too wet, so we moved on down the canyon. Now the walls stood farther apart. The stream had slowed down.

"The U-shaped stage of the canyon," said the geologist.

No longer was the vegetation of north- and south-facing walls alike, now that they were too far apart to shelter each other from wind and sun. The north-facing wall was still dark green with liverworts, mosses, and bladder fern. But the south-facing wall wore a thin covering of gray-green. That covering was composed of lichens, the typical pioneers of dry rocks.

The mosses that were coming in where lichens had prepared the way were different from the mosses that came in where liverworts had preceded them; they were *Polytrichum piliferinum*, and *Dicranum scoparium*. The first fern was different too; it was purple cliff brake, leathery and tough.

The first abundant herb on the north-facing side was a mitrewort, *Mitella*; on the south-facing side it was alumroot, *Heuchera hispida*. The difference in the feel of these two plants, the one tender and silky, the other harsh and hispid, was the difference in feel between plants characteristic of moist shady places, and those of hot, dry areas.

The canyon continued to broaden.

In places where the edge of the cliff had given way and formed a talus slope, the north-facing talus slopes had young sugar maple clothing them, together with linden and ash, and an abundant growth of hepatica, running euonymus, spikenard, and maidenhair and Christmas fern. Incidentally, when that cliff edge had slid down, the last foothold of the hemlocks was gone.

Opposite this rich talus-slope community, a south-facing talus-slope was sparsely clothed in big-tooth aspen (*Populus grandidentata*).

The canyon had a bottom now, where asters and goldenrods were finding conditions much like those by the side of a road. As the bottom broadened, the stream ambled along, forming a flood plain, first on one side, then on the other, and then on both.

"The meandering stage again," the geologist reminded us.

Here grew plants that could utilize the summer for growing after the spring freshets subsided—nettle, smartweed, giant ragweed.

By the time the stream entered Sugar Creek, it was moving placidly and creating flood plains on both sides. Along these flood plains, smartweed and ragweed occupied the wettest parts, those most recently deposited along the river's edge. The areas that were a little older, a little drier, a little farther back from the stream bed, had as their first woody plant the sand-bar willow, which formed a shrubby thicket. Where the willows had prepared the way and the ground had better aeration, the sycamores came in; and after that, the cottonwoods and silver maples.

Black maple came next, together with a rich undergrowth, containing jewelweed and Jack-in-the-pulpit.

No longer was the vegetation abruptly divided into different types of communities by canyon walls. Instead, the tumbled slopes of material that had once been canyon walls graded imperceptibly into the margins of the flood-plain, while the upland forest spilled slowly down the slopes to grade into the flood-plain forest.

Following the black maple came walnuts, with spice-bush, grape fern, and some leatherwood.

Where shade was deepening we found a few young sugar maples and, finally, a scattering of beech seedlings.

The circle was very nearly completed. We were almost back in a beech-maple forest. We had followed the stream from its small beginning under beeches, through its vigorous canyon-forming youth,

CANYON DISSECTING A BEECH-MAPLE UPLAND FOREST COMMUNITY

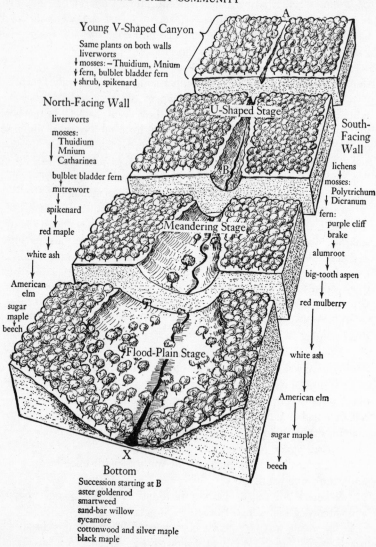

Young V-Shaped Canyon

Same plants on both walls
liverworts
↓ mosses:—Thuidium, Mnium
↓ fern, bulblet bladder fern
↓ shrub, spikenard

North-Facing Wall

liverworts

mosses:
  Thuidium
  ↓ Mnium
  Catharinea

bulblet bladder fern
↓ mitrewort

spikenard
↓
red maple
↓
white ash
↓
American elm
↓
sugar maple
beech

A

U-Shaped Stage

B

Meandering Stage

Flood-Plain Stage

X

South-Facing Wall

lichens
↓
mosses:
  Polytrichum
  ↓ Dicranum

fern:
  purple cliff brake
↓
alumroot
↓
big-tooth aspen
↓
red mulberry
↓
white ash
↓
American elm
↓
sugar maple
↓
beech

Bottom

Succession starting at **B**
aster goldenrod
smartweed
sand-bar willow
sycamore
cottonwood and silver maple
black maple

to its slow-moving old age with the beech-maple forest trickling down around it. The childhood and old age of a stream, like the childhood and old age of a human being, seem to have much in common.

Canyon—Revisited

Unfortunately, the birthplace of the canyon, where we had started tracing the canyon's story some twenty years earlier, was impossible to find when we came back on a grim November day. Had we foreseen that we should be coming back, we could have recorded the spot on a line between enduring trees. Then we could have measured just how far the young canyon had bitten back into the upland, and just how deeply it had bitten downward, in the twenty-year span. We contented ourselves with kicking through fallen leaves, and with stroking old barks, and rejoiced that there were no signs evident of concentrated wear by crowds of people.

Such wear could have been expected, because Turkey Run State Park is a popular place for conventions, reunions, retreats, and especially for accommodation for attendance at the Covered Bridge Festival. The park is in the "Covered Bridge County of the U.S.A.," according to a map provided to all comers. The map shows marked routes to the bridges, and is followed, during the festival, by a steady line of cars, stopping often for displays of handicrafts, foods, costumes. Most of the covered-bridge enthusiasts find little time left over for exploring far into the canyons, or the upland woods. The park headquarters no longer provides a staff naturalist.

The covered bridge within the boundaries of the park has had its work taken over by a stout concrete bridge crossing the canyon of Sugar Creek beside it. A footpath now crosses on the old (1882) bridge. We walked across, looking out of the open sides down into the canyon; we stopped there awhile, imagining that we had come by surrey, and had halted our horse there during a storm, as horses were wont to be halted, and were listening to rain on the roof, and watching the rain make circles in the creek, and perhaps having a bit of gossip with a neighbor who had pulled in his surrey behind us.

As we looked down into the canyon we rejoiced that the Indiana Department of Conservation, in 1963, had opposed any flooding of these state properties. Especially we rejoiced for the failure of the proposal of the Army Engineers Corps, which would have created a reservoir on Sugar Creek up to 655 feet deep and extending from Turkey Run State Park to The Shades State Park.

BIBLIOGRAPHICAL NOTES

"Factors Favoring the Persistence of a Relic Association of Eastern Hemlock in Indiana" by Rexford F. Daubenmire. *Butler University Botanical Studies* 2 (August, 1931), 29–32.

"Studies in Forest Ecology: I, Factors Concerned in Hemlock Reproduction in Indiana" by Ray C. Friesner and John E. Potzger. *Butler University Botanical Studies* 2 (November, 1932), 133–143.

"The Relation of Certain Ecological Factors to the Inhibition of Forest Floor Herbs Under Hemlock" by Rexford F. Daubenmire. *Butler University Botanical Studies* 1 (January, 1930), 61–76.

"A Study in Soil Moisture, Acidity, and Evaporation, in an Upland Woods at Turkey Run State Park" by Mary Fritsche Cundiff. *Butler University Botanical Studies* 9 (May, 1949), 108–123.

"The Mechanical Action of Crustaceous Lichens on Substrate of Shale, Schist, Gneiss, Limestone, and Obsidian" by E. J. Fry. *Annals of Botany* 41 (1927), 437–460.

"The Ecological Succession of Mosses, as Illustrated upon Isle Royale, Lake Superior" by W. S. Cooper. *Plant World* 15 (1912), 197–213.

The Deciduous Forest of Eastern North America by E. Lucy Braun. Discussion of Turkey Run State Park, 310–311. Blakiston, Philadelphia, 1950.

"Starved Rock State Park" by C. O. Sauer, G. H. Cady and H. C. Cowles. *Bulletin of the Geographic Society of Chicago* 6 (1918).

"Natural Areas in Indiana and Their Preservation" by A. A. Lindsey, D. V. Schmelz, and S. A. Nichols. *Indiana Natural Areas Survey*, Dept. of Biological Sciences, Purdue University, 1969.

4

Picnic in a Gritty Wind

OR

THE SAND DUNES OF INDIANA

A SURE way to insight into the life of the Indiana dunes is to attempt to eat lunch there, on the beach, on a windy day in late October.

One has to give up, of course.

We had to give up one October day. And as we worked our way inland, across the dunes, in unhurried search for a more static, restful luncheon spot, we found ourselves reading the story of the dunes in a particularly intimate fashion—identifying ourselves with them, so to speak.

The facts and theories that forty years of intermittent botanizing in the dunes have taught me seemed, on that one day in the gritty wind, to become transmuted into reality.

Probably, in the "old days" when we waded at the edge of the lake, under Doctor Elliot Downing's direction, scooping up nets full of tiny creatures for examination, we were too soggy to have any empathy with a dune. Our viewpoint at that period might have been the viewpoint of a crayfish or a clam. Later, on the many trips when with eager ears cocked forward we followed in the quick footsteps of Doctor Cowles, we were still much too young and vigorous, and too enchanted with the new field of ecology, to care about sun or wind, or sand between our teeth. Our viewpoint was that of pioneer plants, such as marram grass and wormwood and tough cottonwoods. And, some years later, when we meandered in the incandescent wake of Jens Jensen, Danish landscape man, and of Harriet Monroe of *Poetry Magazine*, our heads were too high in the clouds for us to be conscious of the assault of quartz grains. Our viewpoint then was akin to that of gulls and wheeling terns. And on a recent December a field trip through the dunes under the leadership of E. L. Palmer of Cornell and Edwin Way Teale, naturalist and author, our minds were too busy for our bodies to notice much. Our viewpoint here might be likened to that of inquisitive and acquisitive crows.

But when we came to the dunes on an October sketching trip, and wanted, before we started painting, to eat lunch, we were enough older to want peaceful shelter, and earthy enough to want our food without quartz sand. Our viewpoint had become that of the shaded and sheltered maidenhair fern, or of white trillium. Then the story of the dunes, reading from the shore of Lake Michigan inward, became revealed to us as the story of gradual preparation for maidenhair fern— and for elderly, hungry botanists.

As we started off eastward from Waverley Beach, where we had left our car, we walked on the hard wet sand at the water's edge. Out under the water we could just see the first sand bar, and we could remember the succession of sand bars that lay beyond, from the many summers when we had gone swimming from that beach.

Those sand bars were part of the material that Lake Michigan had gnawed off of its western shore, and was dumping there. That sand was destined to become dunes after the water handed it over to the wind to carry still further.

Back beyond the wet beach, where it was dry underfoot, we saw the sand-bar shape repeated in the ripples in the sand—but modeled there by wind instead of water.

That shape—the long gentle slope on the windward side and the abrupt slope on the leeward side—was to become very familiar to our feet before we could eat lunch in a cool sheltered peace.

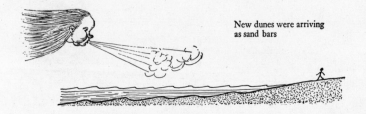

New dunes were arriving
as sand bars

There was a battered Monarch butterfly in the lee of one ripple.
But we needed more of a shield than that ripple.

A more generous bit of shelter lay ahead of us.

A great beam had been rolled in by the waves—part of a boat,
perhaps. In the shelter of its leeward side a mound of sand had accumulated. In that improbable situation two little plants were growing, both the same kind, a tough little annual called sea rocket, *Cakile
americana*. It had to be an annual to survive on this part of the beach,
which, though dry in the summer, is washed by winter waves. It had
exactly the qualities that might be expected of a plant able to survive
sun and wind and moving sand. It was dwarf, distorted, gray-green. I
tasted it, and found the bitter, horse-radish pungency that belongs to
so many plants of sun-beaten places. The whole plant had the fleshy
smoothness that tells of water storage. We pulled up one of the plants,
and revealed roots that were surpringly long and bushy and moist.

The roots made us realize that the sea rocket had probably not really required the windbreak formed by the beam, or had needed it
only during the first few days of its life.

But we needed more shelter than that, our entire expanse being
above ground.

We moved on across the beach, toward a mound that would have
caught the eye of any sketcher, however hungry.

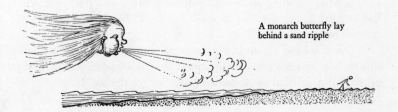

A monarch butterfly lay
behind a sand ripple

Two pioneer plants grew
behind a wooden beam

The gentle rise was topped and held by a photogenic tuft of mar-ram grass (*Ammophila breviligulata*), that was pencilling arcs in the sand that it itself had accumulated.

Here was the real pioneer of the dunes. The sea rocket's display of hardihood is ever destined to be wiped out at summer's end, but marram grass can perennially spread underground, enlarging its clump, catching and holding sand in its intricate network, and grow-ing ever higher up through the mound of sand that it accumulates, until it forms a small dune. In fact, both this pioneer and its close rel-ative of English dunes, *Ammophila arenaria*, show a decline in vigor when the sand surface is stabilized.

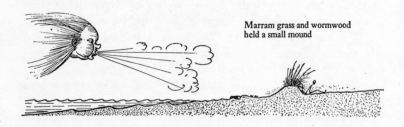

Marram grass and wormwood
held a small mound

"Enough shelter for lunch?" we wondered, and tried sitting on the leeward side of the long mound. We could hear sand grains being stopped by the grasses. But they were not all stopped, so we moved on.

Before we left we noticed something else that had benefited from this shelter. It was a gray-green mound of wormwood (*Artemisia cana-densis*). We nibbled at its famed bitterness, and thought of its sun-baked western relative, the sage-brush.

These two dune pioneers, marram grass and wormwood, both have greatly extended and much-branched root systems, out of proportion to their tops.

We moved inland toward a higher mound.

It looked as if this mound might have been started by marram grass. It was easy to imagine that the wind might have deposited a seed of sand-dune willow on the leeward side of the marram-grass mound, and a bird might have brought a seed of sand cherry. At any rate, there was a thriving clump of sand-dune willow (*Salix syrticola*) and a smaller one of sand cherry (*Prunus pumila*). The thick small leaves of the willow were eloquently different from the leaves of willows found in our river bottoms.

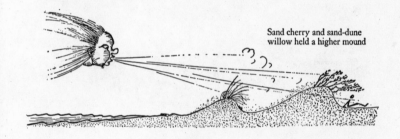

Sand cherry and sand-dune willow held a higher mound

The willow-cherry dune was high enough but hardly long enough to give shelter to the five of us. The gritty wind came around the ends and found us.

Then we came across a strange thing in the level sand—two parallel rows of cottonwood seedlings. Evidently a wagon or a jeep had left ruts there, ruts that had cut down into the moist water table. Cottonwood seeds must have lodged in those ruts and prospered in their shelter and moisture, while other seeds landing on the open sand failed to make a start.

Those moist ruts were serving as miniature "pannes." Panne is the name ecologists give to an area from which the sand has been blown out right down to the saturated sand of the water table. This wet sand does not blow away. It forms an important stage in the stabilizing of the dunes by vegetation.

Many plants germinate and get a good start in such pannes. But most of the plants are doomed. The sand inevitably fills in around them and chokes them out, *unless they can make adventitious roots*.

Cottonwoods *can* make adventitious roots. They can grow right up with the growing dune, because they can make new roots at consecutively higher levels as the sand builds up around their trunks. The cottonwoods that appear to be perched on top of a high dune actually have their original roots far below in a moist panne. Sometimes the whole story is revealed when a dune moves off and leaves a long-necked cottonwood behind.

We looked again at the little rows of cottonwoods at our feet, realizing that they might one day be the backbone of a tall dune, and hikers might walk up there among their tops and wonder why these trees grow in rows.

Cottonwood seeds
had found
wagon ruts

In fact, the cottonwoods at the top of the dune that lay just ahead of us looked suspiciously like the tops of buried trees. Perhaps they came from seeds that had started in ruts, or in footprints, perhaps in the print of a moccasin.

It was loose bare sand that we climbed through to reach the cottonwoods.

And they in turn were surrounded by loose, bare, and blowing sand. The lakeward side of their trunks was sandblasted to a high polish. We could watch the sand grains tumbling over the crest.

Plainly this first cottonwood dune was a moving dune, and the cottonwoods' hold was a temporary one only.

On the steep leeward slope and in the hollow at its base were a few pale herbs. There was bugseed, *Corispermum hyssopifolium,* a tough little annual like the sea rocket of the beach, with the rather plump narrow leaves and the pale-green color that seems to belong to

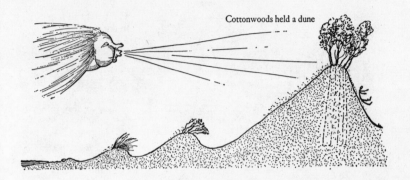

Cottonwoods held a dune

sand pioneers. And there was a sparse colony of false Solomon's-seal, *Smilacina stellata*.

Here certainly was a height adequate to shelter us from the wind, but the leeward slope was too hot. We did not want to sit facing the sun. And the slope was too steep. We tended to slide like the sand grains.

So we sat down on a hump that had been built by sand collected by a clump of sand-reed grass, *Calamovilfa longifolia*, and emptied our shoes—a futile operation.

How dry it looked there at our feet, among those widely spaced plants! But when we kicked away the pale shifting sand of the surface, we uncovered wet-looking sand of deeper color. It felt moist and cool. Plainly the surface sand is stirred into an efficient dust mulch, as topsoil might be stirred by a farmer to hold the water beneath it.

Plants on a moving dune can drink deeply. The trouble is that wind and sun may drink faster from the leaves than roots can drink from the moisture in the sand. No wonder some of the leaves present a narrow vertical surface to the sun, a surface plump with water storage.

The next slope filled our shoes again, fast. It was bare and high. The sand went up and over faster than we did.

The ridge above us was ribbed with battered cottonwoods and lindens, sandblasted and sparse. We were glad to notice a dip in the top of the ridge.

As we headed toward this break, we could see a new darker green ahead. Then we realized that the break that was saving us a few steps

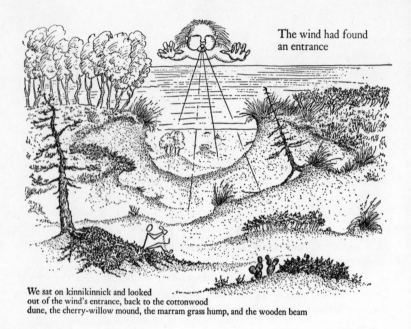

The wind had found
an entrance

We sat on kinnikinnick and looked
out of the wind's entrance, back to the cottonwood
dune, the cherry-willow mound, the marram grass hump, and the wooden beam

and puffs was costing the vegetation, on the other side of the ridge, dearly.

This was plainly a "leak in the dike," where the wind had worked in one finger, then a whole hand, and now was using all its hands and feet and teeth.

We puffed up over the top, between a linden with a great saucer of common juniper at its feet, and a clump of sand cherry with a tuft of sand-reed grass at its feet.

Ahead of us lay a great bowl, holding many small mounds within its rim. The coloring was dramatic in comparison with the mousiness of the lakeward side of the ridge. Reds and oranges marked poison ivy and aromatic sumac, and the berries of kinnikinnick and bittersweet. Their brilliance was heightened by the stern deep green of evergreens.

We had come too late over the ridge. We could have eaten lunch there in great comfort, seated on an evergreen ground cover, in evergreen shade, sheltered from the wind by a ridge held static by evergreens, if we had come earlier—a year, or two or three years, earlier.

If the evergreens had been granted just a little longer respite, before the wind got its foot into a crack of the door, and *if* the cottonwood dune on the lakeward side had been given time to grow a little higher, and *if* that cottonwood dune had been sheltered by a younger cottonwood dune, perhaps accumulated by that row of seedlings in the wagon track, then this hollow might have become serenely clothed with a well-established forest.

As to the composition of that forest we can only speculate, on the basis of developments in other similar situations in the dunes. Certainly those developments have not always been the same.

Probably black oaks would have appeared among the evergreens. Their shade would gradually have eliminated evergreen seedlings. Under the black oaks would probably have been blueberries. This partnership, especially in the event of occasional fires, might have held the situation indefinitely. But, on the other hand, given surcease of fire, and good protection to windward, the black oak might have been replaced gradually by a forest of white oak, red oak, and ironwood, with sugar maples sprouting in its deepening shade.

But the "ifs" did not happen in time, and the wind *did* get its foot in the door. The vegetation was losing ground, actually losing ground. Common juniper was holding mounds of sand with its roots; but we could see where the wind was prying its fingers in under a jack pine. It would topple soon.

The others are doomed too—the few white pines, the carpets of kinnikinnick, and the scattered black oaks. As they go down, one by one, this will become another great dune blowout. Then winter will bring skiers who will appreciate the lack of obstruction; and summer will bring flower-arrangers who will appreciate the attenuated sand-blasted root-tips clawing the blue sky, and will sigh over the possibilities for their picture windows.

Perhaps in time this blowout, like others in the dunes, will reveal remains out of the past. Some have revealed ancient pine forests buried long, long ago, perhaps on the beach of Lake Chicago. Others have revealed "kitchen middens" with their brittle baked and blackened stones. And, recently, there has been an interesting unearthing of mammal bones.

Jawbones and teeth made identification possible, not only of common mammals like rabbits, white-footed mice, and muskrats, but also of mammals long since gone from the dunes.

Of these earlier residents were found bones of white-tailed deer, elk, fisher, and bear. The bear remnant was "an incomplete skull with one complete maxillary tooth row and one incomplete one. From the amount of wear on the teeth it represents a young adult. Though considerably perished, the bone has little brown stain on it. It seems probable this material is more than 100 years old. It was found under a fallen dead tree of a forest that had been smothered by an advancing line of dune and is now nearly uncovered. The skull parts were recovered on two different trips, but fit together, indicating but one animal was involved."

On a collecting trip to one blowout in the Dunes State Park, in 1951, it is reported that four people searching for two hours found jaws and teeth of one mole, one chipmunk, one fox squirrel, four white-footed mice, two meadow mice, one muskrat, one porcupine, one cottontail, three or four Virginia, or white-tailed, deer.

But our blowout was not yet ready to reveal the past. The evergreens were still holding their own fairly well. And this was one of their most buffeted days. That was why we decided not to eat lunch there, but only to empty our shoes again.

But we were careful about choosing a place to sit, because there was cactus in the blowout. It seemed to be on south-facing sides of the mounds. So we chose a north-facing side, and sat on kinnikinnick at the base of a jack pine.

Where else in America could one sit amid dark green that is wont to hobnob with ptarmigan and Eskimo and midnight sun, and look down upon the pale green that is the familiar of horned toads and Joshua trees and Navajos?

But the unlike appearances of these two plants speak of problems that are surprisingly alike. The jack pine in its arctic homeland has to survive the thirsty winter sun. The cactus, in its desert homeland, has to survive the thirsty summer sun. There is plenty of water around the roots of the northern jack pine, but water is not available when it is frozen. The cactus does not have water available either. One faces a physiological drought, the other faces a physical one.

The jack pine endures the winter drought of the far north because of all pines it has the best adapted leaf. The cuticle is so thick that it forms half the bulk of the leaf; there are strong protective palisade cells inside, and the stomata openings are sunk into the lower surface.

The cactus has leaves that are altered much more drastically than those of the jack pine. In fact, the leaves are hardly noticeable on the fleshy gray-green stem.

It is not surprising that these two strangers can both endure the drying wind and sun of the dunes. The surprising thing is that they should be in the dunes at all.

For the presence of the cactus, there is a choice of two explanations. It is one of a group of plants from the southwest that is found in the dunes, and along many sandy areas and dry, rocky ledges, between the dunes and the southwestern desert. The areas the plants inhabit are not too far apart for a normal migration by way of wind and birds; but, on the other hand, they may represent groups of plants left behind at the close of the "xerothermic," or hot-dry period, that followed the glacial period.

The jack pines of the dunes represent the most southerly extension of that species. Not only is it the most southerly, but the colony in the dunes is an *island* of jack pines, separated by more than a hundred miles from the nearest outpost to the north. A disjunct community, such a situation is called.

This colony is a "relict" of the last glacial invasion. The evergreens that moved south before the oncoming glacier crept north again as the glacier retreated. The deciduous forest crowded them out of places that were fit for deciduous trees, and might, possibly, have already superseded them here had not the persistence of pines been favored by occasional fires and other disturbances.

The only places in the Midwest that the evergreens could hold on to, in the face of the northward march of the deciduous trees, were the difficult places, such as the edges of canyons (illustrated in Chapter 3, the "Canyon Story"), the edges of acid bogs (Chapter 5, "History Book with Flexible Cover") and the shifting sands of the dunes.

We reread the story

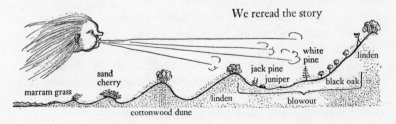

We got up from our rest among the evergreens, and started across the blowout.

I paused to squeeze a leaf of the aromatic sumac to enjoy its pungency. The leaves in the dunes were broader, I noticed, and not so thick-feeling as the leaves on the stunted specimen of aromatic sumac that I had been surprised to find once growing at my feet, far from any other plant, on a sterile gray expanse in the Badlands.

The dunes are certainly a good place for travelers to visit, to revive old friendships with plants met in diverse and distant places.

We continued across the restlessness and threat of the blowout, and climbed the next ridge. It was higher than any ridge we had climbed, and we could look back and reread the chapters up to this point.

At our feet lay the long blowout. Beyond it, we could see the gap where the wind had entered. And through the gap, we could see the cottonwood dune, then the sand-cherry dune, then the marram grass mound, and (with the aid of bird glasses) the beam that the lake had rolled ashore.

Then we turned our backs on the lake, and looked steeply down the leeward slope. We continued to look, for a long time. It rested our eyes.

Beneath us lay a peaceful deep hollow filled with familiar woodland. We had turned our backs on pioneers and relicts and invaders from the arid southwest. We had turned our backs on reduced leaf surfaces and aromatic oils and succulent leaves; also on milky juices and thick skins and leathery surfaces; and on pubescence, and other characteristics of plants that endure gritty wind and unrelenting sun.

We had turned our backs on the xerophytes, the dry-land plants, because we had found shelter from wind and sun.

We slid down among the mesophytes, the plants occupying the middle ground between dry and wet.

Here were lindens and sugar maples, bitternut hickory and red oak and ash. Underneath them were ironwood and shadbush and witch-hazel in bloom.

Underneath the ironwood and shadbush and witch-hazel were great patches of running euonymus and bellwort and Christmas fern.

Here was peace, and a look of stability and permanence. Certainly the gritty wind did not find its way into this hollow.

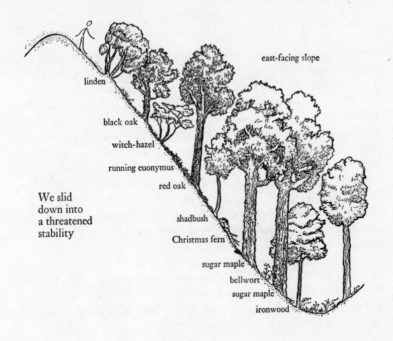

east-facing slope

linden

black oak

witch-hazel

running euonymus

red oak

We slid
down into
a threatened
stability

shadbush

Christmas fern

sugar maple

bellwort

sugar maple

ironwood

But the peace was doomed. As we stood at the foot of the slope that we had slid down, and looked back up to the top, we could see a thin mist of sand. A little sand was plainly beginning to tumble down that slope. The wind that had come in through a keyhole, and was playing havoc with the evergreen slope, had gained strength in its rush across the new blowout, and was beginning to move the dune that marked the end of the blowout.

Sugar maples, ironwoods, Christmas ferns, for all their look of peace, were marked for an enfolding doom. But some day they may be uncovered again, gaunt skeletons with writhing, sandblasted roots up-turned.

But we knew a bank where ebony spleenwort and partridgeberry grew under great old white pines, beside a dark-brown creek. It was not far away. So we kept going, all nibbling hungrily at the twigs of the sassafras thicket we passed in a cut-over section.

We were soon crossing areas dominated by black oak above and blueberry below. According to a recent study, these are old dunes. It was long ago that they saw the waters of the lake, so long ago (according to the records of lime leaching downward through the sand) that some of them were dunes along the margin of an ancient lake of the glacial period. A specimen collected from dunes at Dolton, Illinois, was radiocarbon-dated by Willard F. Libby as having died 3,496 (plus or minus 230) years ago.

Such well-established black oak and blueberry stands on old dunes may be a record of the xerothermic period, which would have favored their development. Once established, this partnership often forms a sort of "closed shop," acid, exclusive, holding land for a long time in its grip.

In some places the wind held sway again, and was prying out established stands of plants. We saw a black oak that was plainly being dispossessed, even though it was far inland.

We skirted swamps fringed with sour gum, and rounded the end of a moving dune. Our feet seemed to remember the way to Little Fort Creek, and before long we were on the path that runs along and above the deep-brown creek, and at the base of a north-facing and sheltered slope.

A black oak was
being dispossessed

Flowering dogwood spread its flat branches there. A few tulip trees grew nearby, and a few small beech trees. The beech trees were important. They were the western outposts of the eastern beech forests. Just so far they advance toward the prairie peninsula, and no farther.

Finally we came to a place where the steep slope beside the path was rich with the shining leaves and red fruit of partridgeberry and wintergreen. We found the patterned leaves of rattlesnake plantain, and patches of trailing arbutus. Great white pines curved up along the creek side of the path. All these plants represented a rich collection of relicts from the glacial period.

Then we found the delicate little ebony spleenwort, and a big clump of maidenhair fern. There would have been masses of white trillium, if it had been spring.

It was the maidenhair fern that marked the end of the story that we had been reading. When we saw that, we knew that we had come as far from the conditions of the windy beach as it was possible to be, in the dunes.

We ate our lunch, seated in welcome shade, on pine needles. It tasted good, and no sand blew into it.

Here, finally, was a stabilized part of the dunes. Actually, we were well aware that a more stabilized part, where the cold spring and the mallows once had been, lay about 200 feet away—encased in concrete. This section of the dunes was now part of the Dunes State Park, and acres of parking space for the cars of swimmers, ball players, and picnickers had become necessary. I was careful not to catch a glimpse of that ominous stabilization lest it spoil my appetite. I could remember dunes on the north side of Chicago, dunes where our family would put up a tent on a summer day, under scrubby trees, in preparation for a day on the wild beach. (Botanizing today among childhood memories, I should identify the trees as black oaks.) There was an imposing high dune that I remember as a tragic site because my sister broke the handle of her ruffled pink silk parasol there as she used it to slow a headlong slide. (From this distance I should identify that as a moving dune.) The Edgewater Beach Hotel, many tall apartment buildings, acres of cement walks and highways now fill that flattened surface, and even the edge of the lake has been engineered far away to make a place for a newer highway.

We knew that what remained of our quiet path had not changed noticeably, except to widen a bit with use, in forty years. But we could see evidence that it could not remain stable much longer unless human erosion of the crest of the dune above the path were immediately halted.

After lunch we separated, to sketch all afternoon. Each one, turning away from shelter and security, followed the beaten path of the arts to subjects that evidenced insecurity, conflict, change, tension. One went back to the dispossessed black oak, another climbed high and wove a pattern of advancing waves of water and sand; another sought out exhumed sandblasted roots; another found a partly undermined shack, standing askew, but with diapers on the clothesline; another painted a bare sand wall poised high over living green.

No one drew the wind. But each redrew some selected detail from the masterpiece that the wind had drawn—and was still drawing.

Sand Dunes—Revisited

On the first weekend of June, 1973, I went back to the dunes to see how they had changed (or not changed) during the seventeen years since our "Picnic in a Gritty Wind." As my guide I had George Svihla of the Save the Dunes Council, who had been living in the dunes during the last twenty-five years, and watching and photographing the changes.

The super-highwayed brevity of the trip from Chicago, and across the dunes, from black oak–blueberry ancient ridges to newborn marram grass foredunes, was itself a clue to the extent of a major change—the spread of three residential developments: Ogden Dunes, Dune Acres, and Beverly Shores.

Most developed of the three is Ogden Dunes. Its development has followed a succession as definite as the one that Henry C. Cowles found in the dunes in 1899.

People came, at first, to live there *because* of the dunes; and came to terms with them, shaping their roads and homes to fit the contours. They respected the natives, especially the grasses, sand cherry, and cottonwoods, if they lived near the beach; and the jack pines, white pines, oaks, dogwood, shadbush, and maidenhair fern, if they lived further from the beach. Feet and houses were at home with sand.

As roads grew harder (they were just sand at first) and wider and faster, people began to come because this was reputed to be a good place to live, offering swimming at a private beach, and coasting and skiing in blowouts and slopes. Some came *in spite* of the dunes with their restless blowing sand. The acreage of pavement and lawn was expanded. Jack pines with their nonconformist gestures were replaced by imports from other places: Colorado spruce, Norway spruce, Austrian pine, Japanese yew, Russian olive, Siberian crabapple, Nanking cherry, French lilac.

Gradually there came residents who were less and less interested in preserving the natural aspects of the dunes, and more and more interested in getting help with their taxes, even if that help was dependent on replacing neighboring dunes with steel mills. In some places the wind-shaped curves of the dunes were reshaped by bulldozers, and held firm and static by high concrete retaining walls, stepping up the slope, with clipped Japanese yews topping each step.

We looked into gardens with strawberries and lettuce, asparagus, raspberry bushes, grapevines, and vegetables; and were shown native treasures, rescued from the advance of drooling bulldozers, and given their appropriate microclimates: yellow lady's slippers, and pink ones, bloodroot, wintergreen, downy gentian, and cactus. On some slopes, the common locust tree, introduced to stabilize the sand, has thrived and spread.

Along the curving roads, drifts of lupine and puccoon made their remembered harmonies, and sassafras buds tasted as they always had.

Then we curved out past the watchful eyes at the gatehouse, and turned east past an area where I remembered ranks of dunes taut under the tension between wind and sand, and sun and shade. Those dunes had been obliterated. I had seen their sand being brought by barges up to Evanston, and being used to extend the Northwestern University campus into Lake Michigan. Further sand-mining and bulldozing had flattened the area; and pavement, and tracks, and buildings had encased it in drawing-board rigidity, to serve the operations of the Bethlehem Steel Company and the Midwest Steel Company.

The encased area is about three miles long on the lake shore, and two miles wide. (Midwest Steel has left an area as yet not encased, but it is starting to lease parts to other industrial companies.)

This industrialized area is not unappreciated. Night motorists appreciate the display of lights, breaking the monotony of the dark dunes. Bank accounts from Florida to California to Switzerland grow fat on the steel mills that have replaced sand dunes along many miles of Lake Michigan shore. Local residents appreciate the jobs that are available, and the contribution to taxes.

From watching how realtors and industry were stabilizing the dunes, we went next to observe the unstabilizing effects of another force. Lake Michigan herself is attacking. Nineteen seventy-three was a time of phenomenal flooding and high water and winter storms; the lake is taking back what it had brought over a long period.

George Svihla showed me a section of lakeshore near his home, where he had watched a wide foredune develop. It started as the unusually high waters of 1952 receded. Wind swept the sand across the widened beach, and the marram grass held it, and mounted steadily through the increasing depth by putting out shoots at a higher and higher level. Finally marram grass covered the entire wide foredune, as far as a row of cottonwoods which marked the furthest extent of the last (1952) invasion by the lake.

Now the lake is slicing off the front of the foredune, making an abrupt straight cliff. The eight-foot high perpendicular face shows the layers of old marram-grass shoots. Evidently the water is higher this time. A few of the marker cottonwoods are starting to topple.

On that section of the shore, the incursion of the lake was only an interesting example of nature's inevitable rhythms. At other points it was drastic and tragic. In Beverly Shores, beachfront houses had been toppled or severely undermined. The main road had been damaged; septic tanks flooded. No beach remained, only a slipping sand cliff. Some residents are attributing the misfortunes to the long jetties extended out into the lake at the steel mill area to form the new harbor called The Port of Indiana. In *Frail Ocean*, Wesley Marx, writing about a breakwater at Santa Barbara, says,

> Below the breakwater the shore receded as much as 245 feet. Ten miles downstream a row of houses slumped into the sea.

In the *Smithsonian* of June, 1973, Gary Soucie says,

> When man, like King Canute, attempts to referee the game between waves and sand, the waves usually win and beaches vanish.

During the years in which the dunes have been destroyed by some forces, they have been given a possible future by others. In 1922 the Indiana Dunes State Park was established, including within its

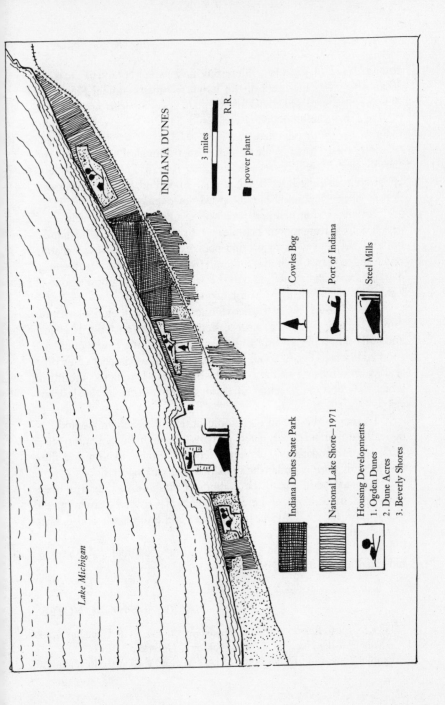

Lake Michigan

INDIANA DUNES

3 miles

R.R.

■ power plant

Cowles Bog

Port of Indiana

Steel Mills

Indiana Dunes State Park

National Lake Shore—1971

Housing Developments
1. Ogden Dunes
2. Dune Acres
3. Beverly Shores

domain some of the most interesting and varied botanical areas. In 1966, after 50 years of effort, the Indiana Dunes National Shorelines Act was finally passed. The master plan, together with amendments proposed by Representative Roush and Senator Hartke of Indiana, includes the following changes.

The three "islands" of homes, Ogden Dunes, Dune Acres, and Beverly Shores, will be reduced in area. Beverly Shores will perhaps be entirely acquired by the National Shoreline. It has the lowest density of development. The other two towns may follow in time.

An area of the national park west of Ogden Dunes is to be converted into a recreational complex, with abundant space "to handle 2,196 cars," and with swimming pools, two beach houses, a skating pond and a warming house, interpretive center, picnic areas, group day-use areas, and a pavilion. All this will be edged by a buffer zone of natural duneland, with paths for hiking.

Immediately east of Ogden Dunes there is a stretch of natural dunes, showing the stages of succession. It includes an active blowout, and good stands of oaks and white pine and Jack pine, and would be a good addition to the national lakeshore, both as a compact study area and as an extension of the beach to the Burns Ditch, the mouth of which has become a center of coho salmon fishing in the last few years.

To reduce the pressure on some of the more vulnerable and botanically important areas, such as parts of the Indiana Dunes State Park, recommendations include the fencing of these, with access limited to study groups under the guidance of a park naturalist.

Proposed additions to the National Lakeshore include: the open water and marshlands of Long Lake east of Gary, an easement for water travel on the Little Calumet River and Salt Creek, and further acquisition of old glacial lake dunes.

Only the land already included in the National Lakeshore is indicated on the map on page 71.

BIBLIOGRAPHICAL NOTES

"The Ecological Relations of the Vegetation on the Sand Dunes of Lake Michigan" by Henry C. Cowles. *Botanical Gazette* **27** (1899).
"Mammal Bones from Dunes South of Lake Michigan" by A. L. Reed and A.

Stanley Reed. *The American Midland Naturalist* **46** (November, 1951), 649–659.

"The Ecology of the Spiders of Xeric Dunelands in the Chicago Area" by Donald C. Lowrie. *Bulletin of Chicago Academy of Sciences* **6** (March 16, 1942), 161–189.

A *Naturalist in the Great Lakes Region* by Elliot Rowland Downing. University of Chicago Press, Chicago, 1922.

Downs and Dunes, Their Plant Life and Its Environment by Edward Salisbury. G. A. Bell and Sons, Ltd., London, 1952.

"The Disappearing Sleeping Bear Dune" by Frank C. Gates. *Ecology* **31** (July, 1950), 386–392.

"Vegetation Substrate Relations in Lake Michigan Dune Development" by Jerry Olson. Doctorate thesis (unpublished), University of Chicago, 1953.

"Rates of Soil Changes on Southern Lake Michigan Sand Dunes" by J. S. Olson. *Botanical Gazette* **119** (1958).

"Where Beaches Have Been Going into the Ocean" by Gary Soucie. *Smithsonian* **4** (June, 1973).

"Indiana Dunes State Park" in *Natural Areas in Indiana and Their Preservation* by D. V. Schmelz, A. A. Lindsey, and S. A. Nichols. Indiana Natural Areas Survey, Purdue University, Lafayette, Indiana, 1969.

"A Master Plan for Indiana Dunes National Lakeshore" National Park Service, Dept. of Interior, Washington, October, 1967.

5
History Book with Flexible Cover

OR

THE RECORDS IN A QUAKING BOG

"You're walking on a history book," said the professor. "It happens, you may notice, to have a flexible cover."

"And to be extremely absorbing," added the undergraduate, using both hands to pull his other foot out of the ooze.

That was my introduction to the Mineral Springs bog—to any bog.

A member of the class broke through the flexible cover that day, up to her waist, and had to lie down on the sphagnum moss and cranberries before we could pry her out. She never did retrieve her shoes, but that was because she had, unfortunately, taken the professor seriously, on the day before the field trip, when he answered our question of "What shall we wear?" by saying "Better wear pumps."

On a later ecology field trip to that same bog, one of the male students killed a rattlesnake there.

On a still later trip, my companion, a young nonbotanical advertising man, cut a walking stick and carried it all day; and I thought nothing of it until, the following week, he called me from the hospital where he lay, his eyes swollen shut with poison sumac.

On that first trip to the bog, we all sat for a while on the end of an old black oak sand dune among columbines and bird's-foot violets while some students put on boots against the water or gloves against the poison sumac; and some put on protection against the mosquitoes (it was citronella in those days); some told tales of teams of horses that had disappeared in bogs; and inevitably someone mentioned "The Slough of Despond."

Then we crossed the narrow old corduroy road, which is said to have once carried stagecoaches from Michigan City to Chicago.

We passed the fringe of sour gum trees and took a few steps down, down among the cinnamon ferns—textured acres of them.

Those three or four steps down from the road transported us magically from that bog in northern Indiana to the woods of northern Wisconsin or northern Michigan. The trees around us were yellow birch, white pine, red maple, arborvitae. The shrubs were red-berried elder and winterberry (*Ilex verticillata*). On knolls about the tree roots we looked down upon a rich carpet of goldthread, wintergreen, bunchberry, starflower, Indian cucumber root, partridgeberry.

The two sides of the road seemed to have nothing in common, until we found, on a low branch above the cinnamon ferns, the hummingbird's nest with its two oblong eggs. That structure made a link. It was built of wool from the stipe of the cinnamon fern, and encrusted with lichens from the base of the yellow birch, and some of the food-energy for the building of it had doubtless come from the long nectar sacs of the wild columbine back there on the end of the dune where we had rested.

We swished ahead tenderly through the waist-high ferns to the point where their ranks thinned.

Then we found ourselves having to jump from the hummock at one tamarack's base to the hummock of the next tamarack. In between was black ooze. And in that ooze we found treasure—a clump of showy lady's slipper, *Cypripedium reginae*.

From this spot, the jumps between tamarack roots became longer and longer, and just as we would grab for an outstretched helpful-looking branch, someone would yell, "Look out! Poison sumac."

Between and beyond the poison sumac stretched open sunnier areas. Here we spent a joyful time jumping up and down to see the poison sumac several yards away jumping up and down with us, until the girl with the pumps broke through the surface. After she had been extricated, we still advanced gingerly, step by step, on the unstable mat. We were young and competitive, but we gave up among the cattails.

From the yellow birches to the cattails we had been reading the story of a bog backward.

Now, as we stood, where our eyes could go farther though our feet could not, we began to consider the story of a bog chronologically. This story, from open water to forest, is written over and over again. It is the story of undrained depressions.

Many such undrained depressions are kettle holes in the moraine, places where masses of ice were left behind as the glacier receded. But the Mineral Springs bog lay in a long lagoon of an ancient beach.

Probably this long inland lake started filling with vegetation like any other lake, with submerged plants attached to the bottom near the edge of the lake.

Probably the second stage, too, was like the second stage of other filling lakes—a few waterlilies attached to the bottom and floating their leaves on the surface. These first two stages, however, had long ago disappeared from the Mineral Springs bog. Their existence here could only be assumed because of their presence in other bogs.

It was at the edge of the third stage that we turned back, for lack of footing. Probably this stage had got its start long ago when, somewhere along the margin of the water, some chance surface—a floating lily rhizome, a log, a thin mat of sedges, a bit of debris perhaps—offered an adequate though shallow seed bed for pioneer plants. This group of floating pioneers soon offered a seedbed for others. Each time some root or rhizome or runner or arching branch, rooting at the tip, added a slight bit of substance to this thin mat, there was more support for more roots and rhizomes and arching branches. The mat was

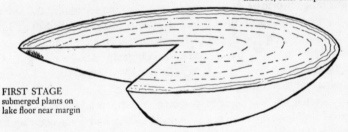

Idealized bog without bays, shallows, other complications.

FIRST STAGE
submerged plants on
lake floor near margin

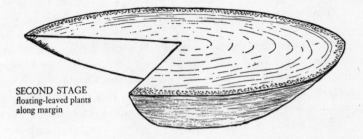

SECOND STAGE
floating-leaved plants
along margin

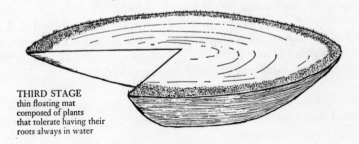

THIRD STAGE
thin floating mat
composed of plants
that tolerate having their
roots always in water

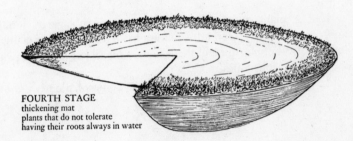

FOURTH STAGE
thickening mat
plants that do not tolerate
having their roots always in water

thickening. Bulrushes rode its wobbly surface, and cattails, and sphagnum moss, and swamp-loosestrife (*Decodon*), with its habit of arching and rooting from the nodes of the stem, and reed (*Phragmites*), and water speedwell (*Veronica anagallis-aquatica*), and water purslane (*Ludwigia palustris*), and forget-me-not (*Myosotis*). We, however, could not ride that fragile surface.

Even if we had been light-footed enough to advance farther, we should not have arrived at open water. That had long been arched over by the bulrush-decodon mat.

As soon as we had turned our backs on this insecurity, our oozing, muck-heavy footgear began to find a firmer foothold, but we felt as if we were treading a soggy spring mattress.

We had entered the fourth stage, often called the sedge, or the fen, stage. No longer were we surrounded entirely by sun-tolerant plants that can grow with their roots ever in water. On this thicker mat there was opportunity for sun-tolerant plants that do not grow with their roots always in water. We lifted our ponderous feet past a variety of plants, including such well-known water-edgers as chairmaker's rush (*Scirpus americanus*), as well as such inhabitants of dry places as aster and goldenrod. In this varied group appeared grass of Parnassus (*Parnassia caroliniana*), white fringed orchid (*Habenaria leucophaea*), grass pink (*Calopogon pulchellus*), blazing star (*Liatris spicata*), Joe-Pye weed (*Eupatorium purpureum*), blue-joint grass (*Calamagrostis canadensis*), and water-hemlock (*Cicuta maculata*). The fern of this fen stage was marsh shield fern (*Dryopteris thelypteris*).

In the fifth stage, where we had our fun jumping up and down to watch nearby shrubbery bobbing in unison, the bog began to develop a distinctive personality.

At that point we noticed that four major changes had appeared on the mat:

1. The plant society changed from an assemblage of familiar plants of a wide and general distribution to an assemblage of plants of a limited distribution, some of them found only in bogs: pitcher plant, poison sumac, sphagnum moss.

2. Shrubs became a part of the mat. Some of them were out-

standing examples of a limited distribution: cranberry, dwarf birch, poison sumac.

3. Something definite seemed to be happening to leaf form and texture. Many low shrubs showed small, thick, leathery, hoary leaves: cranberry, leatherleaf, bog rosemary.

4. Carnivorous plants had arrived, a strange pair of them: pitcher plant (*Sarracenia purpurea*), and sundew (*Drosera rotundifolia*).

Each of these four changes bespoke a changing condition in the bog:

The presence of plants of limited distribution spoke of conditions not generally a part of a plant's living conditions.

The coming in of shrubs spoke of a thickening mat.

The presence of small, thick, leathery, hoary leaves would ordinarily suggest a lack of water, but here they were growing on an oozing mat resting on water. In this instance they indicated that the water, though present, was not readily available, that this situation, while *physically wet* was *physiologically dry*.

The carnivorous plants were long an enigma. It has taken the work of a succession of famous botanists to arrive at our present understanding of the ways of these plants, and of their presence in a bog. If we were to look at the pitcher plant and sundew, as early botanists looked at them, through a gradually clearing fog of mystery, to witness the unfolding of what Emily Dickinson called "truth's superb surprise," we would see a succession of observations and experiments.

The story started long ago, before 1600, when someone made a drawing of the unique pitcher plant. That unexplained drawing traveled to Lisbon and Spain, before 1600, and then to Paris. There the botanist Carolus Clusius published a woodcut of it, in 1601, in his "Rariorum Plantarum Historia." In 1631 this woodcut was copied in Gerard's Herbal in England. Then, in 1640, an actual specimen of the pitcher plant arrived in England, brought home by the botanist, John Tradescant, from America. In 1699 Morison wrote about this enigmatic plant, but he apparently did not inspect it carefully, for he wrote that the lid of the leaf was hinged and movable. At about the same time, Dr. M. S. Sarrazin sent a pressed specimen on a long trip by sailing vessel, from Quebec, to the French botanist, Tournefort. In 1700 Tournefort gave the plant a scientific name. He called it *Sarracenia*, after Doctor Sarrazin. By 1737 the system of Linnaeus was just beginning to gain acceptance. Linnaeus kept the name of *Sarracenia* for this plant, and added the species name of *purpurea*, for the purple coloring. The plant finally had its present scientific name *Sarracenia purpurea*.

But finding a name was easy compared with finding the function of the adaptation of this plant with leaves shaped like pitchers, with red-veined lips and watery contents where dead insects often floated.

In 1743, Mark Catesby, in the Carolinas, had a try at an explanation. He wrote that the pitcher-shaped leaves made a refuge for insects, so that the frogs could not eat them.

In 1791, two good Quaker botanists, William Bartram and Peter Collinson, objected to this interpretation. The insects seemed to be captured by the leaves, they argued, rather than protected. Those two were catching a gleam of light, but the fog of mystery was still thick, evidently, since Bartram added that the water in the leaves was "for the refreshment of the plant."

Presently two physicians, working independently more than fifty years apart, looked hard and long into those baffling pitchers. Doctor James MacBride noticed hairs, on the lip, pointing downward into the tube formed by the leaf; and also a viscid, fly-attracting substance at the mouth of the leaf. This was in 1817. The other physician, J. H. Mellichamp, tried an experiment. He cut some bits of venison, placing part in one of the pitcher-like leaves, and part in a container of distilled water. He observed that the venison broke down faster in the pitcher-plant fluid, and decided that bacteria must be at work in the fluid. He noticed too, that flies did not seem able to escape from the pitcher-plant fluid so easily as from water. He concluded that the fluid had an "anaesthetic action." He noticed one other feature of the leaf, a sort of luring pathway of nectar leading up the outside of the pitcher. The work of Mellichamp blew away considerable fog in 1875.

Working at the same time as Mellichamp, Sir Joseph Hooker studied and made a summary of the findings of previous botanists. (Hooker's summary is the basis for the preceding account of studies of the pitcher plant.) Then he proceeded to inspect the leaf more minutely than anyone else had done. He saw that there were four distinct zones on the leaf, inside the pitcher.

The first zone wore a red color, that same beefy red that seems to mark many flowers that attract flies. Hooker called this the "attractive zone."

Just beneath this zone he saw another one with a surface broken by ridges directing insects downward, with only a little red coloring, and with many glands. This part Hooker called the "conducting zone."

Beneath it was a glassy smooth stretch, with many glands. Hooker called it the "glandular zone."

Beneath the glandular zone, lay zone four, with many long, glassy-smooth hairs, that gave no foothold to an insect. Hooker called this the "detentive zone."

Were this a witches' cauldron tale, instead of the story of an unpremeditating plant, how differently those four zones might be called:

Zone 1   Come into my pretty parlor, my dear.
Zone 2   Right this way, keep moving now, you!
Zone 3   Ha, my proud beauty, in you go!
Zone 4   Bubble, bubble, toil and trouble.

After Hooker, others, notably Francis Lloyd, have helped to brush away the remaining patches of fog.

Lloyd tells that zones one and two are not only attractive, but offer a treacherous foothold, which, together with the glassy surface of zone three, makes the *facilis descensus Averno*. He tells of experiments that showed zone four absorbing materials that zone three completely resisted. He calls zone four the "absorptive zone."

Lloyd recounts his experiment with a blue-bottle fly, and a pitcher plant leaf in a vial of water under a bell jar. The fly followed the nectar path on the outside of the leaf to the rim. Then he began to sip nectar, gradually reaching further and further down, but always hanging on to the lid or the rim with at least one hind foot. But that treacherous surface betrayed him, every time. The reason this fly was privileged to make the trip more than once was that Lloyd had cut a door for his escape, just above the surface of the water. Twelve times that same fly made that same trip.

Other experimenters, Hepburn, Jones, and St. Johns, flushed out the pitchers, emptied them, and then added fresh water. They let this

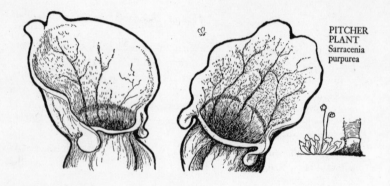

PITCHER
PLANT
Sarracenia
purpurea

stand in the pitchers for several days. Then they poured the liquid out and put fibrin into it. They found that the fluid could certainly digest the fibrin. Then they examined the pitchers for bacteria in their fluid. In open pitchers they found bacteria always present, but working so slowly as to be of little importance in digestion as compared with the fluid itself. These experimenters then added substances that would help them trace the absorption of the digested material. They found that the nitrogenous substances in the fluid were absorbed more rapidly than the water.

While these and many other plant scientists were examining the leaves of the pitcher plant, others were experimenting with the glistening gluey leaves of its small companion, the sundew.

In 1779, Doctor Roth, in Bremen, took an ant in a pair of tweezers, and placed it carefully in the middle of a sundew leaf.

The ant seemed unable to pull away from the gleaming globules at the tips of the hairs. His feet pulled the sticky substance like taffy as

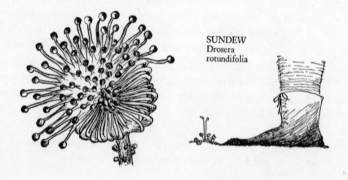

SUNDEW
Drosera
rotundifolia

he struggled. Then the hairs began to bend inward, folding themselves over the ant. He died in fifteen minutes.

In 1852, Milde timed the whole carnivorous operation. He placed small flies on the leaves, and found that the tentacles started bending in five minutes. By the next day the entire leaf was bent around the insect. In five days the leaf was open again.

Later, Darwin and others demonstrated that dead bodies do not provoke so much response as living ones, and inorganic bodies, such as particles of sand, do not stimulate the flow of mucilage, or cause the hairs to move in any way.

Francis Darwin continued his father's investigations, growing sundew plants in two lots, one fed with insects, the other unfed. The fed plants were more vigorous, had more and stronger flowers, and more and much heavier seeds.

The work with carnivorous plants described here, and much additional experimentation, is recounted in greater detail by Lloyd in his book *The Carnivorous Plants*. He concludes his study of the sundew by saying, "There can, therefore, be no sort of doubt that the ability to absorb substances (mineral salts as well as nitrogen) is of significance to the plant."

Are there any other plants that have had as long a line of distinguished plant scientists concerned in building up an explanation of their mechanism? With these investigators revealing that the plants do trap insects, do digest them, do absorb nitrogen and other nutrients from their bodies, and do profit by that absorption, the operation of carnivorous plants is no longer an enigma.

Understanding *how* they work makes it not too difficult to find a probable reason *why* they work in a bog—a place where there exists a deficiency in the nutrients that they obtain from insects.

That deficiency is caused by lack of drainage. The lack of drainage causes poor aeration, resulting in a deficient growth of bacteria, and the consequent accumulation of plant debris, and the gradual development of an acid condition. As the bacteria population is reduced, the nitrogen becomes less available; and, as acidity increases, the ability of the plant to absorb through its root hairs, by osmosis, is decreased.

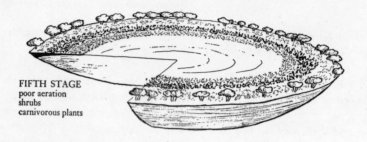

FIFTH STAGE
poor aeration
shrubs
carnivorous plants

Existing under these conditions there could only be a limited assemblage, plants that cannot compete with others in more favored situations, but can have a place here if they can tolerate it. Each plant must have some special adaptation to be a part of this group; the carnivorous plants just happen to have the most dramatic adaptation.

In that tough community we lingered awhile, realizing that we should not be meeting these specialized individuals for a long time, probably. We fed mosquitoes to the pitcher plants, and irritated the tentacles of the sundew. Then we dug up a plant of each to see if their roots were as insignificant as might be expected of plants that had established a new intake. They were, and the plants were easy to set back into their small soggy places.

As we continued on our way, we found ourselves not so much walking as jumping, from root hummock to root hummock. These were the roots of trees, the first tree to come in on the bog mat, the tamarack or American larch.

Each island of tamarack roots gave us a foothold that was less

SIXTH STAGE
shade
tamarack trees
root hummocks

soggy than the area we had left behind. We were in the sixth stage of the bog. A new element was shade. On the hummocks shade-tolerant plants such as jewelweed (*Impatiens biflora*) appeared. Among the mosses, sphagnum was replaced by the moss, *Mnium*. Among the ferns, marsh shield fern was replaced by royal fern (*Osmunda regalis*).

We could see that these hummocks were formed by a surprisingly shallow root system, because the wind had recently toppled two trees over, tipping on edge a flat platter of roots, the shape of the brown pool they had uncorked in the mat.

In the low places between the root-islands, a few poison sumacs still persisted, as did several other plants of earlier stages.

We were soon through with hummock-hopping, and moving on to earth that felt firm beneath our feet. This was the seventh stage of the bog. The mat had thickened considerably, and supported a rich forest, with abundant yellow birch, white pine, red maple, and arborvitae. Shade was more dense, and shade-tolerant plants abundant: serviceberry (*Amelanchier canadensis*), white violet (*Viola blanda*), showy lady's slipper (*Cypripedium reginae*), stemless lady's slipper (*Cypripedium acaule*), wild sarsaparilla (*Aralia nudicaulis*), cinnamon fern (*Osmunda cinnamomea*) most conspicuous of all, spinulose wood fern (*Aspidium spinulosum*) and an assemblage of typical northerners. That assemblage included partridgeberry (*Mitchella repens*), starflower (*Trientalis borealis*), Indian cucumber-root (*Medeola virginiana*), bunchberry (*Cornus canadensis*).

From among the ferns and northerners we climbed up on to the road, and then to the welcome dryness of the dune. We sat among

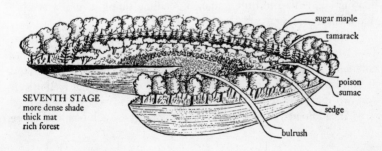

SEVENTH STAGE
more dense shade
thick mat
rich forest

sugar maple

tamarack

poison sumac

sedge

bulrush

black oaks, blueberries, and sassafras, removing black muck from our footgear and looking back down at the bog.

What was that assemblage of northerners doing, across the road from black oaks and sassafras?

To find a similar assemblage we might have traveled either to another bog of our area, or to the north woods.

These bog spots of northern vegetation are considered glacial relicts left behind in the midst of conditions that the natural vegetation of the area cannot tolerate, but that the vegetation of the north is able to tolerate. Evidently plants that are able to survive when soil water is locked up by freezing can survive just as well when it is locked up by acidity.

Not all bogs lie, like the one described here, in deep depressions. In southern Michigan are several bogs that lie in shallow depressions, demonstrating that it is lack of drainage rather than depth of depression that is the essential feature for bog formation. Because those sand-locked depressions are so shallow, they do not show the successive stages of a bog in a deep depression, but have one and the same stage overall. Near Stevensville, Michigan, one may visit a bog that is in the waterlily (second) stage; another that is in the sedge (fourth) stage; another that is in the leatherleaf-cranberry (fifth) stage; and another that is already completely covered with tamarack, representing the sixth stage.

In northern Wisconsin, as a part of summer field work, we once spent an amazing day on a great bog that showed another variation. We set out in the morning on the open water, in rowboats, each boat containing three botany students.

Ahead of us were islands, an imposing flotilla of them.

An island came bobbing alongside our rowboat. It consisted of a floating log, with a minute tamarack seedling riding it, in a crack beside a knob of moss.

Then we passed another island and hauled it close for inspection. Two logs, some branches, and some brown matted vegetation were entangled to make the base for this island. Riding it was a good stand of bulrush, a handful of sphagnum moss, a small plant of leatherleaf, and two minute rosettes of sundew.

Ahead floated islands with trees—tamaracks. Each boatload chose

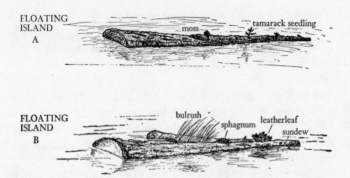

FLOATING
ISLAND
A

moss   tamarack seedling

FLOATING
ISLAND
B

bulrush   sphagnum   leatherleaf   sundew

an island for its own special study. Then someone landed to test the island to see whether it would support three people without bobbing too precariously. If it would, then the other two disembarked, and the identification and listing of every bit of vegetation were begun.

When we had completed the listing on our island, we could not resist a gleeful ten minutes of jumping up and down on opposite sides to make a sort of see-saw. Then we left, and joined the other islanders to compare lists.

FLOATING
ISLAND
C

They were almost identical, and almost the same as our lists from the Mineral Springs bog. The bog conditions were the same, but the mat of the Wisconsin lake was being formed in patches, as well as by extension from the edges.

That was in 1914.

We took great pleasure in reading the story written in bogs where we found them. We did not realize that we were reading only a small part of the available record. We did not know that our book was upside down and we were reading only the events recorded on the last few pages.

Today, when you talk about a bog to a botanist, he is very likely to ask, "Has it been bored?"

No one asked us that in 1914, because no one was conscious of the fact that we were walking over layer upon layer of ancient pollen, scattered through peat formed of plant remains—pollen waiting to reveal its record.

But over in Sweden, G. Lagerheim had already suspected the existence of this record, and had written about it, in Swedish, in 1909.

By 1916, another Swede, von Post, was working out the methods for boring bogs and deciphering their story.

During this phase, Auer bored a Canadian bog. And then started a line of bog investigations, with Fuller, Sears, Potzger, Hansen and Cain leading in this country. This has been a rich field for Master's Degree papers, and for Doctor's degrees. In 1927, according to Cain, there were about 150 publications on this subject and in 1944 about 2,500.

The procedure in a bog investigation is, in general, like this:

A plant scientist goes out on a bog, carrying a peat borer, some bottles for samples, and provision for washing the borer. He has previously spent some time ascertaining the deepest part of the bog.

He starts boring at that spot. The borer is a hollow cylinder surrounded by a movable sleeve. This sleeve has a cutting edge at the opening in the side of the cylinder. He bores the cylinder down to just one foot below the surface, and reverses the handle. That closes the opening. He brings the borer out.

He takes a sample from the core, being careful to take it from the center to avoid any danger of its being contaminated.

He puts the sample into a bottle, and labels it with the name of the bog, and the depth. Then he washes the borer carefully, and takes a second boring, two feet down, treating it in the same way.

Again and again he takes his sample, one foot deeper each time. Finally he runs into gritty sand or mud. There he stops boring. He has reached the original bottom of the depression.

Now he takes his borings into the laboratory. He examines the last one first—the one taken perhaps twenty, thirty, fifty, or one hundred feet down.

He prepares the peat sample by placing it in a solution of 95% alcohol or 12% potassium hydroxide. Then he inspects it under a high-powered microscope. There may be as many as 50,000 to 1,000,000 pollen grains in one gram of the peat. But he does not consider all of them. He counts out 200 of them. (Some investigators count only 100 for each foot level.)

The plant scientist now is ready to identify the kinds of plants (usually trees) that these 200 pollen grains came from. He probably has slides of labeled pollen grains at hand for comparison.

After he has counted out and identified 200 grains from each specimen of peat, that is, one from each foot level, he is ready to read the story of the bog, or rather, he is ready to read the story *in* the bog. For this is the record that the bog has kept of the vegetation that has marched past on the surrounding hills.

In his first specimen the pollen grains may be chiefly of one kind, balsam fir (*Abies balsamea*). If he is working on an Illinois bog, he realizes that conditions must have been very different when that pollen sifted down into the water. Not only does balsam fir fail to grow naturally in Illinois, but it also refuses to thrive for all the vacationers who bring home vigorous young trees from northern Wisconsin, shriveling instead, before the prairie winds.

There is probably some spruce pollen together with the fir pollen, and perhaps a small quantity of pine, and hemlock.

Those pollen grains fell like rain onto the open water of this lake soon after the glacier receded. They were probably laid down about 10,000 years ago. The forest that had been driven south by the glacier was moving north on its very heels. Around the lake the hills were covered with the narrow spires of the balsam fir. Probably little life had begun in the cold waters of the lake.

As the investigator reads the record in his pollen grains, he finds

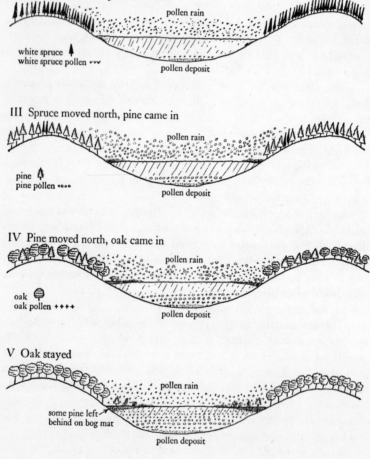

I After the glacier retreated, balsam fir came in

pollen rain

balsam fir
balsam fir pollen

pollen deposit

II Fir moved north, spruce came in

pollen rain

white spruce
white spruce pollen

pollen deposit

III Spruce moved north, pine came in

pollen rain

pine
pine pollen

pollen deposit

IV Pine moved north, oak came in

pollen rain

oak
oak pollen

pollen deposit

V Oak stayed

pollen rain

some pine left
behind on bog mat

pollen deposit

that the fir pollen soon begins to decrease, and the spruce to increase. There is not much pine. Remembering that it is much easier to grow a healthy white spruce tree in northern Illinois or Indiana today, than to grow a healthy fir, he visualizes the conditions then as being still cold, but a little less moist.

As he continues to read upward through the pollen record, he finds fir dropping off in importance from foot level to foot level, with spruce decreasing, too, and pine increasing, and oak beginning to be a part of the count. Probably, he concludes, the climate is growing warmer and drier.

By the time he has examined the record in one fourth of the bottles, he finds that fir and spruce pollen are no longer present. Pine has increased greatly, and there is more oak pollen than any other kind. It is growing still warmer and drier.

Then oak pollen increases in importance and pine decreases. As the pine forest moves north, leaving the hills to an oak forest, and hickory, a few pines are left, together with other relicts, on the bog mat.

The forest stays just about the same up to the present time, with a slight tendency toward an increase of pine pollen, indicating that there is a slight change in the climate toward a cooler, moister period.

Peat bog records agree in their story of the past. Whether they are in North America or in Europe, their story is essentially the same, and includes the following major events:

1. When the glacier receded there followed a *cool, moist period*, indicated by *fir* pollen.

2. Then came a period of *increasing warmth*, indicated by increase of *pine pollen*.

3. Then came a warm, dry period (often called the xerothermic period), indicated by an abundance of pine pollen in one bog, oak pollen in another, and pollen of dry-land herbs in another, depending on the location of the bog.

4. Then came a long period of stability, comprising about three fourths of the total record—a period of warmth, but not so dry as the preceding period, indicated by pollens of the same kind as the present forest of the area.

5. And recently there has been a hint of decreasing warmth, in-

dicated by a slight increase in pollens representing a more northern vegetation.

In all bogs there is some unidentified pollen, and some pollen in too small quantity to be of any importance. Some allowance must be made for pollen that blows in from a distance; and for the fact that some pollen is more perishable than others; and for the fact that some trees produce pollen in greater quantities than others; and for pollens that are insect-borne rather than wind-borne.

Some bogs have shown a thin black page in their records, a "black bookmark," one of the outstanding bog authorities calls it. This is interpreted as being the record of fire.

As we read the pollen record of bog after bog, we naturally begin to wonder, "How long did it take for all these layers to accumulate?"

Since pollen records have indicated that the forests may have come in within 50 miles of the edge of the retreating ice sheet, we could be justified in figuring the age of bog pollen from the time of the retreat of the ice sheet.

But our dating of the ice sheet has recently been revolutionized. Trees, buried by the glacier in southern Wisconsin, were examined in order to learn how much radioactivity had been lost from their radioactive carbon. The results indicated that the glacier that killed them came, not 25,000 years ago, but only 11,000 years ago.

Why not let this tell-tale "Carbon 14" date some of the pollen from a bog?

That is exactly what is being done. Samples of peat from eight feet down in the Quetico-Superior region were sent to Dr. W. F. Libby and Dr. J. R. Arnold of the University of Chicago. The answer came back. The pollen in that eight-foot layer drifted down from the trees 7,128 years ago, possibly 300 years earlier, possibly 300 years later. From that figure Potzger estimated that it took 500 years (on an average) to lay down one foot of pollen in the Lake Superior region. This, he points out, shows us "that several generations of forests developed and died while one foot of peat was laid down."

And now that scientists have gradually deciphered these bog records: the plant succession on a floating mat; the meaning of carnivorous plants; the northward march of forests; the changing climate; the time-clock; and archeologists have made use of pollen analysis for dating such relics of the past as a ruin in Mexico, and a human sacrifice of 2,000 years ago in a Danish bog—now one is inclined to wonder if that is all, or if there is still more to be learned from this "history book with the flexible cover."

The Bog—Revisited

As we turned north on to Mineral Springs Road and crossed the tracks of the South Shore Electric on our way to the bog, I recalled the times our ecology class from the University of Chicago, led by Dr. Henry Cowles, had alighted there, each of us with a green metal vasculum (for specimens) hanging from one shoulder, and a knapsack full of lunch and a *Gray's Manual* hanging from the other. As soon as the train pulled out, the knapsacks would hold the skirts of the women of the class, which were shucked off to reveal riding breeches and high shoes, and were put on again before we got on the train at the end of the day. Because we walked then, we carried all our supplies.

More than 50 years after the trip to the bog as described in the foregoing chapter, I was arriving in an air-conditioned car. The drifts of bluets that I remembered were still there in the meadow to the west of the road, and Michigan holly grew as abundant as ever in the ditches beside the road.

Across the open field to the west I searched for the tamaracks. At first I could see only a few bleached trunks of trees left from a fire several years ago. But beyond them were the living ones, stepping out on the bog as they used to.

Beyond them a white pine stood tall. I knew it must be growing in the sandy edge of the bog. The pine shape was familiar, but next to it was a shape strange to see across the old bog—the chimney of the generating station of the Northeast Indiana Public Service Company, trailing smoke across the sky.

That company, I had read, had been dumping ash, iron oxide, and other solid wastes at the western edge of the bog, defending their action by pointing out that the dumping was being done on their own property. There was no doubt about that. The property line between the plant and the national lakeshore unfortunately ran through water. However, in 1971, the company constructed a sand dike to retain its dumping.

We parked the car near the entrance to the old bog road. The police in the Dune Acres gatehouse did not stop us, as they might have done a few years ago, because this section has now become a part of the Indiana Dunes National Lakeshore.

The bog has been designated a National Natural Landmark. I stood beside the marker with its bronze plate, proclaiming the name "Cowles Bog," and thought how he would have grinned his wide grin, and then perhaps have sat down on the marker to empty the sand out of his shoes. How amazed he would have been at the size of the old bog road which he had watched growing wider and wider under the use of various kinds of vehicles. It has now narrowed down until it is not much more than a footpath, shady and lush.

A most important factor in saving the bog was its inclusion for some years in Dune Acres, with police in the gatehouse refusing entrance to vehicles of any kind.

The cinnamon ferns were six feet tall, and as abundant as ever. The sour gums, and yellow birches, and red maples were the same individuals I had known. Their root hummocks still displayed the same rich northwoods assortment of partridgeberry, cucumber root, star flower, goldthread. The woodthrush call was as mellow, and the tips of the spicebush as tasty as ever. The bog, and its pitcher plants, sundew, sphagnum, and lady's slippers, all have had the benefit of inaccessibility, and the protection of poison sumac and swamp rattlers. The display of cinnamon ferns has escaped the gatherers by their frailty, wilting when picked, dying when transplanted.

BIBLIOGRAPHICAL NOTES

"Problems and Working Lines in the Post-Arctic Forest History of Northern Europe" by L. von Post. In *Report of Proceedings of the Fifth International Botanical Congress* (48–54), University Press, Cambridge, 1930.

"Pollen Statistics" by G. Erdtmann. *Science* **73** (1931), 399–401.

"Pleistocene Forests of Illinois" by John Voss. *Botanical Gazette* **94** (1933), 808–814.

"Postglacial Migration of Forests in Illinois, Wisconsin, and Minnesota" by John Voss. *Botanical Gazette* **95** (1934), 33–43.

"Types of North American Pollen Profiles" by Paul B. Sears. *Ecology* **16** (1935), 488–499.

"Postglacial Vegetation of the Lake Michigan Region" by George D. Fuller. *Ecology* 16 (July, 1935), 473–487.

"Pollen Study of Five Bogs in Price and Sawyer Counties, Wisconsin" by J. E. Potzger. *Butler University Botanical Studies* 6 (May, 1943), 54–64.

"A Comparative Study of Three Indiana Bogs" by Carl O. Keller. *Butler University Botanical Studies* 6 (May, 1943), 65–80.

"Pollen Analysis as a Paleoecological Research Method" by Stanley Cain. In his book *Foundations of Plant Geography*, Harper, New York, 1944.

"Pollen Profiles from Southeastern Alaska" by Calvin J. Heusser. *Ecological Monographs* 22 (1952), 33–352.

"Regional Aspects of the Late-Glacial and Post-Glacial Pollen Succession of Southeastern North Carolina" by David G. Frey. *Ecological Monographs* 23 (1953), 289–314.

"Radiocarbon Dating of Late Pleistocene Events" by Richard Foster Flint and Edward S. Deevey, Jr. *American Journal of Science* 249 (1951), 257–300.

"Pollen Analysis and Mexican Archeology" by Edward S. Deevey. *American Antiquity* 15, 135–149.

"On the Power of *Sarracenia* to Entrap Insects," a letter by James MacBride (read before Linnean Society on December 19, 1815). *Transactions of The Linnean Society of London* 12 (1818), 48–52.

"Notes on *Sarracenia variolaris*" by J. H. Millechamp. *Proceedings of the American Association for the Advancement of Science* (1875), 113–133.

"Address" by John Dalton Hooker to British Association for the Advancement of Science, in Belfast, 1874. *Report of the Meetings of the British Association for the Advancement of Science* (1875), 102–116.

The *Carnivorous Plants* by Francis Ernest Lloyd. The Chronica Botanica Company, Waltham, Mass., 1942.

"The Biochemistry of the American Pitcher Plants" by J. S. Hepburn, F. M. Jones, and Elizabeth Q. St. John. *Transactions of the Wagner Free Institute of Science* 11 (1927), 1–95.

The Bog People; Iron-Age Man Preserved by P. V. Glob, translated from the Danish by Bruce Mitford. Cornell University Press, Ithaca, New York, 1969.

"The Bogs of Denmark" in *Reading the Landscape of Europe* by May Theilgaard Watts. Harper and Row, New York, 1971.

"Cowles Bog and Dunes" in *Natural Areas of Indiana and Their Preservation* by A. A. Lindsey, D. V. Schmelz, and S. A. Nichols. Indiana Natural Areas Survey, Purdue University, Lafayette, Indiana, 1971.

6

Prairie Plowing Match

OR

THE MAKING AND BREAKING

OF THE TALL GRASS SOD

THERE was not a "Whoa!" to be heard at the Plowing Match this year. Farmers, especially the older farmers, talked about that.

They talked about several sounds, and sights, and smells, that were missing. Not because they were suddenly missing—there was no drastic change this year—but because this year's match was the

Seventy-fifth Anniversary of the Wheatland
Plowing Match
with
Special Festivities
and
Special Exhibits of Old-Time Machinery,

people's thoughts tended to turn backward.

96

There was a lone plowman with a walking plow and two horses. But he was carved on granite, on the newly erected marker at the corner of the farm where the matches were being held.

All comers stepped up briskly to inspect the new marker, and then lingered to talk of the past.

Our family had driven to the Plowing Match, as we have been in the habit of driving on the morning of the second Saturday of each September, down a straight road that crosses the section lines at right angles and offers a clear view to the flat horizon.

Such a surface is to be expected, of course, on the way to a Plowing Match taking place in a township named *Wheatland*, near one town called *Plainfield* and another called *Plano*.

We had time to inspect the new marker while the plowmen were having their "drawing for lands."

"This, to me, is Illinois," rolled out a seasoned voice beside me, and I turned to see one of our local politicians making an inclusive gesture with his cigar.

My eyes followed the arc of his gesture.

"Illinois? *Just exactly where?*" I wondered.

Not the granite marker. That was Vermont.

Not the expensive evergreen planting that had been hastily installed. That consisted of Mugo pine from the mountains of Switzerland.

Not the big basket of garden flowers set at the base of the marker

(evidently one of the entries in the Flower Show of the Ladies' Fair). The flowers were marigolds and zinnias and dahlias, whose ancestors all came to us from Mexico, by way of Europe, where they went to finishing school; and petunias from South America; and gladioli from South Africa.

Not the sparrow that alighted long enough to mark the marker. He was English.

Not the freshly clipped grass at our feet. That was bluegrass from Eurasia.

Not the weeds in the grass. They were chiefly dandelions and plantain (said to have been called "white-man's foot" by the Indians), both from Europe.

Not the plowmen who were driving their tractors onto the field. They, too, were sons or grandsons of Europeans.

I glanced further off.

Not that Norway spruce in front of the nearest farmhouse, nor the European larch beside it.

Not those lilacs from Asia Minor.

Not the Black Angus cattle from Scotland.

Not even the small pin oaks and honey locusts recently planted along the highway. They are native further south in Illinois, but not here.

But yes, the two tall cottonwoods and the line of willows in the drainage ditch—these are natives in this area. But even they had come in recently, only after men had dug the ditch.

The plowmen were beginning, slowly, painstakingly, to turn the

Prairie plowing match—
chiefly foreigners going under

important opening furrows, establishing a straight line and setting the required depth—between five and six and a half inches—no more, no less. Presently they were making the important return furrow, folding a ridge to meet the first one exactly and to cover all trash.

There was one plowman who looked back and shook his head because a line of foxtail grass, another European invader, showed clearly down the entire length of the opening furrow. On the next plot a pigweed stuck out its thick green European tongue between the black furrows. On all the plots, we could watch foreigners being turned under; barnyard grass, alsike clover, timothy, red clover, English plantain, yellow sweet clover, Canada thistle. There was an occasional native going under, chiefly ragweed and smartweed.

We went over to watch the plowman Graeme Stewart at work; he was National Level Land Champion, the second national champion from Wheatland. There were neither natives nor foreigners sticking up out of his shapely furrows—just folded satin blackness.

Still searching for Illinois, we wandered toward the farmyard where tents and counters had been set up.

We passed a prize tall corn plant, tied to a Scotch pine. Its tassels were up among the orange branches where starlings from Europe were noisy. We inspected the prize-winning vegetable exhibit. It contained pumpkins, popcorn, squash, yams, beets, beans, watermelons, peas, lima beans, tomatoes, turnips. Nothing there was Illinois.

Tied to a post was an 18-foot sunflower plant with its great head hanging. A "Russian Sunflower" it was labeled; but here was a descendant, at least, of a native—a descendant of the wild sunflower of the prairies, hybridized, selected, and named in Europe it is true, but now returned, tall and big-headed to look down over garden fences upon its wild relatives.

We bought a souvenir program and went in under the big tent for a dinner of chicken, ham, beans, coleslaw, mashed potatoes, rolls and coffee. No Illinois natives on that menu.

Would there, perhaps, be something in the souvenir program that might help to explain where, and when, the natives had gone?

We decided to read back through the record of seventy-five years of plowing matches. The editors of the program had gathered together, out of old newspapers, old programs, and old memories, a few interesting facts about each match.

Return of a native

Embedded among the accounts of enthroning and dethroning champions, of changing equipment, reports on the Ladies' Fair, two wars, and the assassination of a president, we found occasional references that cast some light on the changing face of the prairie.

SEVENTY-THIRD MATCH—1949

David King, grand-nephew of James King, winner of the original plowing-match title in 1877, won the Boys-15-to-18-year-old class with a 90½ score.

Whenever three generations have worked the land proudly, it is usually safe to assume that the land has not been abused. Confucius said, "The best fertilizer for any land is the footsteps of the owner."

SEVENTY-FIRST MATCH—1947

For the first time, the grounds were sprayed with D.D.T. before the match, resulting in their being free of flies and other insects. . . . Several flying farmers flew in to attend the match.

New wings had come to the prairie, bringing farmers from a wider area and making possible the dusting of great fields.

We brushed a few flies off of our apple pie. Perhaps they were of the new resistant strains that we had been reading about. Will there be eventually a new tough race of insects that will be considered, as Edgar Anderson considers weeds, "artifacts"—man's unwitting artifacts? That question, however, concerns the future of the prairie, and we were attempting to unravel its past.

SEVENTIETH MATCH—1946

In the grain show a prize was offered for the tallest stalk of corn, the winning stalk being eleven feet tall.

What a grass! Illinois grew its grasses tall before the plowman came, but not that tall.

Is such tallness a gain? Dr. William Albrecht of the University of Missouri says: "While the bushels per acre of both corn and wheat have been going upward, the concentration of the protein within each of these grains has been going downward. . . . Corn which had a protein concentration ten years ago of nearly 9.5 per cent, has an average figure of 8.5 per cent today (1948). While our crops have been yielding bushels per acre bountifully, those bushels have consisted mainly of the photosynthetic product, starch."

Dr. Albrecht also states that, as soil wears out, plant breeders and farmers find methods, such as the use of hybrid strains, for "hijacking" the mineral stores that are left; and produce crops that are higher in bulk but lower in essential minerals.

SIXTY-FIRST MATCH—1937

One of the newer exhibits were several booths at which hybrid seed corn was shown.

From that time on, crops reached down deeper, and took out more, from the rich storehouse of the prairie.

FIFTY-NINTH MATCH—1935

This was the first year in the history of the Wheatland Plowing Match in which no horse-drawn plows were entered, all being tractor drawn.

And so the work of these grasslands was no longer to be done by the animal that had evolved with the developing of the world's grass-lands. It was when the rising continents, with their drier and colder conditions, made grasslands where had been forests and swamps, that the horse developed longer legs, concentrating the weight on the one central toe, and gaining strength from the keeled-and-grooved joints that replaced ball-and-socket joints. These legs made possible a longer stride and increased speed over smooth ground. The longer head and longer neck probably developed simultaneously, making it possible for the long-legged animal to graze. Along with the development of the harder, drier foods of the plains, came the horse's elongated tooth crowns, with their hard projecting ridges of enamel backed inside by dentine and outside by cement.

George Gaylord Simpson says:

> These horses were learning to eat grass and acquiring the sort of teeth . . . that enabled them to do so. They were changing over from brows-ing animals to grazing animals, still herbivorous but with a profound change in their way of life. It is not likely to be a coincidence that at the same time grass became common, as judged by fossil grass seeds in the rocks.

The 1935 Plowing Match saw the end of power that came from the land and was returned to the land as fertilizer.

FIFTY-THIRD MATCH—1929

Six weeks drought before the match baked the ground and made plow-ing most difficult.

FORTY-SIXTH MATCH—1922

Unprecedented drought and intense heat made conditions for plowing about as bad as had ever been experienced and greatly reduced the at-tendance at this match.

But the Indians and the buffaloes and the big bluestem grass could have told that the drought was *not* unprecedented.

THIRTY-THIRD MATCH—1909

Alvin Stark was disqualified, because his horses became un-manageable, having been frightened by the sight and noise of au-tomobiles arriving for the match.

Probably the furrows that Alvin Stark's unmanageable horses plowed were curves that were much more native to the prairie than the straight lines and mathematical right angles that men have super-imposed on its face.

THIRTY-FIRST MATCH—1907

The Wheatland Match had now become the political forum and joust-ing grounds for the northern section of the state. All candidates and important office-holders from near-by counties were on hand for each match.

But they were not plowing.

It was the accumulated black riches of the old prairie that caused the gathering of parasites, as accumulated riches cause the gathering of parasites everywhere. I remember the mountain-top tundra. There were no accumulated riches there. And there was not apparent a single parasite, saprophyte, or even a clinging vine.

THIRTIETH MATCH—1906

Interest of the crowd was divided between the skilled plowmen, and an innovation to the match, a great steam-drawn gang plow, which turned ten furrows at a time. It was likened to a Mississippi river steamer, plowing up waves, as it went down the field.

As plowing was made easier and easier, more and more Illinois soil would be drained away, until Mississippi river steamboats would, in time, actually be plowing through waves of prairie soil, but they would not need to leave the Mississippi to find that soil.

TWENTY-EIGHTH MATCH—1904

Interest was drawn to earliest models of the "horseless buggy," a few being seen at the match.

Bumping across the ruts toward the Plowing Match, without benefit of filling stations, or numbered roads, or even "Blue Books," those first "horseless buggies" drew behind them, across the face of the prairie, the first string of a network of roads whose strands were to increase in width, number and strength, and enmesh an ever-increas-ing number of foreigners, both plant and animal.

FOURTEENTH MATCH—1890

Over 1,000 rigs and vehicles were hitched along the fences and around the barns.

What kind of fences?

Osage orange

They might have been the then recently-invented barbed wire (1874). The invention put bounds to the seemingly boundless prairie. It enabled farmers to move farther west. A handbook for emigrants from the East, in 1835, said, "Much of this land must lie unoccupied for generations for want of fencing."

On the Illinois prairie the coming of barbed wire meant the gradual grubbing out of miles of Osage-orange hedge.

SEVENTH MATCH—1883

The weather was hot and dry, and the fields were hard and packed. Great interest was shown in the riding-plow events, because farmers were realizing that everything should be done to free themselves and their sons from the more arduous work of the farm.

Each change that made plowing easier, even the change from walking to riding, extended plowland further into the prairie.

SIXTH MATCH—1882

The season had been very dry and it was hard plowing for the contestants.

It was this sort of summer that had sent prairie roots deep, deep down, long before plowing matches had been thought of, or plows.

SECOND MATCH—1878

> Hot dry weather had baked the ground extremely hard. Good plowing under adverse conditions resulted. Wm. Castles won the highest prize, a pair of silver-mounted bridles.
>
> Ladies were invited this year, and brought picnic lunches, and over 500 enjoyed the noonday meal in a beautiful grove near the field on which the match was held.

Those same "adverse conditions" had long ago determined the winners among plants on the prairie. The winners were the ones we now call "native." Those conditions had probably determined also the kind of tree that would furnish shade for the ladies when they opened those picnic baskets. A stand of trees given the name "grove" at that period was usually composed of bur oaks.

THE FIRST MATCH—1877

> The committee reported concerning this match: We learned among other things that a furrow can be plowed straight; that there are men who are masters of the plow; that while we live we progress; that sulky plowing is a great step in advance of all hand plowing.
>
> Factory representatives of plows were on hand with their latest models. Sulky plows were new, and were tested for merit on the grounds.

All the contestants walked, but they dreamt of riding in one of those modern sulkies some day. This innovation would enable them to extend their plowland farther into the prairie, and leave them more time for digging ditches and building fences.

There was probably an occasional purple turkey-foot (the seed-spike that gave the name "turkey-foot" to the big bluestem grass) reaching out from the unsuccessful furrows at that first match, if any puny specimens were left as survivors of former plowings.

At the far end of the field, in a corner that was too hard to plow, the six-foot high bluestem, or turkey-foot, may have whisked the flies from the horses as they made the turn. A prairie chicken probably flew off here, or a whole covey of quail there, or an upland plover, or a flock of passenger pigeons that had paused to rest or to glean a few seeds.

We had finished reading the program, and were ready to visit the

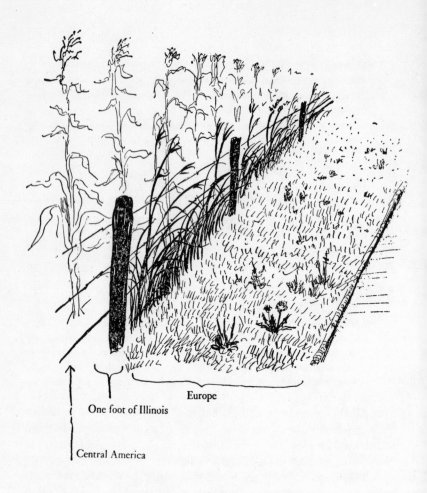

One foot of Illinois

Europe

Central America

Ladies' Fair, and the Wheatland School exhibit; to cast our ballots in the straw vote for president of the United States; to examine the old plows and the new tractors, washing machines, and television sets.

As we walked, we continued to look for Illinois natives—without success.

Later we drove off, still searching, down the straight quarter-section road.

Suddenly I caught a signal from the natives—a waving signal.

"Oh! there they *are!*" I shouted, pushing hard on imaginary brakes.

"Where?" probably the size of my shout had left my family half-expecting something dramatic like buffaloes, or Indians.

But the natives I had seen had found a hiding place that the Indians and buffaloes could not use. They were not in the green strip along the road. That autumn greenness belongs to European plants, adjusted to a lingering autumn that oozes halfheartedly into winter. Nor were my natives in the fields beyond the fence. That hybrid corn of Mexican and Central American ancestry was too tall, too dun, too stiff, to be a native.

But there in the fence row They stood!

Their sanctuary was only a foot wide. But it was a quarter-section long. They were safe because the road worker's mower does not reach there; and the farmer does not plow there.

We got out, and crossed the green strip of Europe, to the fence row; the purple claws of the turkey-foot grass waved above our heads, just as they waved above the heads of the first Spaniards, the first Frenchmen, the first trappers, the first oxen drawing the first covered wagons on the long journey from the East.

Nor was the big bluestem entirely bereft of its ancient companions. As we walked the fence rows, we found colonies of switch grass and cord grass, little bluestem and wild rye.

At first we could not find the other contemporary that belonged with these—the Indian grass. But, finally, we located it, too, in a different sort of sanctuary, the slope behind the fence of a little German-Lutheran churchyard.

Above the slope, in the shorn precision of the burial plot, there were plant foreigners. Below the slope, on the plowed land, there were foreigners, too. But the steep slope in between could be neither plowed nor mowed, and there a few bunches of Indian grass stood tall. They were hobnobbing, these outcasts from the prairie, with that outcast from gardens, the bouncing Bet, or lady-by-the-gate.

The sun set, then, on natives and foreigners alike, and we drove home, talking about fences.

At home we turned at once to the old books to see what we could find about the coming of fences to the prairie—contemporary comments such as we had been reading in the Plowing Match program.

The first reference that we unearthed overlapped the period of time covered by the program. In 1885 a State Law was passed, in an

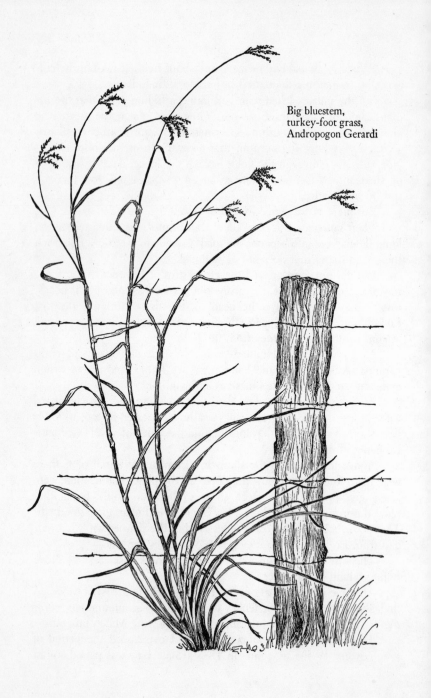

Big bluestem,
turkey-foot grass,
Andropogon Gerardi

attempt to keep swine and cattle from running at large within the corporate limits of local communities. "Although a woman had been gored in the village streets, Naperville had paid little attention to the law . . . the less affluent citizens . . . contended that the streets were the poor man's pasture."

Naperville is our town.

Rufus Blanchard, writing of this area in 1882, told of the wide-ranging cattle on the prairie. "The writer once knew one of them [referring to a cow owner] to move six or eight miles and build a new cabin at the spot because his cow had chosen her range there."

We were fortunate to come across a little paper-bound booklet published in 1857, with a cover showing six oxen pulling a plow, and with this title:

The
Illinois
Central Railroad Company
offers for sale
Over 1,500,000 Acres
Selected
FARMING AND WOOD
LANDS
in tracts of Forty Acres and Upward
To Suit Purchasers
On Long Credit and At Low Rates of Interest
Situated
On Each Side of Their Railroad, Extending All The Way
From the Extreme North to the South of
The State of Illinois

On the subject of *Fencing* this booklet told the settler,

An abundant supply of lumber, or timber for building or fencing, can be easily procured, but the Osage Orange plant has been extensively introduced, and is rapidly supplanting all other kinds of fencing. Being at the same time more permanent and more secure than any other, and highly ornamental, it must soon be universally employed. It can be raised by contract at from fifty to seventy-five cents per rod, parties making a business of preparing the ground, setting out the plants, and cultivating and trimming them until a perfect hedge is produced for the settler. For this, one third of the contract money is paid out upon the setting of the plants, and the balance when the fence is completed, without interest.

Those were the Osage oranges that have been so conspicuous in our northern Illinois scene as their brilliant orange roots have been grubbed out of the black soil that proved too valuable for them, after barbed wire came.

There are still left a few short remnants of Osage-orange hedge. But of the fence that preceded it, there is no trace.

B. G. Roots wrote, on December 27th, 1855, in a letter published in that same Illinois Central pamphlet:

Fencing is the hardest work which a settler here has to perform. Good white oak rails, laid up in fence, are worth from 2 dollars to 3 dollars per hundred. To lessen the cost of fencing it is desirable for several friends to settle together, so that the land may at first be enclosed in one common field.

The angles of a rail fence made plenty of havens for prairie natives.

In an account of an 1846 wolf hunt, not far from the Plowing Match site, we found a reference to another kind of fence:

The new settlers had commenced fencing their lands, and at several places the party had been obliged to dismount and remove the obstruction, but here they found a ditch fence.

The ditches and the mounds beside them have long ago been leveled.

"Were fences the first of the straight lines, and the right angles, on the face of the prairie?" wondered one of the family. "It is hard to visualize Wheatland township without that network of power lines, and roads, and fences—and furrows."

"Probably the furrows were the first straight lines," suggested another, and we turned back again to the old books, to see what contemporary writers had had to say about the first furrows on the face of the prairie.

At once we learned that settlers did not speak of "plowing" when they made those first furrows. They spoke of "breaking the prairie."

C. G. Taylor wrote, in 1856, from Rock Island, Illinois, in that same little Illinois Central pamphlet:

> The breaking of prairie is mostly done in May or June, though it can be carried on at any season when the frost is out of the ground. Many farmers use the heavy breaking plough, cutting a furrow from eighteen to twenty-six inches wide, and about three inches deep, requiring a force of from three to six yoke of oxen: of late, however, so many improvements have been made in the form and draught of ploughs, that the prairie can be readily broken, at the rate of one and a quarter to one and a half acres per day, with a single pair of horses.
>
> Sod corn, if planted in the month of May, and followed by favorable weather, viz. warm and dry, will yield from twenty to fifty bushels per acre. The planting is done by sticking an axe or spade between the layers of sod, and after dropping the corn, applying the heel of the boot freely. Only a small portion of prairie is yet broken.

Mr. James Phillips wrote, from Washington County, Illinois, in 1855:

> All we have to do is to turn down the sod with a plough, at the rate of two or three acres a day, stick in the corn with an axe, and come out in Fall for the crop.

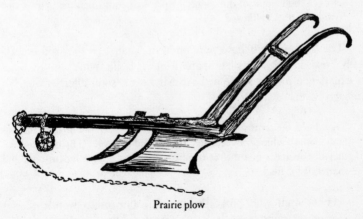

Prairie plow

C. B. Johnson, M.D., in memories of his childhood in "Illinois in the Fifties," recalled that:

Six yoke of oxen opened a furrow 2 feet or more in width, and the ox-driver carried a long whip of twisted raw-hide, which he was fond of flourishing with a sharp retort.

We found numerous references to breaking the prairie. They all agreed that the prairie sod was *deep* and *tough,* and that the prairie was rich and productive when the sod had been broken through.

That deep sod must have been broken occasionally before the oxen came. Gophers must have broken it, and perhaps an occasional woodchuck. Sometimes Nature must have taken advantage of such breaks. I believe that certain wide-spreading oaks that I pass every day, standing alone in a field, a stone's throw beyond the forest margin, may have got their start in gopher holes. Such a break in the sod would have made it possible for the new root thrusting downward out of the acorn to reach soil in the first season; whereas other acorns could not put out, in a single season, enough growth to penetrate to soil.

We can only speculate on the beginnings of those lone oaks, but we have records that men took advantage of gopher holes.

In 1820, Schoolcraft wrote:

. . . the white hunters of Missouri and Arkansas frequently avail themselves of the labours of the gopher by planting corn upon the prairies that have been thus mellowed.

The Indians must have punctured the prairie, if they did not actually break it, for Tonti, companion of La Salle, wrote, in 1686, of an experience on the shore of Lake Michigan, soon after leaving the Chicago River:

They lived on acorns and garlic found under the snow in the Pottowatamie village which they reached only to find it deserted. By good fortune they discovered a quantity of frozen squash and a little Indian corn and roasted it for food.

"Those men who broke the prairie," one of us wondered, remembering the wind, and the sun, "where did they live?"

"In the woods," the rest of us answered unhesitatingly, with knowledge gained from the many references we had come across, while reading about the breaking of the prairie.

We looked up those references again, and others.

In a small book compiled by the board of supervisors of Dupage County, in 1877, we read:

> After the close of the Black Hawk War the tide of emigration again turned to Illinois. . . . The first settlers selected, of course, the best locations, which were adjacent to timber. Scarcely any were to be found upon the prairie prior to 1837. All the timber land was claimed before 1835, but some of the prairie land in our county, which at that day was considered almost worthless on account of its being inconvenient to timber, was never claimed by the squatters.

The Big Woods Claim Protection Society, in 1836, began its resolutions thus:

> Be it remembered, that we, the undersigned, inhabitants of the east side of the Big Woods, and its vicinity, have settled on lands belonging to the United States, and who have severally made their respective claims, including timber and prairie.

The old books referred constantly to "groves," and we noticed that most of the first settlements were called after them, Downer's Grove, Walker's Grove, Holderman's Grove, Babcock's Grove, and others.

An early account of French explorers told that they

> likened the Illinois River to the Seine at Paris, . . . its bordering hills covered with fine trees, . . . they climbed to behold from their summits the prairies extending further than the eye could reach studded at regular intervals with groves seemingly planted in regular order.

Tonti, in his memoirs of 1684, said:

> . . . it is for the most part a great plain adorned with clusters of trees.

During the Black Hawk War, some ten to twenty miles west of the Plowing Match area:

Major Stillman was permitted to make a tour of inspection up the river. . . . They continued their march to a small stream, where, on the 14th of May, 1832, a little before sundown, they dismounted in order to encamp for the night. Their encampment was judiciously selected in a beautiful oak grove, destitute of underbrush.

When oaks stand well spaced, "destitute of underbrush," and making an inviting camp site, those oaks are, in northern Illinois, almost inevitably bur oaks.

On a bright winter morning in January, 1834, a man named Charles Fenno Hoffman, according to his own account, set out on a trip from Chicago to St. Louis, by stagecoach, "in a handsome four-horse coach." The coach was given up for a sled with hay in the bottom, at Lawton's Grove. And night brought them to "Walker's Grove, which then consisted of two or three log huts, sheltered from the north wind under an island of tall timber."

The bur oak trunks

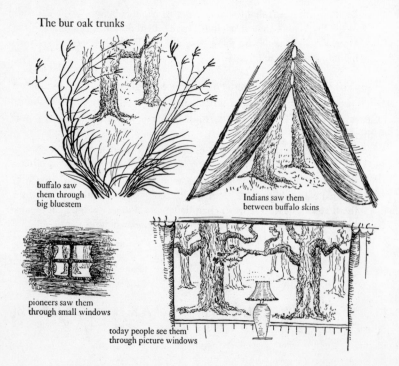

buffalo saw
them through
big bluestem

Indians saw them
between buffalo skins

pioneers saw them
through small windows

today people see them
through picture windows

Since Walker's Grove lies, or lay, just south of the present town of Plainfield, nearest town to the Plowing Match, we made a trip over there to see it.

A typical "prairie grove" we saw, with its great bur oaks standing well spaced.

Ranch houses are coming in under those massive branches now. And people look out through picture windows at the furrowed trunks. Pioneers saw such bur oak trunks, through much smaller apertures; Indians saw them between flapping buffalo skins, and buffalo saw them through tall turkey-foot grass.

We felt the thick bark and the corky twigs of the old bur oaks, and understood how this oak, rather than the red oak, or the white oak, could have withstood the Indian fires that swept the prairies and licked at the margin of the forest. It was easy to believe that the cambium (tissue-forming) layer would not have been so easily cooked under that corky insulation, as would the cambium of the thinner-barked trees.

The fires continually wiped out the thin-skinned underbrush, and so the prairie groves became a savannah type of forest, with a grassy floor.

"Do we know, for sure, about these Indian fires," came the question, "or do we simply assume their existence because of the evidence?"

Each of us instantly remembered some reference that had turned up in the old book while we were hunting material on prairie groves, or on "breaking the prairie," or on fences. We hunted up those references, and found many others as well. And incidentally, we learned that three things went together. When we found a record of fire, we found at the same time, a record of Indians and of buffaloes.

In 1834, according to an account published in 1857, Indian fires were still to be expected in the Chicago area.

> . . . the first attempt at actual farming of which the writer has any account, was in the fall of 1834. Mason Smith and Hezekiah Duncklee cut and stacked a few tons of hay near Salt Creek, to keep a small pony—which they had brought all the way from Detroit. Their stack was completed after several hard days' labor, and they were advised to burn the grass for several rods around it in order to protect it from the annual fires set by the Indians.

In 1823, an English farmer, making a tour of the United States, to see the "prospects for British emigrants" was rather depressed by the fires. He, William Faux, wrote:

The season called Indian summer, which here commences in October, by a dark blue hazy atmosphere, is caused by millions of acres for thousands of miles around, being in a wide-spreading, flaming, blazing, smoking fire, rising up through wood and prairie, hill and dale, to the tops of low shrubs and high trees, which are kindled by the coarse, thick, long prairie grass—darkening the air, heavens, and earth, filling the whole horizon with yellow, palpable, tangible smoke, ashes and vapour, which affect the eyes of man and beast, and obscure the sun, moon, and stars, for many days, or until the winter rains descend to quench the fire and purge the thick, ropey air, which is seen, tasted, handled, and felt.

On the following day, near Princeton, Indiana, he wrote,

. . . we rode all day through fire and thick smoke, which met in pillar-like arches across the road, and compelled us to wait a while or turn aside.

A few days later, near Harmony, he wrote:

The everlasting sound of falling trees, which, being undermined by fires, are falling around almost every hour, night and day, produces a sound loud and jarring as the discharge of ordnance.

In 1820, Schoolcraft described the use of fire:

. . . but on the upper Mississippi, where they are destitute of horses they make amends for this deficiency by several ingenious stratagems. One of the most common of these is the method of hunting with fire. For this purpose a great number of hunters dispose themselves around a large prairie where herds of buffalo happen to be feeding, and setting fire to the grass, encompass them on all sides. The buffalo, having great fear of fire, retire toward the center of the prairie as they see it approach, and here being pressed together in great numbers, many are trampled underfoot, and the Indians rushing in with their arrows and musketry, slaughter immense numbers in a short period. It is asserted that a thousand animals have been killed by this stratagem in one day.

In 1682, La Salle saw the Indians using fire in this way, not far south of the Plowing Match region,

> When they emerged from the desolate region of the Kankakee marshes, they found great open plains covered with tall dry grass; and they knew that they had at last reached the land of the Illinois, the prairie country of which they had heard so much. Their expectations of game were disappointed, for the autumnal fires, lit by the natives while hunting, had driven away the buffalo.
>
> In a journey of more than 60 leagues they shot only two lean deer, some swans, and two wild geese, a meager support for so large a party. Two-thirds of the men, dissatisfied from lack of food, planned to desert and join the Indians, whom they saw now and then in the distance hovering about the burning prairies, but LaSalle divined and frustrated the scheme. When their need was sorest, however, they found an enormous buffalo mired on the bank of the river. Twelve men with difficulty dragged the huge creature to the solid ground with their strongest rope, and its flesh furnished abundant supplies.

Such records kept by explorers and early settlers leave little doubt about the existence of prairie fires where there were Indians and buffaloes.

The buffalo might have had a close connection with the Wheatland Plowing Match, if the Marquis de Galissonière, governor-general of Canada, had had his way. In 1750 he wrote to the King of France, urging that "the little colony of the Illinois be not left to perish," and described the country as open and ready for the plough, and traversed by an innumerable multitude of buffaloes, "and these animals are covered with a species of wool, sufficiently fine to be employed in various manufactures." He suggested that "the buffalo, if caught and attached to the plough, would move it at a speed superior to that of the domestic ox."

As we searched for references to these various aspects of the prairie we came across two comments that were of interest chiefly because of the well-known men who wrote them. The more recent comment was by Monroe, written to Thomas Jefferson, in 1786, concerning the Northwest Territory.

> A great part of the territory is miserably poor, especially that near Lakes Michigan and Erie, and that upon the Mississippi and Illinois consists of

extensive plains which have not had, from appearances, and will not have, a single bush on them for ages. The districts, therefore, within which these fall, will never contain a sufficient number of inhabitants to entitle them to membership in the confederacy.

The other comment, the very first account of this region, was written by Father Marquette, in 1684. He was following the Illinois River when he wrote:

. . . they had seen nothing like this river, for the fertility of the land, its prairies, woods, wild cattle, stag, deer, wildcats, bustards, swans, ducks, parrots, and even beaver, and its many little lakes and rivers.

With this account by Father Marquette, our early human records relating to the story of the prairies were exhausted.

To continue our unravelling of the past, we turned, for a picture of the prairie that met the eyes of explorers and pioneers, to plants of undisturbed fence rows, undisturbed sections of old cemeteries, certain railroad rights of way, and whatever other pieces of northern Illinois prairie survived, unplowed, ungrazed.

In such sites, most omnipresent of all plants is big bluestem, thriving best on places that are neither dry nor wet. Its most probable companion is Indian grass, *Sorghastrum nutans*.

In the fence row near the Plowing Match, these two grasses were not accompanied by prairie flowers. But that fence row has not, for a long time, been subjected to fire. Prairie areas subjected to occasional burning have shown a tendency to form a more rich mixture of many species of prairie flowers—probably because the thick accumulation of matted undecayed vegetation, "prairie duff," favors grasses.

Big bluestem and Indian grass are usually a part of a rich mixture composed of New Jersey tea, blazing star, flowering spurge, puccoon, compass plant or rosin weed, blue-eyed grass, and stiff goldenrod, rattlesnake master, smooth aster, and white false indigo.

On drier, usually higher, areas within our surviving remnants of prairie, the little bluestem (*Andropogon scoparius*) is the dominating plant. Its most probable associates are leadplant, purple prairie clover, the goldenrod sometimes called "hill goldenrod" or "dyer's-weed goldenrod," and daisy fleabane.

On moister, usually lower, places the principal grass is cord grass (*Spartina pectinata*), associating with Canada anemone, closed gentian, tall meadow rue, Sullivant's milkweed, wild strawberry, sawtoothed sunflower, black-eyed Susan, prairie dock, and Culver's root.

Whether the prairie is dry or wet or medium, it produces each growing season three successive layers of flowering, each one higher than the preceding one. As the summer progresses there is an ever-increasing feel of denim and calico and burlap in the foliage; a crescendo of the sounds of corduroy, tent-flaps, sails, as one walks through the prairie; a growing pungency; and a multiplying of the flower forms that wear the Composite-family pattern, an image of the sun.

The three types of prairie—dry, wet, and medium—are all represented in fence rows within a three-mile radius of the plowing-match site. The lowest, wettest areas contain not only cord grass, but cord grass in association with sedges and smartweed. At one time it is probable that cord grass was dominant over much of this area. The soil must have become gradually drier through the years, as a result of alluvial deposits; through the development of the drainage pattern in this area where glacial drift had destroyed or plugged old patterns; and through the construction of drainage ditches and the tilling of the fields. As the drying progressed the cord-grass areas were taken over by big bluestem and its associates.

The presence of a few sedges in some cord-grass areas suggests the possibility of a preceding stage, dominated by cattails. The geological map of this area shows a bay of the post-glacial Lake Waubonsee, covering much of the plowing-match vicinity. Along the shallow margins of that bay, the sedge and cord-grass stage may have been preceded by the other stages of a filling lake, as discussed in the chapter "Coming Ashore."

While the cord-grass areas are reminiscent of a post-glacial body of water, little bluestem areas on the drier ridges suggest the great ice-sheet itself, depositing those ridges.

But the story of the prairie reaches back even farther than to the time of the glacier. The record in rocks tells of prairie before the cold interlude of invaders from the north, as well as afterward—prairie in the high places, prairie in the low places, prairie in the medium places.

But why did these low places, these high places, these medium places, become prairie?

Why not forest?

With that question we step out onto a battleground, an old scarred battleground of midwestern botanists, where many a shiny theory has met defeat, and where raw material has been assembled for many a thesis offered toward a Master's degree, or Doctor's degree. (Most of the arguments in the following controversy are discussed by Transeau, in the first of the references at the end of this chapter.)

Men have said, in essence:

It is a matter of *rainfall*. More rainfall makes forest; less rainfall makes prairie.

Others have answered:

Under the same annual rainfall, some regions produce forest, others produce prairie.

Men have said:

The reason prairies are found, where, on the basis of rainfall, forests might be expected, is that *the soil is too fine*. Forest trees need a coarse, loose soil.

Others have answered:

Trees grow anywhere in Illinois where they are planted, and there are prairies on many textures of soil.

Men have said:

It is a matter of *soil constituents*.

Others have answered:

Prairie remnants are found on hilltops, and in marsh land, on cliff edges, and in bogs, on sandstone, outcrops, and on limestone, on sand dunes, and in ponds.

Men have said:

Prairies mark the sites of filled lakes, or of a continuous chain of *water drainage*.

Others have pointed out:

Some prairies are high, some are low; some are well drained, some are poorly drained.

Men have said:

Prairies inhabit areas that are *geologically young*.

Others have answered:

There are younger regions that are covered with forest.

Men have said:

The prairie is a deciduous forest temporarily without trees, the trees having been eliminated by hardships that have long ago ceased to exist. The natural forest would have returned if man had not kept the prairie open by farming.

Others have answered:

It is true that forests preceded prairies in this part of the country (certainly bog pollen records seem to indicate such a past), but that was thousands of years ago, before the uplift of the western mountains robbed the west winds of their moisture. Fossils from the Late Tertiary period show an abundance of dryland grasses already inhabiting the plains.

Then men have said, pointing to the trees that are now growing on prairie soil, especially on the wet prairie:

If *they grow there now,* it is to be supposed that they might have grown there formerly.

But others have said, pointing to the extensive system of drainage ditches, and the thousands of miles of tile:

Most of the rainfall is run off into the rivers now, so that the water table is seldom raised, and so that the farmers have had three times to deepen their wells. The wet prairie is not so wet as it was formerly.

Men have said:

This part of the country has seesawed back and forth *between prairie and forest*. When there has been a dry period, the prairie has pushed the forest back; when there has been a wet period, the forest has pushed the prairie back.

Others have answered:

That is, in part, true, but only in small part. There were thousands of oaks that died in the intense drought of 1914–1915. But the typical prairie earths, that are deep as far east as central Ohio, speak of a long, continuous prairie tenancy.

Many men have said:

Indian fires made the prairie.

Others have answered:

It has been observed that the result of fires in forest is scrub forest; the result of fires in prairie is maintaining the prairie. It has never been observed that a fire made a prairie.

And there is no conclusive difference between the vegetation on the west bank of our larger streams, as compared with the vegetation on the east bank. In our prevailing westerlies, a large river would have given enough protection to the east bank to have kept more forest remnants there, if Indians made prairie out of forest.

Men have said:

The Indians may not have made prairie out of forest, but, after some extremes of Nature made the prairie, the Indians maintained it by fire—else it would long ago have returned to the original forest.

Others have answered:

When the glacier receded, the northern vegetation that had moved south before the glacier left behind many relict communities, of pine, and tamarack, and hemlock, in states of the Midwest, especially in bogs; but not a single relict community was left behind on the Prairie Peninsula, though there were plenty of depressions that might have held bogs. Evidently, then, trees did not thrive here, even without the influence of Indians or fires.

Men have said:

It is a matter of competition, and grasses got there first. Whenever prairie soil is disturbed, as along ditches, cottonwoods abound. During our present climate the prairies east of the Mississippi delay invasion by forest only by the nature of their prairie soil.

Others have answered:

In some places where prairie land has been plowed and subsequently abandoned, it has gone back to prairie; not in all places—there are many exceptions in Iowa, for example, especially in valleys, and on stream margins. The prairie shows more and more stability against invasion by forest the further west it lies.

Bohumil Shimek, in "Papers on the Prairie," says, "The breaking of the prairie turf is sufficient to cause most of the prairie plants to disappear from the broken surface, but there is abundant evidence to show that it requires continued cultivation to keep them out. Their return is rather slow and is preceded by a transitional mixture of species, but it is quite certain, provided man does not interfere." He concludes a study of certain tracts with this statement: "The views that prairie will disappear for all time if broken, and that, with cessation of prairie fires, the forest will take possession of the prairie, are untenable in the light of these and similar prairie tracts."

Homer Sampson recounts the story of a strip of farm land on his father's farm near Wheeler, Illinois. A railroad right of way that had been fifty feet wide was, in 1897, made eighty feet wide by the addition of a fifteen foot strip on each side. To this strip came back the big bluestem prairie.

Today some men are saying:

The outstanding factor in making prairie on the Prairie Peninsula, east of the Mississippi extension of the prairie, is the ratio between evaporation and rainfall.

Certainly the relative humidity is lower on the Prairie Peninsula than it is to the north and to the south of this area that reaches, like a hand with many long fingers, eastward from the Iowa prairie. Occasionally that ratio is so extreme as to make a severe summer drought. Those summer droughts have been a potent factor in shaping the prairie.

To this theory of relative humidity and drought, some others have answered:

Yes, it is ever demonstrated that the extremes determine what is to be the native vegetation. The averages are not nearly so important as the extremes. It is plain that prairie grasses can wait. They can seize the good years, and lie low through the bad ones, putting out a minimum of growth.

And the different kinds of grasses can take turns at prosperity. The kind of grass that the shoe fits can put it on. Some wet years it fits the cord grass. Some dry years it fits the little blue-stem.

Grasslands can endure fire, whether made by man or lightning or meteor, because the grasses can rise again from their roots. And they can shade out a forest seedling, if one should succeed in putting down a root long enough to pierce the sod.

A prairie, then, is shaped by many forces: by fire, water and wind; by Indians and buffaloes; most of all, by the ratio between rainfall and evaporation; and by occasional periods of extreme drought.

A prairie is vanquished by two forces: domestic grazing animals and the plow.

Cows ate the tall grasses off too close to the ground. Lower grasses could endure that close cropping. Consequently the tall prairie grasses were gradually replaced.

If the prairie was dry, the turkey foot was replaced by bluegrass, from Eurasia. If switch grass was the dominant grass, it, too, was replaced by bluegrass.

If the prairie was wetter, with cord grass dominant, or switch grass, they were replaced by redtop, from Eurasia.

Both of these replacements form a low turf.

We drove out to the plowing-match site again, in October—not directly, but in a wide arc, because we wanted to enjoy the fall color in the fence-row strips of prairie.

The little bluestem was exquisite with turquoise and garnet and chartreuse; and the big bluestem waved its turkeyfeet of deep purple high against the October sky, past the warm russet of the Indian grass.

In one long strip, a farmer was at work, taking down his fence.

"Why?" we asked.

"Easier to work it without fences," he answered. "If I ever want to turn stock onto this field, it's easy to string up an electric fence."

That will be the end of that colorful rectangle of prairie, one foot wide, one-half mile long, and eight feet deep.

We picked a few purple turkeyfeet to take home. They make pleasant bookmarks in the old books.

Plowing Match—Revisited

In 1973, as usual, September brought the Plowing Match to Wheatland township, and, as usual, we took the same straight road and paused along the way to look at the granite marker. It had been decorated with a bouquet (honoring the memory of a "flying farmer") in a big sprinkling can painted yellow. There were pink geraniums, blue daisies with red centers, petunias, carnations, and roses—all plastic. The can was braced against the prairie wind by a glacial field stone. The Mugo pine had not survived that prairie wind, and had been replaced by two junipers, pruned, from Colorado. Someone had thrust one spray of living goldenrod into the back of the can.

Further along the road, the Plowing Match was about to start its traditional "8:30—Drawing of Lands by Plowmen." Suddenly the farm rang with the lusty crows of a rooster—from a record put on the public address system. When the tractors started rolling into position—the prize winners' class, the men's class, the dealers with their six-bottom plows—I decided to head for the area where that splendid pair of dappled-gray Percherons had been so good to watch, and their proud owner so good to talk to, at a recent match (in spite of the fact that horses had been absent from the seventy-fifth annual match, they had been back again since then).

But that day no horses came, no mules, no oxen, though these were all listed in the printed program. Back at the headquarters tent, the explanation was brief: "No entries."

"Is there a James Patterson here today?" I asked, remembering how the Patterson name had been part of every plowing match, and was on many gravestones in the Wheatland cemetery, and was in fact on the list of "Plowing Judges" in the program in our hands.

"Jim Patterson, come to headquarters!" the call went out on the public address system.

A smiling face appeared, "What have I done now?"

"Lady wants to talk with you."

I asked questions for a long time that morning, and on a later day. Naturally the first question was "Where are the horses? And why didn't we see a single cow, or a chicken, or a pig, on our way over here?"

He answered, "Because general farming belongs to our past; today we farmers are specialists. When I was a child, of course we had pigs, and put down the pork in brine for the winter, and of course we had chickens, and cows. Double-purpose cows, some of them. Do you know what that means?"

"They gave milk and meat both?"

"Yes, and sometimes were hitched up to the plow, too. Now we buy our meat and milk and eggs. And eat different meals. In Wheatland we eat twice as much beef as we used to, and half as much pork. And there's no need to keep up our fences any more; they've been taken down, mostly."

One single apple tree was left on the plowing-match farm, over near the tent where the ladies were having their bake sale.

I asked, "Your apple trees are gone, too, aren't they?"

"Orchards plowed under to make room for more beans," he said. "That's what we grow now, soy beans and corn. Soy bean acreage has more than doubled in the last ten years."

"And oats?" I asked, pointing to the oats stubble that covered the plowing-match site.

"Oh that!—well this farm would certainly be covered with corn and soy beans, if it wasn't going to be used for this affair. But those crops wouldn't mature in time; and oats would. The oats harvested would barely pay the rental of these hundred acres, and the cost of seed and fertilizer, even though the work of sowing and harvesting is donated by local farmers. In the old days oat straw was used for bedding down the livestock, and the oats were used for feed."

"Don't you miss the manure that you used to get from that livestock?"

"Miss the manure!—well one truckload of commercial fertilizer will furnish as much plant food as a whole barnyard full of manure. That stuff can cost all it's worth just to haul it out and spread it, expensive as labor is now. When I was a boy nitrogen cost about 20 to 25 cents a pound. Now it costs as little as 5 cents a pound. The ten pounds of nitrogen in a truckload of manure was worth 2 dollars; now it's worth 50 cents. Doesn't pay to haul it. The rest of the manure is the humus, and that's important. We aren't getting enough organic matter into the soil, even though we plow the crop residue under."

"Speaking of prices, how do farmers in Wheatland feel about the sales of corn and beans to foreign countries lately?"

"Well, most of us were in favor of selling to them, I think. Our gripe was that we sold our corn for $1.50 a bushel and our beans at $4.00, and then after the sale, anyone who had them could sell corn at $2.50 and beans at $11.00."

"Tell me about something I miss about Wheatland, especially in the spring. There is no longer a precise checkered pattern of corn hills across the swells and dips of the land. Why not?"

"It was pretty to look at, wasn't it, and farmers took pride in doing it just so. But it isn't economical, not any more. Now we pack them into the rows, and give them plenty of fertilizer. The old checked pattern was for cultivating two ways across the field. We used to cultivate five times. Now we usually cultivate once."

"But the weeds—what keeps the weeds down?"

"Well (you won't like this), but herbicides are used to keep the weeds down, 24D mostly. If chemicals that control insects, weeds, and crop diseases were outlawed, the farmer would be unable to produce crops economically, and widespread famine would result."

"There's another thing I miss. There is no great giant of a corn plant on display, tied to a tree or a telephone pole; and no perfect ears of corn competing for prizes, waiting for judges to examine the depth of the kernels, the spaces between rows, the coverage of both ends of the ears. Why not?"

"That's just something we don't care about any more. What we care about is yield per acre, just yield per acre. Crowded into the rows the way corn plants are nowadays, the ears aren't going to take prizes for any kind of perfection. But the yield is high—oh, I know that doesn't seem likely. But it's a fact."

"Are there some aspects of farming on which the Wheatland farmers disagree?"

"Plenty! Always were, always will be. Some of us still keep sizeable home gardens; others don't. Some of us keep worrying about putting more humus into the soil; others don't. Some of us read the articles against using 24D and DDT; others don't. And now there seems to be something wrong with the moldboard plow that once seemed to us to be the greatest invention of all. The men from the university are saying that maybe we shouldn't bury all the crop residue, maybe our fields shouldn't look so neat, like velvet, maybe old stalks should stick out here and there from the plant parts that are not buried but just mixed through the soil. That way they could help with the runoff after rains. They're talking about a sort of V-shaped plow that gets dragged along beneath the surface and incorporates the residue into the soil."

"And you—what do you think about this different kind of plowing?"

"Mostly I think that Wheatland farmers would try it out—they have always tried out the new ways—but I am afraid that there won't be time. The suburbs are closing in on us. Our taxes are based on sub-dividing. This land is worth about $4,000 an acre. Much of it is being tilled by members of the third and fourth generations on this land. Have you noticed how the same names crop up on the plowing-match programs, year after year? For instance there is an eleven-year-old named Robert King watching the plowing. I heard him asking his father to promise him that he could enter the Beginners Match next year. His father is David King, now a Plowing Judge. He was the winner of the fifteen-year-old class in the seventy-third match, and a grand-nephew of the James King who won the original plowing match in 1877. Another judge today is Robert Erickson. He plowed in two national and two world matches, and in Sweden in 1955, and in France in 1961, and was a judge at the national match in Sauk Center, Minnesota, in 1973. Well, only three years to go to the hundredth anniversary."

I asked just one more question (James Patterson was needed somewhere else), "Could you tell me where to find some real prairie around here, now that the fence-rows are almost gone?"

"There's a little old abandoned cemetery over beside the railroad tracks. It's being saved."

That cemetery I knew well. Two of us had come upon its riches on a day spent scouting from one small cross to another on a regional map. We had found abandoned cemeteries in the middle of farms, far from any existing roads, some thoroughly invaded by raspberries, gray dogwood, black cherry, and other woody growth; some mown and planted with blue-grass from Europe. And then there was this one, with big bluestem and Indian grass, and switch grass waving high above our heads, and compass plant and rosin weed rustling around our legs. The cemetery ground itself rose high above the surrounding plowland which had been steadily peeling itself off toward the Mississippi under generations of plowmen.

It became a pleasure to visit that cemetery, to observe the stages in the confrontation between natives and foreigners. The old marble tombstones were still fairly intact. The grave plantings of old roses, peonies, lilac bushes, six-inch-high purple irises, lilies of the valley, love-in-a-bathtub, still bloomed on schedule. Springtime was espe-

cially interesting. Then natives, like yellow stargrass, shooting star, and prairie phlox, wove their way among irises and old red peonies; and the prairie pungencies mingled with the nostalgic fragrances of lily of the valley and lilac. The tensions, the advances and retreats of the two elements of the vegetation, were worth watching even though the natives were sure to win out.

It had been a fair confrontation, and I regretted missing the outcome, when it became necessary to enclose the little cemetery in a high cyclone fence. But it did become necessary, because a new thrill had entered this area, and the world—the easy titillation of vandalism in the dark. So the old tombstones, respected by generations, were demolished—even the small ones with doves, or lambs, went down. Finally the graves were being rifled for bones, and then the fence went up. Now there is a padlocked gate, and some may come to study prairie plants, and some to scatter or gather seeds, or to replace with natives any surviving Europeans, or to burn the whole thing off on a regular schedule in order to keep the grasses from taking over to the exclusion of other plants. Anyone who enjoys peering through the grating in the spring to see the low-blooming flowers that greeted the pioneers after their first hard prairie winter, or looks up to see the tall spikes of blazing stars and the turkey feet of big bluestems waving above the fence in the autumn, should be grateful for this sliver of the past, grateful not only to the dedicated volunteers who preserved it, but also to the pioneers who kept it from becoming plowland by being buried in it.

BIBLIOGRAPHICAL NOTES

"The Prairie Peninsula" by Edgar Nelson Transeau. *Ecology* 16 (July, 1935), 423–437.

An Ecological Survey of the Prairie Vegetation of Illinois by Homer Sampson. Illinois Natural History Survey 13, State of Illinois, Urbana, 1921.

"The Vegetational History of the Middle West" by H. A. Gleason. *Annals of the Association of American Geographers* 12 (1922), 39–85.

Découvertes et établissements des Français den l'ouest et dan le sud de l'Amérique septentrionale (1614–1698) by Pierre Margy. Maisonneuve, Paris, 1879.

Indiana as Seen by Early Travelers; A Collection of Reprints from Books of Travel, Letters, and Diaries Prior to 1830 edited by Harlow Lindley. Indiana Historical Commission, Indianapolis, Indiana, 1916.

History of Du Page County, Illinois by C. W. Richmond and H. F. Vallette. Steam presses of Scripps, Bross and Spears, Chicago, 1857.

History of Du Page County, Illinois by Rufus Blanchard. O. L. Baskin, Chicago, 1882.

[The Illinois Central Railroad Offer for Sale of Selected Farm and Wood Lands in Illinois] Rand and Avery, Boston, 1857.

Narrative Journal of Travels Through the Northwestern Regions of the United States; Extending from Detroit Through the Great Chain of ·American Lakes, to the Sources of the Mississippi River. Performed as a Member of the Expedition under Governor Cass. In the year 1820, by Henry Rowe Schoolcraft. E. and E. Hosford, Albany, 1821.

Travels in the Central Portions of the Mississippi Valley; Comprising Observations on Its Mineral Geography, Internal Resources, and Aboriginal Population by Henry Rowe Schoolcraft. Collins and Hannay, New York, 1825.

Chicago's Highways, Old and New by Milo Milton Quaife. D. F. Keller, Chicago, 1923.

"The Invasion of a Planted Prairie Grove" by Raymond J. Pool. *Proceedings of the Society of American Foresters* 10 (January, 1915), Number 1.

The North American Buffalo; a Critical Study of the Species in Its Wild State by Frank Gilbert Roe. University of Toronto, Toronto, 1951.

"The Indian as an Ecological Factor in the Northeastern Forest" by Gordon M. Day. *Ecology* 34 (April, 1953), 329–436.

Eight Months in Illinois, with Information to Emigrants by William Oliver. Walter M. Hill, Chicago, 1924 (originally published at Newcastle upon Tyne, 1843).

The North American Prairie by J. E. Weaver. Johnsen, Lincoln, Nebraska, 1954.

Horses: The Story of the Horse Family in the Modern World and Through Sixty Million Years of History by George Gaylord Simpson. Oxford, New York, 1951.

Plants, Man and Life by Edgar Anderson. Little, Brown, Boston, 1952.

Papers on the Prairie by Bohumil Shimek. Studies in Natural History 11, Number 5, University of Iowa, Iowa City, 1925.

"Structure of Prairie Vegetation" by T. L. Steiger. *Ecology* 11 (January, 1930), 170–217.

"A Prairie Continuum in Wisconsin" by J. T. Curtis. *Ecology* 36 (October, 1955), 588.

Chapters from Illinois History by Edward G. Mason. H. S. Stone, Chicago, 1901.

The Prairie World by David F. Costello. Thomas Y. Crowell, New York, 1969.

"Prairie in a Post-Prairie Era" by Ray Schulenberg; "Notes on Prairie Plant Cultivation" by Elizabeth Zimmerman. *The Morton Arboretum Quarterly* 3 (Summer, 1967).

The Prairie, Swell and Swale by Torkel Korling, 1972. Published by author, Dundee, Illinois.

7

Readin', 'Ritin',
and Recess

OR

TREE RINGS IN A COUNTRY

SCHOOLYARD

THE first time we passed that corner was during the summer. Someone in the back seat said:

"Look! There! Isn't that a little cupola, or bell tower, or something, in that thicket?"

"Schoolhouse, probably," grunted the driver. "Shall I back up?"

We decided to investigate next time.

It was November when we came that way again. The little
bell tower and half-boarded windows squinted out through weedy saplings.

As we pushed through the thicket it became apparent that, within
the last few days, the roof had been mended with a few shingles, and
several of the saplings that grew out of the very foundation had been
sawed off.

"This school must have been closed some years ago," said one of
our group, feeling the thickness of the saplings around the front stoop.

133

"Let's see if we can read the clues well enough to tell just when the school closed down," someone suggested, and we all agreed. "We" were one geologist, one teacher, and two botanists.

The geologist turned at once to the stout masonry walls of the school building, and to the cement floor that indicated the former position of a coal shed. There was still coal dust, and a few chunks of coal, left.

The teacher found a board that others had used, and braced it against the side of the building beneath a window and scrambled up and over.

We two botanists turned to the plants.

Presently, the geologist, tongue in cheek, narrowed time down cautiously out of the past.

"We can safely assume that the building was constructed well after the Silurian (some 300 million years ago), inasmuch as Niagara limestone, laid down under a Silurian sea, has been used at the corners and for window lintels. We can further narrow it down to post-glacial times on the evidence of the schoolyard's being glacial drift containing bits of Canadian rocks; and also on the evidence of the masonry walls, which are built of glacial boulders, bigger ones within, and small fist-sized ones carefully collected and laid up in rows on the outside finish.

"But a careful inspection of those ingredients of the wall reveals lime mortar, and also the fact that not all those cobblestones are natural ones; a few are man-made, and those green glassy lumps might have been bottles. That narrows us down to the industrial age, even without the help of the two boards over the entrance that bear the inscription:

S. S. DICKINSON

A.D. 1855

"Those two artifacts bring us right down to the September morning when the president of the Board of Directors, probably S. S. Dickinson himself, tied his horse to the hitching post beside the mud road, and went around to the other side of the surrey to help the probably high-collared, long-sleeved, pompadoured, young teacher get her several long skirts over the wheel.

Relicts inside,
pioneers outside

"So much for the opening of the school, but when it comes to dating the closing, I find few clues that speak to a geologist. There is the coal that still remains on the floor of the former coal shed, and there is no coal in the crack that has formed in the foundation. That crack, however, seems to have been made by a tree root, so that I should be encroaching on the field of my colleagues if I were to include that among my clues. There is a worn place on the window ledge—a form of differential erosion—that might indicate how long people have been entering through the window. But it is probable that the windows held against the public for several years after the school closed."

Then we added a little differential erosion to the window ledge, as we four scrambled up and over.

Evidently the schoolroom equipment, stove, desks, organ, cupboard, had, as with most schoolhouses hereabouts, been sold at public auction. The blackboard had not been sold because it was no more than a black painted strip across the front wall, above the built-in recitation benches. But, when buyers removed cupboard and desks, they evidently dumped their contents on the floor. No books were there; those, too, must have been sold. But there were scraps and torn fragments; enough for us, who had each been a teacher at some time, to piece together the educational era that had been in sway at the time the school closed.

Palmer-method writing, for one thing, with its rows of fifteen capital As to the line, pointed back at least twenty-five years, even allowing for a possible educational lag out here in the country.

Phonetic reading (back in style again today), from flash cards with "hop, top" or "fond, pond" on them, was there. We found no sign of the next era that started right in with whole sentences such as "Run with me to the tree."

Among the scraps was a bluejay picture, in outline, colored in with crayons. A soiled, stepped-on card cheerily said, "It is a bright, sunny morning." There were two Perry pictures, "The Return of the Mayflower" and Corot's "Spring"; but no colored pictures, unless the coloring had been done by the pupils, as suggested on the page torn from a Second Grade Reader:

"RIDDLES"

"I am little.
I am brown.
You are good to me.
You give me bread and water.
I like bones, too.
I find your ball for you.
What am I?
Draw me. Color me. Draw what I find for you.
            Color it red."

Two clues here! 1. A dog talking like a human! Anthropomorphism, educators would stamp it today, with a shudder. 2. "Color it red." No chance for a child to express himself, by coloring it chartreuse, or putting square corners on it, or a mustache!

Another clue, mixed with fallen plaster, was the nature of the titles that appeared on scraps of textbooks—titles such as "Africa," "Inventions," "Seeds." In a modern textbook such subjects might, or might not, be touched upon under a larger concept, such as "The World We Live In," or "Finding New Ways To Do Things," or "How Men Get Along." (The same difference between titles would probably crop up today between the answers of teacher and pupil if asked, "What are you having in your class?" The teacher might say, "How Living Things Rest," while the pupil, unprodded, or the teacher, if tired, might blurt out, "Seeds." But we have long ago learned to look for primitive characteristics in unprodded children and tired adults.)

Remnants of "busy work" lay in one corner—a card punctured into a picture of a Sunbonnet Baby, for sewing; a mat woven out of narrow strips of wallpaper. As I automatically started to put right the strip that had skipped a place, I visualized the small hands that had left the mat unfinished, baffled by that strip; the backs of the hands I visualized were stiff with chilblains, as hands had been stiff in the country school where I had taught forty-odd years ago.

There was no trace of "meaningful activity"—no orange crates, no hammers, no balsa wood, no test tubes.

The teacher gave her verdict on the date of the school's closing. Between eighteen and twenty-five years ago, she said.

We wandered out into the entry where the coat hooks still made a neat row, and a stout bell cord still hung. But the cord had been tied to a rafter when the bell was sold. We found the shelf for the water bucket, the ruffled parts of what had evidently been ruffled dotted swiss curtains, and a corner of a school flag.

Then it was the botanists' turn to show how well plants can record the passing of time.

We turned first of all to the three bur oaks. They looked like old settlers, but not old enough to have passed the crest of their muscular vigor.

One of the oaks was a natural "climbing tree." Many a pair of stout, home-knit, ribbed wool stockings held up by garters from a Ferris waist must have suffered from that ridged bark.

Those trees must often have served as "gools" for games; and their acorns must have been handy ammunition for schoolground battles. We walked on ground that was pebbled with them.

But what of the three acorns from which these trees had grown? When and how did they get their start? They must have germinated after Indians and their prairie fires were gone from this area. They would not have been big enough or corky-barked enough to resist those fires as mature bur oaks are able to resist them.

But how at that time did they escape being cropped off, with the grass, by wandering cattle? Fences were scarce; osage-orange hedges were small; and barbed wire and lawn-mowers were not yet available.

We turned away from the oak, undecided about its place in the chronology of the schoolground; and gave our attention to the elm that stood in the middle of the side yard. About fifty or sixty years ago someone must have planted it there, and given it adequate protection against damage during games at recess—else it could not have survived.

Two trees on the schoolground might well have been Arbor Day trees. In 1872 Arbor Day was started, in Nebraska, and soon spread to Illinois. One of the trees was a sugar maple; the other was a Scotch pine. Both had been well located to leave the front part of the ground open so that farmers could pull their rigs in off the road there, when they came to Speaking Schools, or Spelldowns, or Box Sociables.

Two other plants had been brought in, a black locust out beside the road on the west, and a lilac bush near the northwest corner of the building.

There were two gaps in time represented by the trees of the schoolground: one large gap between the age of the bur oaks and the pine-elm-sugar maple-locust-lilac group; one smaller gap between this group and the tangle of saplings. Many young elms made up that tangle, as well as young locusts, several young bur oaks, a few young ash, and a close thicket of young wild black cherry.

Among the young trees, one size predominated, the size of the largest specimens. We concluded that this dominant size indicated the group that started to grow on the schoolground in the first year after the school was closed down and the grass was no longer kept cut. We concluded further that the gap between the ages of mature bur oaks and the thicket trees represented years during which the grass had been kept cut. On the west side of the grounds alone, there were twenty-five trees of dominant size.

We counted some of their bud-scale scars, starting at the tips of the highest twigs and going downward. These scars, left when the protective scales are shed by an opening winter bud, were easy to count for the last eight or ten years, but scars of previous years had become obscure. By estimating that the earlier growth would have been only a little more rapid than the later, we concluded that these trees had started growing about eighteen to twenty-two years ago.

Then we turned to the five trees that had very recently, probably within the last week, been sawed down. Two of these were close against the foundation on the east side, so that they must have been growing directly up past the windows there.

We counted their concentric rings—nineteen.

There were several trees growing up close around the front stoop. All of them were of the dominant size, the same size as the elm that had been cut down on the east side of the building, and two locusts that had been cut down on the west side.

Beside those two locusts a pear tree had also been cut. All three of these showed nineteen rings.

A sprawly apple tree, uncut, was growing up out of the foundation on the east side. A few wormy, distorted apples lay on the ground under it.

At first thought the trees that blocked the entrance seemed to be the most telltale ones. Certainly they would not have been tolerated there when school was in session, and they would have been trampled to death as seedlings.

"Granted that they would not have been there while school was in session," said the teacher, "but how do you know that they came in immediately afterward?"

"And how do you know," asked the geologist, "that the grass was not kept cut for a few years after the school closed down? I can show you two country schools not far away that have been closed, but still have their grass cut."

Because of these arguments we turned to the apple tree and the cut pear tree for affirmation of our nineteen-year estimate.

No bird brought those seeds; the fruits are too large. And certainly no human deliberately planted either the pear or the apple, either as seed or sapling, in such a position, six inches from a masonry wall. Farmers have more sense than that. But someone might have thrown away a core, or spit out a seed—possibly spit it out through a temporary gap in the front teeth. Probably it was recess, morning recess, in the fall, and probably, for a little boy who wasn't wanted underfoot in the big boys' games, this east wall was a warm place to lean up against. Probably that boy liked apples better than pears. I remember how, in my country school, the best tidbits were eaten from the lunch box during morning recess. Probably the pear seed for the tree on the west side was spit out during afternoon recess.

This must have happened during the last year that school was in session here, otherwise the tender seedlings would have been mown with the grass, or tramped down during games of tag. True, it had to endure through that last spring session, but country schools closed earlier then, and the big boys with the heaviest feet were not there to play "Andy, Andy, over" and "pom-pom-pullaway" after the planting season started.

As we counted and recounted the nineteen rings of the pear stump, we felt again that we were keeping good company; at least we were hovering on the outermost fringe of the good company that has found interesting records in tree rings.

Venerable in that company was John Evelyn, Esquire, writing, in 1664, his "Sylva, or a Discourse of Forest Trees and the Propagation of Timber in His Majesties Dominions." Printed deep, with wooden type, into hand-made paper, we can read his cautious statement about the rings in trees:

> "It is commonly and very probably asserted, That a Tree gains a new one every year. In the body of a great Oak in the New Forest, cut transversely even (where many of the Trees are accounted to be some hundreds of years old) three and four hundred have been distinguished. In a Fir-tree, which is said to have just so many rows of boughs about it as it is of year's growth, there has been observed just one less immediately above one row then immediately below: Hence some probable account may be given of the difference between the outer and the inner parts of the Rings, that the outermost being newly produced in the Summer, the exterior superficies is condens'd in the Winter."

Outstanding among that company was the astronomer Douglass of Flagstaff, Arizona, extending his vision in one direction with the telescope, toward sunspots; in the other direction with a microscope, toward tree rings, and discovering the same rhythm in both objectives; and then deepening his understanding in the human direction, by a study of pottery patterns, until he was able to find the needed wood for completing his tree-ring calendar that has presented anthropologists with a new tool for dating.

Included in that company was Dr. Henry Cowles, offering as testimony in an Arkansas lawsuit the tree-ring record that proved that lakes had not been where early survey maps had placed them.

Towering, and most recent, in the company is Dr. Willard Libby, first suggesting that cosmic radiation, bombarding the nitrogen envelope of the earth, might split the nitrogen atom, and that one result of the splitting might be radioactive carbon; and then reasoning that this Carbon 14 would become a part of living plants. It was after his Geiger counter had clicked to measure the deterioration of the Carbon 14 in the spruce trees at Two Creeks, Wisconsin, that had been toppled by the glacier, that our estimate of the last glacial invasion had to be moved up from 25,000 to 11,000 years ago. But while the Geiger counter was testing for dates, it was also being put to a test by tree rings. A section from a famous old sequoia tree was used for this test. From this section a bit of the core was taken, because that was the oldest part. The Geiger counter made three counts. The readings were: 3,045 years, 2,404 years, 2,817 years. The rings on the section told the age of the tree as 2,905 years. The average for the Geiger counter readings was 2,710 years. The tree had been cut in 1874.

Farther out toward the fringe of the tree-record readers was Aldo Leopold of Wisconsin, sawing down an old bur oak, and interpreting the story of each ring in his "A Sand County Almanac."

And there was Enos Mills, of Long's Peak, finding records of earthquakes, avalanches, crowding neighbor trees, Indians, heavy snows, woodpeckers, Spaniards, and telling of them in "The Story of a Thousand-Year Pine."

And there is Jesse Stuart, another country schoolteacher, conscious of the importance of recesses, telling the story of a man who was able to keep his land only because of the irrefutable story in tree rings.

In 1953, a great white oak blew down in an eastern forest, and revealed in its rings a fire record that seems to support the idea that stands of oak in regions where the dominant forest trees include beech, and sugar maple, usually have fires in their history. The rings told that this tree had started growing in 1627. They showed fire scars, all healed over by vigorous growth, for the years 1641, 1652, 1662, 1676, 1701, 1711. Settlement in this area was in 1701.

The rest of the vegetation on our schoolground, other than the trees, had only a few comments to make on the past.

Many pioneers had come in. There were thistle, burdock, curly dock, giant ragweed, dandelion, wild roses, black raspberries, aster, evening primrose, catnip, wild grape, plantain. Together they recorded transportation by wind, by fur, by bird, by man. The plantain's ancestors may have come over on the *Mayflower*.

Out under the big elm, where an automobile party might have stopped for lunch, there was a four-year-old peach tree.

Around the coal-shed foundation the trees were younger. Nine years was the age we read on bud-scale scars of trees growing in cracks of the foundation, and between the foundation and the road. We decided that saplings had been cut nine years ago by the person who had bought the coal shed at the school auction and moved it away.

The future of the schoolground, if man did not intervene, was written plainly. Bur oaks were starting up through the thicket, even on the west side, far from the big oaks. Squirrels must have carried acorns to that corner. It was well on its way back to the same sort of forest that it must once have held. In the most dense spots where shade was deepening, grass and sun-loving pioneers were going, and their places were being taken by typical forest ground covers such as bedstraw.

But evidently man had plans other than a forest. The new shingles and the cut trees spoke of a new venture.

A big yellow school bus, bringing the local farm children home from the graded school at Algonquin, turned the corner.

"I thought I felt the schoolhouse shudder," said the geologist, who had been inspecting a pebble of granite from the edge of Lake Superior, set in the old wall.

We started for home, but we turned in at the first farm lane. No one questioned that stop. We wanted to check our reckoning.

The farmer was in his barn. He said, "Well, yes, I guess I ought to be able to tell you a little something about the old school, but it's been sold already."

We assured him that we didn't want to buy the school, we only wanted to know when it had been closed.

"Well," he said, "I guess I can tell you that all right. Let's see now. I graduated from eighth grade there, myself. I was fourteen then. Five years later I was back there off and on, going steady with the teacher, sort of. She was just out of high school, too, and a week of Teachers Institute. Next year they had a man teacher. Kept him two years. Then there was a girl teacher again. Stayed two years and then married a farmer over there on the River Road. That was the year I got married myself. There was some other girl teaching there that next year. I don't remember her much. But that was the last year. We were married in June, and when school closed next spring it was all fixed already for the kids from this district to go to school in town. Some people kicked about it. That was—that was eighteen, no, nineteen years ago."

He looked at us inquiringly.

"The reason we're so pleased is that we figured out it must have closed nineteen years ago, from the tree rings."

"Good for you," he said in a tolerant manner.

As we left, he pointed to the tool shed.

"There's a part of your old schoolhouse," he said. "That used to be the coal shed, I bought it at the auction, and moved it over here— nine, ten years ago, or so . . ."

As we drove home that day, we did not suspect that those school-ground trees would offer us still more tree-ring evidence.

We passed that way again a few years later. The bell tower no longer peered from a thicket. The thicket had been cut, and a big streamer across the face of the schoolhouse invited the public to enter the real estate office of a new subdivision. Shining cars were parked under the bur oaks, the elm, the Arbor Day trees. The lilac bush was gone.

A year later we sought out the schoolhouse again, and thought, when we reached the site, that we had taken the wrong road. A modern service station stood where the biggest bur oak had been. An expanse of cement, punctured by new gas pumps and a sign that said "Progress" in foot-high letters, covered the site of the schoolhouse. In back of the filling station lay the bur oaks, the elm, the sugar maple, the Scotch pine, the original black locust. They had been bulldozed out of the ground.

Then we saw the schoolhouse itself. Wrapped in stout cables, it had been moved on to a new high cement foundation to the east of the former school grounds. The bell tower was gone; the wooden shingles covered with roofing paper, and there were new two-paned windows. Out beyond it and the tumbled trees we could see several new ranch houses.

The upturned roots of the trees answered one of our questions about the bur oaks' beginnings. They held no trace of rich deep prairie earth in their clutches, only the pale clay of oak openings. This corner had probably been cleared to make a school site.

There was one more question—the age of the bur oaks.

bur oak
seedlings

bur oak
seedling

First day—1855

bur oak
elm
bur oak
pine
maple
lilac
locust

Last day—1933

peach
cherry
elms
pear
locusts

Eighteen years later

school
bur oaks
maple
elm
pine

Three years later
One hundred years after first day

We hunted up the owner of the schoolhouse, and found his wife at home. She had been a schoolteacher in the next district, and had come over to the cobblestone schoolhouse for box sociables. She regretted, with tears in her eyes, the passing of the bur oaks, and gave us permission to cut a slice from the largest trunk.

We got the slice, and counted the rings.

The tree was the same age as the school.

Probably the three oak seedlings owed their chance of survival to a thicket that developed on the line between school land and farm land. Perhaps hawthorn trees, keeping cows at bay, made a good oak nursery. A board fence may have helped. By the time the lawn was mowed, the young oaks would have attained enough stature to be respected by the mower.

Life had been easy there on the school ground, the tree rings, broad and evenly-spaced, said, with recesses to eliminate any springtime seedlings that might have developed into competitors for sun and rain, and with long peaceful summer vacations for untrammeled growing.

It seemed not unfitting that the trees that had been born with the cobblestone schoolhouse should die with it. On our way home that day we passed two great heaps of bur oaks that had been bulldozed out so that the land could be flattened for the even spacing of houses in a new subdivision. The time has passed, in that countryside, for country schools and bur oaks.

Country School—Revisited

When next I entered the old schoolhouse, there was no question of going in over the windowsill, as on our first entry—that was fully occupied by an air-conditioner. Nor was there any possibility of finding a scrap that proclaimed "It is a bright sunny day"; nor, indeed, of finding a scrap of daylight, sunny or not. The windows were covered, with shades, or plywood, or air conditioners, or all three of them.

There were desks for three officers (only two were present) of the Village of Barrington Hills Police Department. They showed us around without surprise. "A man stopped in here the other day, who had gone to school here a long time ago. He wanted to see the old

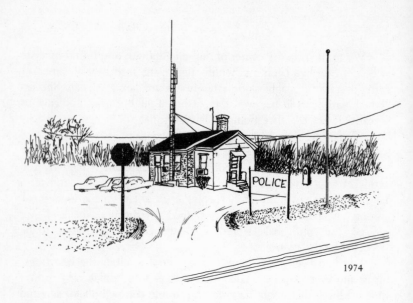

1974

place. Another man told us that farmers had used the building for a while, for storing soy beans."

Thin walls divided the space, and screened off the space heater, and made a wall for notices and "Wanted" posters, and a display cabinet for awards: driving-school diplomas, citations for traffic safety, various target-shooting awards, first place, second place, third place.

The ceiling had been dropped eighteen inches.

Keeping order had always been a part of the old schoolhouse, but the techniques have become more sophisticated than those that the young teacher had available: stay after school and clean the erasers; write "I will not shoot spit balls" a hundred times; stand in the corner.

We went out to the schoolyard, to see the rest of the equipment: cement paving that covered almost everything; three squad cars; a gas pump with a one thousand-gallon tank; a receiving antenna on the roof, and a transmitting antenna about thee times as long as the height of the school; an emergency generator; an impressive flagpole; and three signs: Police, No Truck Parking, and Stop.

A forsythia bush had been planted at the foundation, but it cannot bloom any more, disciplined as it is to conform to the air conditioner. An undisciplined box elder sprawls hippie-style in a back corner. It will be detected.

Rich farmland stretches across the pampered hills, with extensive white fences, and riding horses, and landscaping with evergreens, and swimming pools and patios. Retired land, it is, not supporting anyone, but being supported; and being protected by private lines to the old schoolhouse.

BIBLIOGRAPHICAL NOTES

Sylva, or a Discourse of Forest Trees and the Propagation of Timber in His Majesties Dominions by John Evelyn. Royal Society, London, 1664.

The Story of a Thousand-Year Pine, and Other Tales of Wild Life by Enos Abijah Mills. Houghton Mifflin, Boston, 1913.

"The Trees That Won a Lawsuit" in *Book of Plants,* by Bertha Parker and Henry C. Cowles. Houghton Mifflin, Boston, 1925.

Testimony of Trees, from *Clearing in the Sky* by Jesse Stuart. Whittlesey House, N. Y., 1951.

A Sand County Almanac and Sketches Here and There by Aldo Leopold. Oxford, New York, 1949.

Radiocarbon Dating by Willard F. Libby. University of Chicago, Chicago, 1952.

Sun Spots in Action by Harley True Stetson. Chapter on Tree-Rings. The Ronald Press, New York, 1947.

Tree-Ring Analysis and Dating in the Mississippi Drainage by Florence Hawley. The University of Chicago Publications in Anthropology, University of Chicago Press, Chicago, 1941.

"The Phytosociology of an Oak Woods in Southeastern Wisconsin" by Grant Cottam, *Ecology* **30** (1949), 271–287.

Dating Prehistoric Ruins by Tree Rings by W. S. Stallings, Jr. Revised edition published by The Tree-Ring Society with the cooperation of the Laboratory of Tree-Ring Research, University of Arizona, Tucson, 1949.

"Carbon 14 and the Pre-History of Europe" by Colin Renfrew. *Scientific American* **225** (Oct. 1971), 63–72.

"Upgrading Radiocarbon Dating" *Science News* (Aug. 30, 1969), 159–160.

8

Watching the Islands Go By

OR

BLACK HAWK'S PERSPECTIVE

OVER THE RIVER

"AND SO-O," the great professor would conclude, stacking his notes, and pushing his spectacles down so that he could peer over them at his audience—

"And so, the natives can sit on the shore and watch the islands go by."

That was the closing line whenever Dr. Henry Cowles gave his River lecture in Physiographic Ecology.

It had been many years since I had thought of that last line. Then it came back suddenly one day.

We had pulled off on a shoulder of the road for a view of the statue of Black Hawk, chief of the Sacs, silently dividing, with his upright blanketed stature, the clamor of autumn oaks on the opposite bluffs, and thrusting deep into oak reflections in the Rock River. No wonder he had fought and burned and massacred to hold such wooded hills, such rivers, such prairie, against the white man's treaty that demanded all these lands east of the Mississippi.

No sooner were we out of the car than our two bird watchers were away up the shore, murmuring something about "the waders."

The sketcher was off in the other direction, holding her card with the peep-hole in it, and squinting selectively at the opposite bluffs, and Black Hawk, the river, the little boy who was fishing, and at the island.

The boy's rubbery fingers needed help in coping with the plump night crawler; and his mother and father were still eating lunch and listening to the radio in their car. I put the worm on the hook.

"You fish, too," he invited. So I took his father's pole from the bank and gutted another worm. It was pleasant there on the bank with the autumn sun on our backs.

A shout was whispered from upstream, as only bird watchers and head librarians can whisper a shout. No pointing; that was taboo in their ritual.

"Blue goose—on end of island!"

I saw him there, on the blunt, upstream end of the island, a lonely looking individual, especially for October, when geese are seen in great congregations.

"Male, immature," breathed the first watcher from behind the gleam of binoculars.

"Juvenal plumage," exhaled the other watcher.

But just then the blue goose, male, immature, hurtled off precipitously. And where he had walked, an elm tree was lying down, in a tired sort of way, on one elbow first and then with its head in the river.

The water must have been undercutting that elm for a long time, and the straw that broke the camel's back apparently was laid on before our very eyes, even though the river looked so smooth.

The last yellow and brown leaves of the elm were dipped into the water. Many floated free. We watched them go.

They followed the long shoreline of the island. A few were caught in a tangle of low branches along the margin; some went on down the river.

But most of them gathered on the long tapering downstream tip of the island. There they stayed, bright among three green glass bottles that lay in a row, stem end upstream, along the side of that gritty tip.

That was the moment when I suddenly heard again that last line about watching the islands go by, and realized that I was seeing one in motion.

The elm leaves showed plainly enough how the substance of the island was traveling, how it was removed from the upstream end and deposited on the downstream tip. The green bottles were evidence that the island was growing by new deposits from the river.

The story of an island should, obviously, be read from the downstream tip, where there is perennial renewal, to the upstream end, where the chapter ends. Just exactly what was the succession of plant life out there, reading from low tapered bow to high blunt stern?

Just back of the bare tip, we could see a low dark-green patch. What was that? Back of it was a wine-colored drift. What was that? At this point the bird glasses came in handy. The dark-green patch proved to be rushes; and the wine-colored mass, lamb's-quarters.

How do rushes and lamb's-quarters arrive on an island? Both have minute seeds, without wings or other traveling devices.

A killdeer, coasting to a landing on the bare tip of the island, suggested a solution of the riddle. Lamb's-quarter seeds are known to be capable of lying dormant in mud for years. A killdeer might have landed in such mud, and carried seeds on his feet to this place.

Back of the lamb's-quarters was a tangled mass. In it we could detect milkweed, goldenrod, and thistles. The little fisherman's line had accumulated a mass of milkweed seeds. When it was time for a new worm, I plucked off one of the seeds to inspect it.

Here was a parachute for flight, and something more. It looked as if the seed were wearing a life preserver, a ring of corky material that might enable it to float. The seeds were coming down the river like boats under full sail. Many of the parachutes had become detached from their cargo and were floating free, but enough were complete. It was plain that milkweed might have arrived on the island either by air or by water.

Behind the tangle of milkweed, goldenrod, thistles, and other airborne pioneers, was a tall jungle of giant ragweeds. Beyond the ragweeds came the first of the woody plants. These were willows—all willows, in a dense, weedy mass of shrubby growth, six to ten feet high.

That would be sand-bar willow, *Salix interior*, chief pioneer of the soggy frontiers—sand bars, mud banks, downstream tips of islands. Wherever a river, slackening its speed, drops its load, the sand-bar willow is likely to be the first woody-stemmed opportunist to appropriate the new-made land. The thicket that we were observing was probably composed of only a few individuals, perhaps not more than one, sending up many trunks from wide-spreading roots and creeping stems.

Willows have two means of transport to an island. The seeds are air-borne, and the twigs have a habit of snapping off at the base and floating downstream, broad end first (as those three green glass bottles must have done), and becoming lodged in debris along the shore, where they take root. A willow's tendency to root from a twig is easily understood by anyone who has seen a springtime bunch of pussy willows develop roots in the water.

Behind the sand-bar willows, upstream, were bigger willows, actual trees. Beyond those were taller, wider, older willows. Mingled with the willows were silver maples, *Acer saccharinum*, showing the same many-trunked broad shape that seems to belong to the riverside fraternity always, and to the upland aristocracy not at all.

A few cottonwoods, those cosmopolitan pioneers of both wet and dry situations, were present.

There were a few box-elders and ashes, too. Those may have arrived on the wind, but I have seen their seeds often, in winter, skating over the ice, so they may conceivably have skated to the island.

Along the side of the island, near the upstream end, was a single hawthorn tree. How does a hawthorn arrive on an island? Probably this seed arrived in the intestine of a bird. If so, the parent tree could not have been too far away on the mainland, since a bird's digestion is rapid. Probably, out of the many hawthorn seeds that were brought thus, this particular one throve because it happened to be on the drier part of the island, in the sun, and in the hawthorn's usual habitat, the forest margin.

The upstream end of the island was entirely dominated by elms. Here again was a tree that used air transportation for pollen and seeds; one that had a wide-spreading top, and that could thrive with wet feet—but not such wet feet as the willow can tolerate.

The elms were the final chapter, with the elm that toppled over

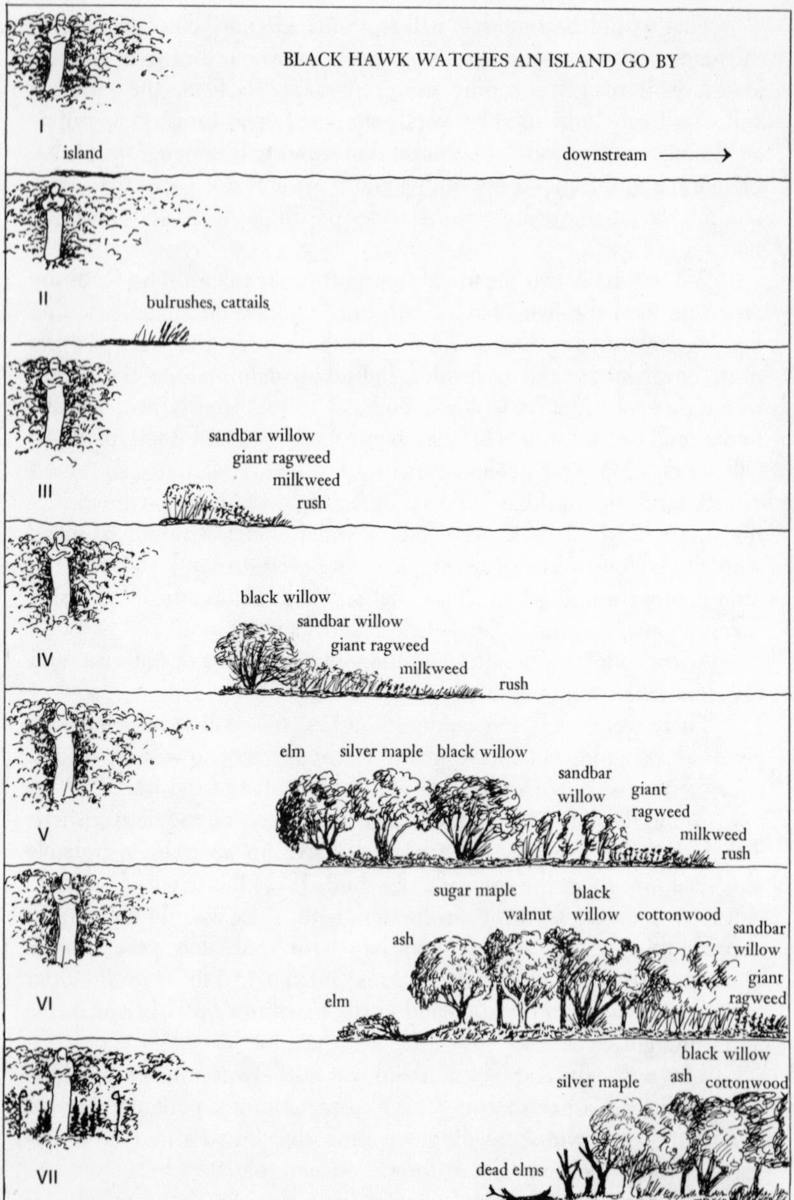

BLACK HAWK WATCHES AN ISLAND GO BY

I
island   downstream ──→

II
bulrushes, cattails

III
sandbar willow
giant ragweed
milkweed
rush

IV
black willow
sandbar willow
giant ragweed
milkweed
rush

V
elm   silver maple   black willow
sandbar
willow
giant
ragweed
milkweed
rush

VI
sugar maple   black
walnut   willow cottonwood
ash
sandbar
willow
giant
ragweed
elm

VII
black willow
silver maple   ash   cottonwood
dead elms

into the river as the final sentence and the depositing of the upstream substance onto the tapering downstream tip, as the first sentence of the next chapter.

Along the river road from Rockford to Grand Detour we listed, with the aid of bird glasses, the vegetation on each island in the Rock River. The succession from tip to butt end was the same on island after island. Some of the smaller islands did not attain the elm stage before their upper end was shifted to their lower end. Islands in a wide, shallow stretch of the river showed both ends tapered.

As we drove south along the river, we tried to visualize the sort of trip that our island below the Black Hawk statue might take, if there were no dams, no rush of tributary waters to alter its course, nothing but placid, steady advance.

Before many miles some new passengers would certainly come aboard. Sycamore would be first, rearing the layered patches of its bark and the bleached antlers of its boughs high above the upstream end, perhaps having time to form a huge hollow trunk for opossums and racoons to inhabit, before it would inevitably be toppled off into the river.

Somewhere between southern Illinois and Missouri banks, the catalpa and the river birch would quietly take passage. Farther down the river the sweet gum would unobtrusively come aboard.

Then some of the passengers would disembark. Silver maple, and catalpa, and elm, would leave before the end of the trip; but the sandbar willow would probably ride the prow the whole way.

Presently bald cypress would raise its bony knees along the margin; there would be scrub palmetto, and draperies of Spanish moss, and great white egrets nesting.

The final passengers would have to endure, not only excessive moisture, but also the bitterness of salt spray in their faces. The live oak seems able to tolerate both conditions, and Black Hawk's island might conceivably end its final chapter under the widespreading branches of fine live oaks.

There was one moment in our "islanding" when we felt a sudden kinship with the illustrious men out of the past who have devoted study to islands. That was the moment when we discovered our island's "mystery." Each renowned island the world over has seemed to present a mystery—or, at least, a problem.

On Easter Island, in the South Pacific, it was a matter of 550 statues, cyclopean masonry platforms, stone houses, that formed the "unsolved mystery of the Pacific."

On Crete it was the beginning and end of the advanced Minoan culture that formed the mystery.

On New Zealand it was the presence of wingless birds.

On Australia it was the lack of mammals, and the fact that marsupials were filling each ecological niche.

On Galápagos, it was the giant reptiles that interested Darwin first and Beebe later; and the finches that had developed to fill each ecological niche that would usually have been filled by some other kind of bird.

On Krakatoa it was the return of vegetation after the great volcanic eruption.

On our island in the Rock River, it was the summer home of a squirrel, high in the tips of an elm tree.

Why should he have built there where there was not a single nut tree? Did he swim back to shore every time he remembered the taste of acorns? Did he come swimming home again, with his cheeks bulging like two shopping bags? It was a squirrel's nest, plainly enough. It showed clearly in the bright rays of the setting sun. The whole island, and Black Hawk, were ruddy with sunset.

The little boy had caught a bullhead, and his father had come to admire it. The bird watchers had caught a glimpse of a spotted sandpiper, fall adult.

So we left Black Hawk to watch the islands go by.

The Islands—Revisited

As we stood again on the shore opposite the Black Hawk statue, we could see that the island had made little progress in its journey down the river. The placidity of the water above the dam not far from the downstream tip took care of that.

An elm had recently toppled off of the upstream tip, in the same position as that other elm of twenty years ago. But no leaves could have floated downstream off its branches. The tree had been dead, with broken branches and stripped bark, before it was undercut. The elm which would be next to go, and the next one and the next one—all were dead. Dutch elm disease had come to the island since our last visit.

Presently we were standing at Black Hawk's feet, and looking down at the island. The base of the statue had been landscaped with evergreens, and floodlit, and protected with barbed wire against climbing children's feet. We could see how wide the long island had grown. At the downstream tip the river had deposited not only bottles and cans but also two whole elm trees.

Up in the woods behind the statue, at the steadily enlarging Lorado Taft Field Campus, two friendly professor-naturalists told us about another change that had come to the island.

"Thieves have cut the black walnuts," they said.

Walnuts!

I and my field glasses had failed to see them from the opposite shore simply because I had not expected them to be there. The difficulty of perceiving the actual, through the foggy barrier of the expected, evidently had been too much for me. But someone else had been sharper-eyed, and had come back to work in the nights, felling and trimming and stacking the valuable boles. But they were discovered before a chance came for taking them away. One of the naturalists told me that he had been present at the auctioning of an especially fine log of black walnut, in Indiana. The highest bidder was a Japanese man who paid $15,000.

The mystery of a squirrel's nest would have been solved by those walnuts, but it no longer needed solution for me. For years I have watched the squirrels eating maple seeds, and ash seeds, and box-elder seeds, and much more. The foggy barrier that had kept me from seeing walnuts had evidently been thickened by third-grade-reader stories about squirrels and acorns. Out of such fogs mysteries can grow.

BIBLIOGRAPHICAL NOTES

Journal of Researches into the Natural History & Geology of the Countries Visited During the Voyage Round the World of H.M.S. 'Beagle' Under Command of Captain Fitz Roy, R.N. by Charles Darwin, John Murray, London, 1912 (original ed. 1845).

Galápagos, World's End by William Beebe. Putnam, New York, 1924.

"Trees for the Aleutians" by David Bruce and Arnold Court. *Geographical Review* (July, 1945), New York.

"Darwin's Finches" by David Lack. *Scientific American* **188** (April, 1953), 66–74.

"Small Mammal Populations on the Islands of Baswood Lake, Minnesota" by Beer, Lubens, and Olson. *Ecology* **35** (October, 1954), 347–445.

Darwin and the Beagle by Alan Moorhead. Harper and Row, New York, 1969.

Aku-Aku by Thor Heyerdahl. Rand-McNally, Chicago, 1958.

"Navigation of the Green Turtle" by Archie Carr. *Scientific American* **212** (May, 1965), 78–86.

9

Coming Ashore

OR

AS LAKE CHANGES TO LAND

How many times had my canoe slid to shore with that identical sequence of sounds!

But I had not been conscious of the sequence, until one windless evening when I rested the paddle to wonder what had suddenly made me think of Denmark. What feature of a starlit Wisconsin lake had summoned up the memory of Fru Gormsen hurrying to the window to peer into the narrow strip of mirror fastened to the outside of the window frame? It wasn't her checking on passersby that was memorable. Every house along that cobblestoned street had a similar mirror for that purpose, outside the lace curtains. It was what she had said, even before she looked, breathing it softly because the windows were open:

"Americans!"

"But how did you know?" we asked when they had passed.

"Silk petticoats," she explained. "I heard silk petticoats." (That was in 1920.)

Silk petticoats! They must have been the link between the canoe

157

and the memory. The canoe was sliding across lily pads with a silken sound.

But hardly had I realized the sound before it was succeeded by a different one. The bow was separating cattails with a subdued rustling, like that of a popcorn sack at the movies.

The cattail rasp seemed so inevitable after the silken sliding over the lily pads, so obviously one of a series of sounds, that I asked myself what had preceded the sliding.

Was it the dip and drip of the paddle in open water? Was the sequence, *drip, slide, rustle?*

No, there was something missing in that sequence. Something between the *drip* and the *slide.*.

There was an interval filled with a sort of tangled dripping, the stretch between open water and waterlilies—that stretch where submerged pondweeds enmesh the paddle and change the clean drip to a muffled spatter.

The sequence was: *drip, spatter, slide, rustle.*

I pushed off again, and went to test this sequence at another landing place—and another. The darkness seemed to help me hear the changes in sound, as keel and paddle stirred the surface of the lonely lake. *Drip, spatter, slide, rustle.*

But next day I went out to use eyes as well as ears on the situations that had shaped those sounds. I took along a fish pole.

Out in the area of clean *drip* the water was dark and clear. It looked devoid of life, but a microscope would reveal myriads of tiny transparent plants and animals. I knew the coldness of that deep water, because we used to dive into it from the seat of a row boat. The boys would bring up what they could in their hands. It was not much; it was, for the most part, sand and gravel, with a little trace of blackness, probably the residue of the dead bodies of microscopic floating life, and of material washed out toward the center from the margin of the lake. Once, long ago, immediately after the glacial ice had melted, the entire bottom of the lake must have been clean and free of all life. Then began the long slow process of filling in, the first stage being the appearance of microscopic forms of plant and animal life.

In addition to the microscopic life of that area of open clear water, there were a few algae floating free. I scooped up a handful of the filmy threads.

This free-floating life below the surface of the water seems to have a minimum of problems of protection, of survival, of food supply. Thin, permeable membranes, bathed continuously in an everlasting supply of nourishment, need no mechanical tissues for standing against the wind, no insulation against the thirsty sun, no roots for anchorage or food intake. And when winter comes, they need only sink to the bottom and await the warmth of spring. There is no need for floral structures fitted to bees or moths or wind or water, even, for reproduction is accomplished by one body's splitting into two, or by a simple emptying of one cell into another, all under the water.

FIRST STAGE in a small filling lake

free-floating microscopic plants and animals; and algae

cross section of margin

bird's-eye view

I paddled out of the *drip* area into the *spatter* area. Now I could look down into a rich growth of plants and see perch and bluegills swimming among them. With the long fish pole I poked down to learn the depth of the water. In most of the area it measured from ten to five feet.

After I had measured in a few places the fish pole became encrusted with the gritty scum which covered the surface of the water. Actually, this scum consisted of flowers, millions of them—the pollen-bearing flowers of the eel grass, *Vallisneria*. These had been released from a short stalk, far below on the floor of the lake, and sent bobbing to the surface. Most of them were drifting uselessly about, but here and there I saw some flowers that were fulfilling their destiny.

These flowers had been drawn into tiny dimples in the surface

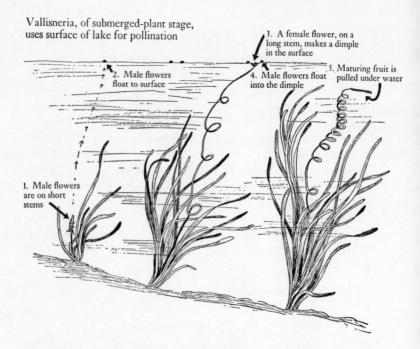

Vallisneria, of submerged-plant stage, uses surface of lake for pollination

3. A female flower, on a long stem, makes a dimple in the surface

2. Male flowers float to surface

4. Male flowers float into the dimple

5. Maturing fruit is pulled under water

1. Male flowers are on short stems

film—dimples made by the female, or pistillate flowers. The female flowers were not nearly so numerous as the male ones, nor were they floating free. Each one was attached to a long corkscrew stem. One that I managed to pull up into the canoe was twelve feet long, flexible, gummy.

Pollen-bearing flowers that floated into a dimple were sure to rub some pollen against the stigma of the pistillate flower. Around the canoe I could see plenty of pistillate flowers that gave evidence of having been successfully pollinated. They had pulled in their lines. The long corkscrew stems had tightened up their coils and were pulling the plumping seed pods down into the water.

The waterweed called Elodea uses the surface of water for its pollinating agent in much the same way that the Vallisneria does. But, like most of these submerged plants, it does not depend on seeds for distribution, but reproduces readily from segments broken off from the parent plant. This ability of Elodea has made it a real pest in Europe. Robert Gathorne-Hardy, in his "Wild Flowers in Britain," tells us that in "the early 1850s a piece of Elodea from the Oxford Botanical Gardens fell into the Cherwell. In 1853 it was seen in the Thames at Folly Bridge. Between 1866 and 1874 it had rendered parts of the Thames almost unnavigable."

Since there are only pistillate plants of Elodea in Europe, it is certain that this invasion has been by fragmentation, not by seeds.

I pulled up several kinds of submerged plants into the canoe: pondweeds, *Potamogeton*; hornwort, *Ceratophyllum*; white water crowfoot, *Ranunculus trichophyllus*; water milfoil, *Myriophyllum*. They were all swathed in algae. The spineless supine plants hung limp in my hands, as soon as there was no water to support them and give them form; and they broke apart easily at the joints. All that flaccid verdure, lying in a collapsed heap across the ribs of the canoe, was evidence of little need for mechanical tissue; of no need for protective structures. These thin-walled leaves are often, in submerged plants, quite as important in absorbing nutrients as are the roots.

The roots that I managed to pull up were unimpressive. As I lifted the mass from the floor to dump it over the side, it seemed to weigh less than might be expected. That was probably because of the big air chambers in the stems, a typical feature of submerged plants. Here and there jelly-like masses clung to the stems. In some of the masses I could see tiny spirals of snail forms developing.

Schools of little fish poured past. A tern dipped close beside me. I knew from experience that a leech was probably biding his time down there among the waterweeds, waiting his long wait for blood.

Except for the plants that were using the surface film as a pollinating agent, and for the snails that took a swallow of air down below with them, life in this zone was still shaped by a water medium, still submerged.

This stage of submerged life was gradually raising the level of the bottom, not only by the accumulation of partly decomposed plant and animal remains, but also, especially, by the slowing down of the currents, thus causing the deposit of inorganic material washed into the lake from surrounding shores.

Now the canoe was starting to slide over waterlily pads. No wonder their sound had been noticeably different in the night. Here was a rigid waxed surface. The leaves that the canoe had passed over did not appear to be as wet as might be expected of leaves that had been pushed down under water. Keeping the surfaces dry above is im-

SECOND STAGE
submerged plants

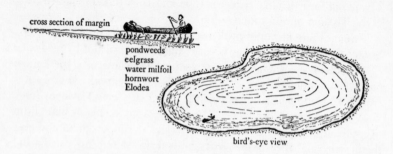

cross section of margin

pondweeds
eelgrass
water milfoil
hornwort
Elodea

bird's-eye view

portant to these floating leaves. Unlike the submerged plants whose leaves, for the most part, have none of the minute openings called stomates, and unlike land plants, whose leaves usually have stomates on their under surfaces, the waterlily bears leaves with stomates on the upper surface. The upturned edges of the leaves, as well as the wax, help to keep the surface dry.

I poked the fish pole down again among the waterlily pads. Here it measured depths ranging from five to two feet. The stems had neither stiffness nor wax. They were stout, flexible hawsers, that allowed the leaves to float freely, rising and falling with changing water depths. The flowers floated, too, on green sepals whose shape might have been the inspiration for the first canoe.

I picked a flower, and pulled it apart carefully, starting at the outside, and laying the individual parts in concentric circles on the floor of the canoe. (They had been growing in a similar concentric formation, but a more compact one.)

The outer parts wore a little white on their edges. The next whorl was less green and more white. Next were several bands of pure, gleaming white. Nearer the center, the white petals began narrowing and dwindling in size. Then there was one bearing a trace of yellow at its tip. The next petal had a bit more of the yellow. Each successive part showed more yellow, and dwindled further in size, until these were not petals that I was pulling off and laying down—they were stamens. But I could not lay my finger on any one place and say, "This is where petals stop and stamens begin."

This arrangement of flower parts suggests that a leafy stem, foreshortened, telescoped, might end up looking something like this. Reading in, from the outside toward the center, might be like reading a tabloid account of the development of a flower from a leafy stem—even to characteristic tabloid inaccuracies.

Looking down on the fluidity of that floral pattern of the waterlily, I was reminded of other flowers that show stamens that are half petal, or petals that are part sepal: delphiniums, peonies, roses, poppies, hollyhocks. Hybridizers, quick to recognize the possibilities of the unstable and, as yet, uncrystallized nature of such floral material, have encouraged the production of petals, at the expense of stamens. The wild rose of the field has become the many-petaled rose of the florist.

Such plasticity belongs to the primitive flowers—flowers from the lower branches of the floral family tree, from the living fossils; and consequently, flowers from the first pages of our systematic flower books.

In flowers from the uppermost branches of the floral family tree, flowers more recently arrived on the earth, the pattern is more rigid, more fixed. These present no such fertile field for hybridizers bent on doubling floral parts. Changes come hard to plants, or people, when their patterns are fixed, inflexible.

A beetle landed to inspect the dissected flower at my feet in the canoe. Then he took off for a growing one, beside the canoe. After he left, another beetle came, and another, then a fly, followed by a bee.

At first glance it looked as if these insects' visits could have no role in seed production, but inspection showed that the pistils were not ready to receive pollen at the same time that the stamens in the same flowers were ready to give off pollen. This meant that these flowers must depend on insects to carry ripened pollen from one to another.

On the yellow pondlily growing nearby, the flower opened on its first day only wide enough to expose the receptive surface of its pistil; later it opened wide enough to expose the stamens that would furnish pollen for another partially opened flower.

I noticed a neat circular hole in a leaf of the yellow pondlily and pulled the leaf in to investigate. On the underside of the leaf, the hole was partly ringed about with a double row of white eggs, arranged radially. These were the eggs of *Donacia*, the leaf beetle. She had bit-

THIRD STAGE
floating-leaved plants

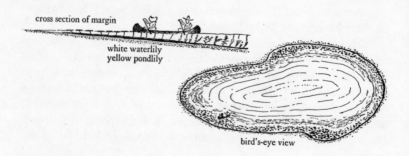

cross section of margin

white waterlily
yellow pondlily

bird's-eye view

ten the hole, and inserting her abdomen through it, had deposited the eggs there. It had probably been a *Donacia* that had gleamed with metallic bronze and green on the floor of the canoe for a moment when she came to inspect the parts of my waterlily.

Like the waterlily, she lives a life that uses both the lake and its surface, as well as the air above it. When those eggs hatch in about ten days, the little larvae will drop down into the water, but they will breathe air during their entire existence. They will attach themselves to the stout stem of a waterlily plant; this they will rasp with their spines, until they have made a hole. Into this hole each larva will push its head and thorax, and breathe the air that is in the air chambers of the stem—the same air that makes bubbles in the water when a waterlily stem is broken underwater. When the time approaches for the larvae to enter the second phase of their life cycle and to become pupae, each one builds a cocoon, silky and watertight, that holds this pupa or resting stage, in a place where air is available. And when the adult emerges from the pupal case, its body, enmeshed in silk and buoyed up by a bubble of waterlily air, floats to the surface, ready to begin again a life in the air.

The donacia eggs were not the only things attached to the underside of that leaf. There was a snail, and two small deposits of snail eggs in jelly, and a few elongated eggs, probably of the damsel fly. And in the shadow of another leaf a sunfish was hiding.

The waxy upper surface of these leaves had become familiar to me by moonlight and by flashlight, because we had come often in the canoe to turn our flashlight beams on the shining bubble of the throat of a swamp cricket frog or of a tree frog. These two, when filling our nights with the sound of clicking stones and sleigh bells, would invariably go right on with their songs even though we paddled close enough to touch them, and turned our lights full upon them. The green frog's banjo twang, and the bull-frog's "jug-o-rum" would pause briefly after we crept close, but they too would soon resume full strength. Amphibian voices, the first voices to be heard on the young earth when animals came ashore, belong in this zone in which plant and animal life has both submerged and emergent phases; and where the frog, beginning his life breathing water and ending it breathing air, is colored below like the water and above like a lily pad.

The floating-leaved plants altogether add considerable bulk to the lake margin, both of their own mass and by their catching of material washed in from the shore.

As I moved in from the *slide* sound of the waterlily leaves to the *rustle* of cattails, I used the fish pole again for locating the bottom in the muck of this emergent-plant zone.

At no place was the water more than two feet deep; in most of the cattail zone it was only six inches, or less.

Cattails, sedges, and bulrushes stood upright, sparse toward the waterlily zone, but densely crowded toward the shore. The leaves, reinforced against wind, sun, and decay, sounded and felt very different from the waxy saucers of the floating plants, the flaccid sponginess of the submerged plants.

The wind is important in the economy of the lake margin. Flowers of this zone depend on it for carrying their pollen. Here is no floating pollen-bearing flower such as the submerged Vallisneria sends bobbing to the surface; no knobby, heavy pollen sticky enough to cling to the hairy parts of insects, such as the waterlily produces. Instead, there is light, winged dust, suited to air travel, and prodigiously abundant, only a minute fraction of which is ever likely to arrive at a working destination. There is no insect appetite to guide this pollen, no chemical attraction, no dimple in the water film.

I examined a cattail. It was brown and thick. The upper part of the spike was shriveled, with all its pollen spent. A few weeks ago that upper part was golden, dusty, and thick. If struck, it would pour forth a cloud of pollen. The lower part of the spike was thinner then. You had to look with a hand lens to see the myriad stigmas held out like tongues. Those tongues must have caught their pollen, because the cattail was now swelling with ripening seeds.

Later in the season the wind will again become important to the cattails. That will be when their seeds are ripe and equipped with fluff for flight.

The erectness of the vegetation in this zone was being utilized by dragonflies and damsel flies. Above the water on cattails and rushes clung many ghostlike empty skins, split down the back. Those skins had contained fierce voracious creatures that crawled on the floor of the lake, seizing and eating anything smaller than themselves, and sometimes tackling living things a little larger. That was during the nymph stage of the dragonfly. Anyone who has put a few of these into an aquarium, and watched them eat up the other inhabitants, then start in on each other, knows how vicious they can appear. The winged creatures that emerge from those whitening skins merely shift the scene of their hunting to the air above.

The surface of the water among the cattails was alive with gyrating battalions of whirligig beetles, and with the water striders, skating on the surface film with each foot in a dimple of water.

FOURTH STAGE
emergent plants

cross section of margin

cattails
bulrushes
sedges

bird's-eye view

The canoe grated slightly on the narrow strip of shore, where clam tracks and clams and the masonry shelters of caddis flies were abundant.

There was the crackle of a fallen willow twig as I stepped out.

Among the willow trees around the lake are a few elms, many silver maples and ashes. There are no oak seedlings among them. Not yet. The hills around the lake are covered with oaks, but those hills are moraines, and their story is one that begins with dryness, not wetness.

The bottomland trees that are now only a fringe around the shallower shores of the lake will some day step out farther onto the mucky bottoms where cattails have prepared the way for them.

Then the cattails will grow out on the decaying remains of waterlilies.

The waterlilies, in turn, will float new leaves where submerged plants, and materials they have enmeshed, have built up the bottom so that it is shallow enough for them to get a foothold.

The submerged plants will then invade areas that have become less deep as materials have been washed out from the shallower margin.

Presently the submerged plants from one shore will meet the submerged plants advancing from an opposite shore, and gradually the water will become too shallow even for them.

Then the waterlilies from one shore will meet those progressing from another, and presently the water will become too shallow for them also.

The cattails will be right behind them.

The willows will lead then in the advancing company of bottomland trees. Eventually violets, Virginia bluebells, and wild ginger will bloom where the waterlily once floated. Orioles will nest where the tern dipped.

If the lake happens to be in the prairie region, the cattail stage will be succeeded by wet-land grasses, instead of willows.

In either case a canoe will be out of place.

This is the story of filling lakes, thousands of filling lakes. But some lakes have different stories. Successions may be changed or modified, accelerated or slowed down, by such features as the nature of the substrata; the material of the surrounding slopes; the degree of

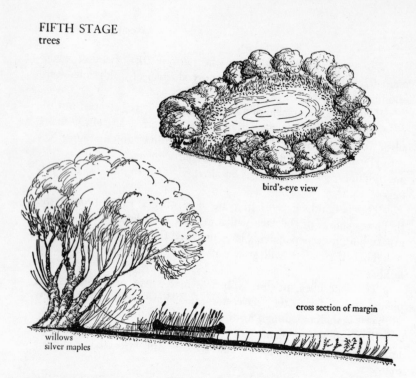

bird's-eye view

cross section of margin

willows
silver maples

slope of the shore, and the basin; altitude; latitude; or the development of the drainage pattern. There is a different story in an undrained, or poorly drained depression. This one is told in the chapter "History Book with Flexible Cover."

Sometimes man inserts himself into the sequence. He may raise water levels with dams. Then waterlilies may float again where violets and wild ginger have been for a time; and terns may dip again where the oriole has nested. Man may decide to halt the successions artificially, and capture a desired stage, instead of allowing the natural course of events to proceed. He does this in cranberry bogs, for example, and in areas flooded to maintain the species that are pasture for waterfowl.

In the end, however much the intervening story may have been modified, events march inexorably toward a time when wheels may turn where the canoe once floated; and the surface may be stirred into a cloud of dust, where once it was stirred into the sounds of *"drip, spatter, slide, rustle."*

Changing Lake—Revisited

During the years since I described the sounds of coming ashore in a canoe in a filling lake, that familiar lake has stopped making that succession of sounds. Instead of *drip, spatter, slide, rustle,* there is now only a clean *drip.*

That particular lake (which has been a part of our family vacations for fifty-some years) is slower to fill up than many. It is a spring-fed lake in a deep kettle-hole among gravelly moraines that rise steeply from a major part of its shoreline. Native vegetation covers a considerable part of the steeper shores.

In natural succession of events, the more-sheltered bays were being taken over by vegetation—with more or less speed according to their size and depth. The outer end of our pier, on a large bay, extended over a pavement of waterlily pads, interrupted only by temporary channels made by the canoe or by the muskrats who sometimes undermined our bank with their homes. The inner part of the pier was waved over by cattails.

Then the weedcutter bought by the lake property-owners association went to work. Anyone was free to use it, and many did, clearing much more than the area at their own lake front, partly because of general neighborliness, and partly because of being tired of tangled fishlines.

The cut plant parts were, largely, driven ashore. Sometimes one shore got it all; sometimes another, according to the wind direction. Whoever got it, raked it in and heaped it up on shore. There it amounted to surprisingly little, when dried out. Some was burned, some used as a mulch, or a fill, or to heap heavily on a patch of poison ivy.

We could swim again, in our own bay; and fish off the end of our pier.

Now, however, the state has made a ruling about weedcutters. They have become illegal unless equipped with harvesting devices.

So began a time of deciding about future action. Some owners lean toward investment in the new, but costly, equipment for cutting and harvesting. Others favor the use of weedkillers in a carefully controlled program. The State Department of Natural Resources is investigating all sales of weed-treatment chemicals to unauthorized individuals.

Meanwhile we watch with special interest the procedures in other lake-dotted areas—in New England especially.

One shallow lake in Massachusetts had its center covered with pink waterlilies that someone had planted not foreseeing such a spread. The edges of the lake (called a pond in Massachusetts) had been invaded by purple loosestrife, a naturalized European. Ducks and boats were finding their areas steadily narrowing. Swimming had been given up. Then the people invested a thousand dollars in a poisoning program. There was a period of revolting sliminess of poisoned vegetation, but now the lake is used by canoes and sailboats and many ducks and migrating wild geese and gulls, and swimmers. The program is in its third year.

Another lake (pond) in Massachusetts had become (according to a newspaper story) "a vile-smelling, weed-infested swamp. Sixty-one ducks died of botulism there. Fish succumbed in the murky, weed-choked water. And the stench made life miserable for the neighbors."

That city had tried weedkillers year after year. The dead weeds, they reported, "would sink to the bottom, clog air circulation of the waters, and exert a demand on the oxygen. This caused the odor."

Then, in 1972, the City Council and the Conservation Commission decided to try something else—costing $8,000. Weedcutting and harvesting machines were used. They loaded 25 truckloads and donated the weeds to a farmer who used them as mulch.

Now the engineers who managed the weedcutting and harvesting program feel that the program has been a success. The town is enjoying boating and fishing again. The Conservation Commission reports that "swimming may even be possible in the future if the Recreation Commission develops the site and the Public Health Department approves."

The second phase, which was to have been aeration of the pond, may not be necessary, because the wind seems to have taken over the aeration now that the heavy mats of vegetation are gone.

To our lake in Wisconsin, another change (not connected with the filling problem) has come, engineered by the Department of Natural Resources.

winter lodges

The lake had one very small enclosed bay from which a trickle of brown bog water sometimes made its way out into the lake over the bar across its mouth. The retreating glacier had left the hills enclosing that shallow kettle; and the northern vegetation, driven south by the glacier and then surging back north on its heels, had left behind a few glacial relics. The ones left on the hills lasted until shade, crowding, or cows finished them off. But down in the acid bogginess of the enclosed bay, some relics survived, especially the leatherleaf, *Chamaedaphne*, a member of the heaths, a family which tends to occupy acid soils around the world, and to take over places where other plants can't grow. Conspicuous against this dark, leathery low shrub, the light-green fronds of marsh-shield fern stood erect. Sphagnum moss carpeted the surface.

The water at the perimeter of the bay was different, not acid. Drainage from the surrounding hills, with their high proportion of limestone bits, was responsible for that. This "moat," as ecologists call it, was filled with cattails.

The small bay was a museum piece, a record of time and change and tolerances.

But the Department of Natural Resources decided to use that site for a "fishery research project." First they "attempted to reduce the leatherleaf density by burning" and then they "seeded in some reed canary grass." They did "limited dredging at the outlet of the bog, and inundation during April and May." (The quoted parts are from a letter of explanation that I received from the headquarters.) They also installed a small dam with a gate, at the narrow entrance to the bay, to hold the water above lake level until fingerling northern pike were ready for release into the lake.

The purpose of the project was to "help provide guidelines for development of other controlled northern pike spawning marshes"; and to "augment the northern pike population in this lake."

"The northern pike normally spawns in shallow weedy areas, a habitat which is adversely affected by man's shoreline development activities; e.g., filling of marshy areas to create cottage sites. This project sought to determine if, under controlled conditions, such incursions on northern pike spawning habitat could be offset, at least in part."

In view of the fact that our particular lake has among its steep-sided moraines a minimum of marshy areas, and an almost complete lack of filling for cottage sites, the project seemed misplaced. Especially since fifty years of fishing there has always produced an occasional northern pike. Probably the fishermen will get more of them for a while after the researchers withdraw, and then the proportion will return to the one established by the nature of the lake.

Our despoiled bay may, however, not have been sacrificed in vain; the research may have earned a masters degree for some student.

During the past summer of extremely high water, when boathouses stood deep in water, it was suggested that some of the excess water might be pumped into the deepened container that the bog had become—after closing the new dam again, and perhaps raising it.

The high water of the lake continues to produce changes. Trees that cannot tolerate standing water around their roots have already begun to die. Pin cherries were the first to go.

The many muskrats of the lake are changing their house-building styles. Through the years they have built none of the characteristic domed winter lodges (except for one or two in a very shallow bay). The steep banks were riddled with the muskrats' channels to the high and dry burrows which are their usual summer homes. In our lake such burrows served for winter and summer both. But not in this year of high water. They are moving out, offshore; and are using as a foundation any partly-submerged tree base, or any undermined tree that has lain down on the water. There they are building, at a great rate, the traditional winter lodges of their species.

The lake gets excellent reports on its water, which must be regularly tested for the Girl Scout camps. A recent report from a company of marine-biochemists says: the water shows good clarity and grades out very good to excellent; the lake has good food value for fish growth, and appears to be stable and is not exhibiting an excessive algae condition. Property owners are asked to keep it clean, by bulletins that make requests that anyone washing hair in the lake use no detergents, and that owners who have lawns not use fertilizers on the slopes toward the lake, and that as much of the shore as possible be left to its native cover of trees and shrubs.

BIBLIOGRAPHICAL NOTES

Animal Communities in Temperate America by Victor Ernest Shelford. University of Chicago Press, Chicago, 1937.

Clean Waters for New York State by James G. Needham. Cornell Rural School Leaflet 13, Number 4, Dept. for Rural Education, Cornell University, Ithaca, N. Y.

Field Book of Ponds and Streams by Ann Haven Morgan. Putnam, New York, 1936.

Field Book of Animals in Winter by Ann Haven Morgan. Putnam, New York, 1939.

"Plant Succession of Long Pond, Long Island, New York" by Dorothy Parker. *Butler University Botanical Studies* 7 (April, 1945), 74–88.

"Plant Succession About Douglas Lake, Cheboygan County, Michigan" by Frank C. Gates. *Botanical Gazette* **82** (1926), 170–182.

"The Development of Vegetation in the English Lakes Considered in Relation to the General Evolution of Glacial Lake and Rock Basins" by W. H. Pearsall. *Proceedings of Royal Society, London*, Series B 92 (1921), 259–284.

The Life of Inland Waters by James G. Needham and J. T. Lloyd. Comstock, Ithaca, N. Y., 1937.

Lands Beyond the Forest by Paul B. Sears. Prentice-Hall, Englewood Cliffs, N. J.

Of Men and Marshes by Paul Errington. Macmillan, New York, 1957.

10

Camp Sites, Fires, and Cud-chewers

OR

HOW THE UPLAND FOREST

CHANGES FROM ILLINOIS

TO WISCONSIN

RUMINANTS and fires played a part in our trip from the very start before we had even reached the place in Wisconsin where we were to pick up our canoe. Fires long dead, and ruminants of two kinds, shaped our first lunch stop.

That was in northern Illinois.

A splendid piece of woodland, four-layered, had red oak and white oak forming the canopy, with ironwood, young sugar maples, spikenard, and bloodroot beneath. We considered lunching there, but we were discouraged, partly by signs, partly by mosquitoes, but most of all by an efficient fence. By excluding ruminants, this was responsible for preserving the four-layered aspect.

We stopped instead in an oak opening, where old bur oaks stood widely spaced, with a few hawthorns, a blackberry patch, and grass beneath.

If buffalo had not grazed out there in the prairie beyond these woods; if Indians had not hunted the buffalo with prairie fires; if the prairie fires had not beaten against the edge of the forest; if the bur oak had not worn a corky bark that kept it from being eliminated along with the thinner-barked trees; if a farmer who came after the Indians had not turned his cows into this oak opening to graze; and if hawthorns had not worn stout thorns that kept them from being grazed by the cows, then we should not have been lunching in a parklike area such as this, and listening to a brown thrasher singing in a hawthorn tree.

After lunch we walked through the oak opening to the pasture where the cows were grazing. There, invading the bluegrass and redtop that had replaced big bluestem and Indian grass under the influence of plows and cows, were many strangely shaped specimens—cow-pruned hawthorns. We could see every stage in that mute drama of a midwestern pasture.

The earliest stage was hardest to find. They were not as tall as the mullein stalks, those tiny hawthorns. We found one that a cow had just been nibbling. It was not more than four years old and seemed to be having a struggle for existence. It would probably have been devoured completely had it not had a few thorns.

Nearby was an older specimen, denser, thornier, with more years

Hawthorns and blackberries under bur oaks mark a grazed forest

of intensive cow-pruning in its history. The perfect cone shape looked almost artificial.

Beside it stood one of a little later stage, wider, higher, but just as dense and trim. Evidently it had managed to do a little growing each year in spite of the intensive clipping of tender tips.

Not far away grew a hawthorn that seemed to be making the first triumphant gesture in this sequence. It had slowly grown just wide enough so that the cows could no longer quite reach the tip of the cone. That was the turning point. Suddenly it was able to pour its growth upward, uninhibited.

Then came the hourglass stage. Several in that stage stood around the pasture, trimmed by cows, as far in, and just as far up, as they could reach.

Up above the cows' reach the branches began to spread horizontally, in the characteristic way of the hawthorn.

Pasture hawthorn
1. tender tips

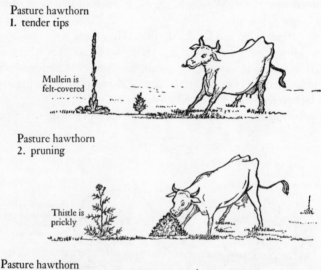

Mullein is
felt-covered

Pasture hawthorn
2. pruning

Thistle is
prickly

Pasture hawthorn
3. slow growth in spite of pruning

Vervain
is bitter

Pasture hawthorn
4. top shoots inaccessible

Pasture hawthorn
5. hour-glass shape

Pasture hawthorn
6. spreading branches

Gradually the wide-spreading branches shaded out the old cone at the base of the trunk. A few broad trees still wore a ring of dead sprouts around their feet—all that remained of the barbed-wire entanglement that made their development possible.

This cow-pruned hawthorn story may have a prelude, also with the cow as the chief factor. Some sort of prelude is needed to explain the survival of the seedling tree during its first two or three years, because thorns on seedlings are much too tender to repel a grazer. I can eat them, and have, as an experiment.

One summer the Morton Arboretum, where I work, was enlarged to include a considerable piece of land, mostly pastured, with many hawthorns.

While helping to make a plant count there (made immediately after the cows were taken out, so that we could record the changes during the coming years), I began to suspect that a cow-pruned hawthorn may owe its existence, as well as its shape, to a cow. The fastidiousness of a cow may be an ecological factor.

This is the way it apparently happened in this field:

1. A cow deposited dung.

2. No cow ate close to that patch in the following season. The cow dung became ringed with ragweed. Ragweed has good seeds for birds. A bird that came to eat had previously eaten a hawthorn fruit.

3. A little hawthorn started to grow in this sanctuary, well-protected, well-fertilized.

4. The cows did not eat close in the second year either. Yarrow and other weeds replaced most of the ragweed. The tiny seedling had sun, shelter, room, organic fertilizer, mulch.

5. The cows seemed not to reach the seedling in the third year. The twigs had a chance to harden their wood and *stiffen their thorns.*

6. The cows seem to have overcome their fastidiousness at about the fourth year. Then the little tree was sharply pruned of all its tender tips, but not exterminated. (Some of the patches had prairie roses in them. A few had wild crab apples. A few had slippery elms, but those had no thorns to stiffen.)

We ate our supper beside a small lake, in southern Wisconsin, on an oak ridge between two kettle holes (as we call the bowl-shaped hollows formed where great chunks of ice were left behind by the glacier). Under these oaks there was grass, as there had been at our lunch stop in Illinois, and blackberries, too, but no hawthorns. Filling the same ecological niche that the hawthorn had filled under those bur oaks of northern Illinois was another tree that, like the hawthorn, was bird-distributed, and prickly, too. This was the red cedar, *Juniperus virginiana.*

All around the lake, on the many hills of that kettle-moraine country, there were red cedars among the oaks. Those hills had been grazed for many years before the farmers started selling off the lakefront plots to summer people. There were different shapes of red cedars, telling something about the different times at which plots had been sold and fenced off from cows.

Around the first cottages on the lake, fenced off more than fifty years ago, the few remaining cedars were a spindly, thin, brownish lot. The growing shade of both tall canopy trees and smaller understory trees had been too much for them.

On our own piece of land, where the cows were fenced out twenty-seven years ago, there were some shapely compact trees, big ones, that had attained a good size in the sunny pasture openings. There were many smaller, spindly specimens, that were being over-topped by twenty-six-year-old oaks. Directly under the branches of several oaks there was a thick stand of small cedars, perhaps a record of a flock of cedar waxwings that perched there after feeding on cedar berries.

Across the lake, where sheep were still pastured, the hills looked parklike, manicured, with short-clipped grass, and with the cedars trimmed as far up as sheep can nibble, standing—with their forefeet braced against the trunk.

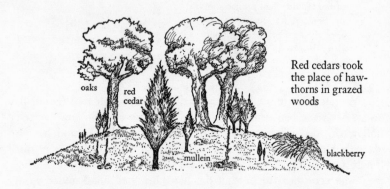

oaks
red cedar
mullein
blackberry

Red cedars took the place of haw-thorns in grazed woods

Any occasional hawthorn that I have found around this lake has been puny, distorted, and dying, with orange spots on its sparse foliage. These orange spots are the mark of the cedar-apple rust. In the fall, each spot develops white beards on the underside of the leaf. These put out spores. Some of them, wind-borne, make a landing on a red cedar. There they slowly develop into cedar apples. By the second spring, these brown "apples" are about an inch in diameter. Then they put out beards, and become orange and gelatinous. At that time their spores are taking to the wind. Some of them land on a hawthorn. The drastic loss of leaf surface suffered as a result, weakens and eventually kills the hawthorn. Because these two trees that may fill the same ecological niche are alternate hosts to this cedar-rust, one does not find them hobnobbing in a grazed woodland.

As we ate our supper there on the ridge between the kettle holes, it was so warm that we discussed going over to the farmer's field, to see if it was true that one could hear the corn growing on warm nights. But it was too warm for any effort, and we fell to talking, instead, about the camp sites we hoped to find. We visualized tall pines and hemlocks, close-ranked, with a deep pile of needles under our sleeping bags, and enough balsam fir for stuffing our pillows.

What we were hoping for was the forest that greeted the early settlers, with marching miles of potential ship masts, beams, clear-grained framing and siding. Such a forest in Wisconsin records two conditions: sandy soil and/or fires. It is not a self-replacing forest. Should enough time elapse without fires, even the sandiest of soils would probably be clothed with a cover of hemlock, beech, sugar maple, and yellow birch. That canopy will have a young forest of the same trees rising up through its shade. The forest will then have arrived at the self-replacing stage. Every ecological niche will be filled, with no room available to outsiders—unless some force such as man, or fire, or wind, opens a place, and lets the sun in again for a while.

When we hoped for balsam fir to fill our pillows, even while we slept on pine needles between uniform tapering columns, we were depending on the habit forests have of interlacing long fingers with neighboring forests. Balsam fir found here could only be a finger poking south from the boreal forest of spruce and balsam fir.

Many years previously, I had botanized in some imposing stands of white pine, red pine, and hemlock in the Lake Superior region. Appallingly often, when we talked to local people, they told us that the forest we admired was to be cut during the next year. The urgency at that time was World War I.

During succeeding years, we made two canoe trips into this area. Twice we had the good fortune, my high-school son and I, to camp under tall stands of pine and hemlock; once on an island in Crab Lake, and once on a high bank overlooking Presque Isle Lake, where the hemlocks were memorable. That was the place where we heard wolves howl one night; and where the arborvitae fringing the shores had been neatly trimmed to the height that deer could reach from the frozen lake. At that time I had failed to see the connection between the wolves and the arborvitae.

World War II, and the building boom that followed, had incited more cutting of forests.

That we might succeed in camping, for even one night, in the forest of my memories, was almost too much to hope for. But I hoped for it, nevertheless, because I wanted to show it to my daughter before it should have disappeared utterly.

In the early morning we hoisted the canoe on to the top of the car, and started north. We had only five days for our canoe trip, and one of those days must be devoted to transporting the canoe from Pleasant Lake to White Sand Lake in the Northern Highlands Forest. Another must be spent in transporting the canoe back to Pleasant Lake. That left us with four nights out, with four different camp sites along the circular route we had laid out on the map.

As we drove north we read the succession of records that rain and sun and soil and man have written across the face of Wisconsin. We were not reading the margins of the highways, because we realized that highway margins are dominated by European plants. Nor were we reading the river valleys. We knew that southern vegetation pokes its long fingers northward up the river valleys. Nor did we read the bogs that we passed, because those held a relict vegetation, left behind by the glacier's invasion. What we did read was the upland of Wisconsin. We were watching eagerly for indications that we were approaching our visualized camp site.

The first change was in the barns. The roadsides were still dominated by bouncing Bet and chicory, and the small towns by hollyhocks, when the big dairy barns, with their plump silos, gave way, somewhat abruptly, to a different type of barn, flimsier-looking, with slits in its vertical siding. Tobacco barns they were. The tobacco, that thrives on cold nights, made dark-green patches here and there in the landscape pattern. The corn, that thrives on warm nights, was no longer dominating the scenery.

The next indication of change was read on signs along the roadsides, hung out near the mailboxes. The signs said, "Maple Sugar for Sale. Maple Syrup for Sale." And when we stopped at a roadside stand we bought not only maple sugar, but also basswood honey.

We ate our lunch late, but we ate it on a high hill overlooking slopes covered with maple and basswood forest. We had planned to eat breakfast in one type of forest, lunch in another, and supper in still another. So far we were running on schedule.

As we started north again we noticed that the dairy barns had taken on a new appearance. Many of them had the upper part overhanging the first story on one side, with arched openings under the overhang. That provision for shelter for cattle spoke of hard winters.

And presently the trees that have become adjusted to longer winters made their appearance. We began to see small groves of evergreens here and there, but we did not find ourselves passing smoothly into the evergreen forest. Instead, for mile after mile, there was a scrubby growth of birch, aspen, and jack pine.

These are the "pioneers," with special qualifications for clothing the burned-over and cut-over areas and for preparing the way for the eventual forest, and, simultaneously, for their own extermination.

Here were jack pines by the million. Nothing stately about them; nothing to inspire the galaxy of poems that white pines have engendered, but with one distinctive character, their cones. These stay closed for a long time, sometimes not opening until touched by the heat of a forest fire, with the result that the fire may automatically help to reforest the area that it is deforesting.

Here, too, were birches and aspens, rising three-fold, or five-fold, from the cut or burned stumps. This root-sprouting habit, and the presence of abundant winged seeds, are important features of these pioneers. The feature that limits the tenancy of pioneers is their inability to tolerate shade.

As we continued northward there was an occasional narrow spire of a balsam fir or white spruce. By the time these began to appear, the big dairy barns had definitely disappeared.

At Stevens Point we unconsciously put on a burst of speed. That was because of a sudden fear that all the woods would be gone before we reached our first camp site—there were such great piles of pine logs along the Wisconsin River. Many of the piles were of small stuff—pulpwood. But several piles were of sizable logs.

We were within the limits of the pine-hemlock forest. On the courthouse lawn in Portage we saw a section of a huge white pine, with a bronze plate, explaining that this was a piece of one of the very last of the Big Pines of Wisconsin. In Wausau there was another section, with another bronze tablet.

We drove along, visualizing the endless upright battalions that had met the eyes of the pioneers, the forest described by Increase

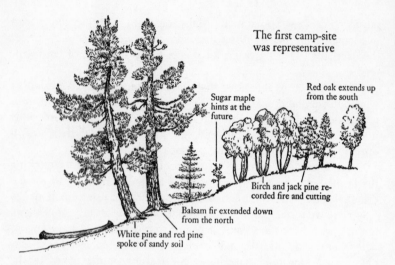

The first camp-site
was representative

Sugar maple
hints at the
future

Red oak extends up
from the south

Birch and jack pine re-
corded fire and cutting

Balsam fir extended down
from the north

White pine and red pine
spoke of sandy soil

Lapham in 1852, by T. C. Chamberlain in 1877, and by C. S. Sargent in 1884. We couldn't help wishing that Paul Bunyan and his blue ox, famed in lumber-camp tales, had been a little less muscular.

We passed the gadget outcrops of the tourist shopping towns at Minocqua and Woodruff, and then left the highway at last, to follow a dirt road to White Sand Lake.

There we found a memorable camp site. Before sliding the canoe into the lake we ate wintergreen and a handful of blueberries as a sort of ritual; and we squeezed and smelled a handful of balsam-fir needles, and a leaf of Labrador tea. Then we cooked our supper on a high spot among jack pines and birches that told of lumbering and fire.

Before it grew quite dark we had time to visit the dark little stream that hurtled along among tamarack trees and alders, and curved around our camp site to pour its mahogany waters into the lake.

We spread our sleeping bags on the sandy shore under a few tall white pines and red pines. Among the pines a few narrow spires of balsam fir and white spruce were outposts of the boreal forest to the north; two small red oaks, northern extensions of the forest to the south. A small sugar maple represented the forest of maple, beech, yellow birch, and hemlock that is destined to clothe this site when sandy soil and man and fire shall cease to dominate.

Folding fans of northern lights, and the voices of a loon and two owls, made sleep unprofitable. I lay and wondered about the two trees that were missing from this assemblage.

There should have been hemlock among the pines; and there should have been arborvitae along the margin of the brook; and, along with the rich undergrowth of wintergreen, clintonia, prince's pine, trailing arbutus, and club mosses, there should have been yew. Where were the hemlocks, the arborvitae, the yew?

Evidently we had not yet achieved our goal of a camp site in the forest that first challenged Paul Bunyan. But, none the less, it was a good first camp site, offering a sampling of all the situations we might expect to encounter.

In the morning we crossed White Sand Lake into White Sand River. For many hours we twisted and turned and ducked among alder, tamarack, and black spruce, wading three times to push the canoe over beaver dams.

Then White Sand River flowed into the swift current of the clean, sand-bottomed Manitowish, and we rode the current into Boulder Lake.

Scowling, growling skies drove all thought of a pine forest out of our minds, and we made a hurried camp among birches, harebells, and bracken fern—not much of anything else in the way of vegetation. The birches were many-trunked, most of them, recording a fire that had followed the obvious lumbering.

The wet margin of our point had the usual wet-edge material—hazelnut, alder—but no arborvitae.

The knob back of the point had a few red pines, and one or two white pines, but no hemlock, no yew.

The second camp-site
recorded lumbering
and fire

hazel and alder   birches   bracken

Across the bay, two does and a fawn came down to the water. They, like the howling wolves that my son and I had heard on a previous trip, were clues that we failed to interpret until later.

Next day, after a portage past the rapids, and a pause to fish the white water, there were long hours on the clean Manitowish, with two imposing beaver dams to cross, and with the discovery that one of the best possible ways to see wild life is to float with the current down a lonely river.

A mink swam along beside us, close to shore, dodging under roots, and bobbing up again. We lost his company because the current carried us faster than he swam. A porcupine thrust out a piggy snout and beady eyes between rushes at the stream's edge. A merganser and twelve young swam sedately ahead of us, and then all silently submerged as we gained on them. A buck scooped up mouthfuls of duckweed, slobbered noisily. On a steep bank lay many shells of turtle eggs, probably the remains of a buried nest rifled by skunks.

Then the current faded as the river merged into the unnatural flowage area with its drowned trees and wildly gesturing upturned roots marking water held by a recent dam. We were glad to be out of that, and into Island Lake, heading for a camp site that the Boy Scouts who had helped us portage at the rapids had told us about.

From a distance, as we approached, it seemed as if we had reached our goal. Certainly we were headed toward a grove of tall pines. But, as we beached our canoe, and climbed up over the bluff, we realized that this was not virgin forest.

The third camp-site recorded thinning, camping

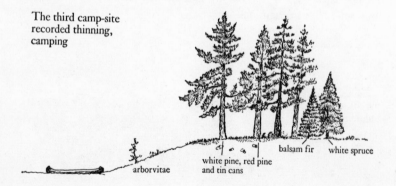

arborvitae

white pine, red pine and tin cans

balsam fir   white spruce

The trees stood far apart, with a parklike aspect, and there was grass beneath them, and—tin cans. The grass and the tin cans explained each other. The grass came after the forest had been thinned by cutting, letting in the sun. That was long ago. These pines had obviously had plenty of elbow-room during most of their lives. The tin cans were there because many large-group canoe trips from the camps on these lakes had found this open site ideal for an overnight stop; and because the animals of the forest had found it easy and rewarding to dig up the buried cans.

The trees were predominantly red pine and white pine, with a few balsam firs and a few white spruces. Still, there was no hemlock, no yew.

There was, to be sure, one single specimen of arborvitae down beside the lake. But it had scarcely any foliage, and looked as if it could hardly last another season.

Next morning we crossed Island Lake, and the motor-churned waters of Spider Lake, and Manitowish Lake, and then started paddling a water path through wild-rice fields.

All afternoon we were in the wild-rice fields, on Rice Lake, Alder Lake, and then on the Trout River, with a pause to eat handfuls of serviceberries where the stream swung close to a bluff, while an osprey ogled us from a high bare tree.

After that approach to the bank, the avenue of open water stayed far from either shore for a long time, so long that we were tired enough to give up all thought of one final camp site in a pine-hemlock forest.

Then suddenly the open path swung over, close to a high bank. We had to beach the canoe and climb the high sandy bluff to see whether there had been a camp fire there. There had been, a small one, with no tin cans.

But it was a long time before we got around to unloading our duffel. There was too much to see.

There were acres of tall close-ranked white pines and red pines. Such a stand of even-aged pines usually records a fire, followed by a good seed year.

But among and under the pines were hemlock trees, smaller than the pines. And, on the forest floor, along with the wintergreen, and pipsissewa, linnaea, lycopodiums, coral mushrooms, and partridgeberry, there was yew.

Having found two of the missing members present, we sought a lower spot back of the camp site, and there the third one, arborvitae, was thriving. We had evidently found our camp site in an intact piece of the Northwoods of memory.

Why was it intact?

We were standing on the bluff, under a hemlock, when I looked down and saw a cartridge shell half-hidden under partridgeberry. It offered the link that I needed.

Standing there, looking down at the cartridge shell, I remembered the camp site, several summers ago, where wolves had howled. There had been hemlock there, and abundant arborvitae.

Now that we had attained our desired camp site, it took us a long, long time to settle down to making camp. There was the glow of the low sun on red pine trunks to distract us; and there was the rich pattern of the forest floor with its embossing of waxed and polished leaves.

Above that rich carpet rose a few young sugar maples and yellow birch, indicating the eventual destiny of this site, when the shade-tolerant hardwoods and hemlock take over. There will probably be, here and there, a venerable white pine left behind, topping the others, but not reproducing itself in that denser shade—not unless there should be a windfall that would let the sun in again, or a fire.

There were strange rectangular holes near the bases of many of the pines. About two inches wide by nine inches long by two inches deep they averaged, with square corners. Some were older and had become less angular as the tree healed the incision. Others were recent, with huge chips, an inch or two long, lying around.

It might have looked as if the last campers on this site had been equipped with sharp chisels and had gone berserk, unless one remembered the existence of the only bird capable of such carpentry—a bird of northern wilderness, the pileated woodpecker, seeking ants. When we finally caught a glimpse of the massive head and showy crest of this great bird we could understand the story that a forester in the Cascades had told us, about the way the Klamath Indians scalped the birds, keeping the upper half of the bill and the crest, and wearing them dangling, to use in the purchase of wives.

We did not find arborvitae in abundance. The site was too high. But next morning, when we took to the Trout River again, it suddenly became swirling rapids with thick gnomelike forest on both sides. Trees, leaning and old and dead, and young and green and upright, were hung with mosses and lichens, and continuously moist with the spray of the white water.

I looked at the map. All afternoon we had been within the bounds of the Flambeau-Ojibway Indian Reservation. These Indians had no closed season on deer. They could shoot when they wanted to shoot.

I remembered that arborvitae is considered the number one deer browse in the winter, and hemlock second; and yew is another favorite. Then I remembered pictures of dead deer in the snow—pictures that Aldo Leopold had shown one evening as he explained the mass starvation of deer in places where the deer population had become too dense to be supported on the natural deer fodder.

The fourth camp-
site recorded
fire, good seed
year, Indians

white
pine

red pine

arborvitae

hemlock

yew

hemlock

seedling
sugar maple

Our first three camp sites had been in areas where the deer were probably hungrily consuming every bit of available hemlock, arborvitae, and yew. The nature of the forest in such areas had been altered by man, who first eliminated the wolf, natural predator on deer, and then protected the does until they had reproduced themselves out of browse.

We finally waded, pushing the canoe, and saw that here was arborvitae in abundance, leaning out from both sides. We were out of the Indian reservation, but evidently not even a deer would walk those violent stony waters for his chosen food.

Suddenly we emerged into the calm of Trout Lake. We had only to cross the lake, walk to our car, bring it to the lake, and put the canoe on top. Then we started south, behind car licenses that said, "America's Dairyland," ruminating as we drove—on the ruminants.

Camp Sites—Revisited

Twenty years later, I revisited the camp sites described in this chapter.

The first stop, as before, was at the small lake in the dairyland of southern Wisconsin, where the old canoe lives, leaking now, but still functioning. The cows and the sheep have all been banished from the lake margin. With them disappeared the last of the open parklike areas, set with mature even-aged oaks and punctuated with single or grouped specimens of red cedar, bird-planted and cow-pruned. Oaks of all ages have been taking over as fast as the grazers have been fenced out—except where lawnmowers have taken over the grazers' operations. Red cedars that had matured in the sunny openings of the grazed groves still lifted compact green spires above the oak canopy. They looked healthy as viewed from the lake; but a closer look revealed all the brown dead branches down below, where the oaks are crowding and shading. The time of red cedars has passed.

Many other evergreens are scattered about on these hills: white pine, Norway spruce, Colorado blue spruce, jack pine, arborvitae. The ones that the Boy Scouts planted throughout their camp before they left are meeting the inevitable crowding and shading of the native

The time for red cedars has passed

shade-tolerant trees. They will not last long. The ones that were planted around cottages, and have been protected from shade—those are thriving.

Shrubs brought along from home gardens have sometimes become a nuisance. We regret the day when it seemed to us to be a good idea to bring along a few plants from the home garden to soften the foundation line of the new cottage that rose so naked from the grassy pastureland of our hilltop. We had no idea how speedily one honeysuckle bush and one mock orange would populate every available inch of those manured slopes with their seedlings; how they would blot out our view of the lake, and require tireless throttling, uprooting, cutting. Other plants from the home garden made no trouble: peonies, daylilies, lily of the valley, irises.

Native shrubs and vines and wildflowers, that never had a chance on that hill while the cows were there, came back. We are grateful for the drifts of wild columbine, and the patches of hepaticas in the shade, and masses of brown-eyed susans in the sun. But we could gladly do without the spiky buckthorn bushes, and the extensive masses of root-sprouting nannyberries, and the poison ivy.

These plants, whether native or introduced, would all be wiped out (hepaticas would survive) by the inevitable march of the deep forest returning to the hills that it once dominated, before lumbermen, and farmers, and vacationers came—inevitable if only we would all go away.

But we all don't plan to leave. We have come to terms with that forest destiny—pleasing terms.

Forests everywhere (like cities) are ever enhanced by sunny openings that reveal their architecture and offer vistas of their avenues, and give access to their charms. The hills are well-clad in native vegetation, down to the water's edge around more than half of the shoreline (for this the wise scout camps are partly responsible). Our sunny openings form a pleasing balance to the mass. And surely the lines and motion of a canoe or a sailboat are as fine as the lines of the bur oak that frames them.

Next day, the first of the canoe camp sites welcomed us as it had twenty years earlier, with tall red pine and white pine at the sandy shore, and with the same small dark-brown stream. But a "wayside" had been provided for parking cars. It reduced the area to a narrow strip, labeled a "canoe landing," and evidently much used for the putting in and taking out of canoes.

The second camp site was covered with many-trunked birch trees and bracken fern, as it had been before. There was evidence of many campfires.

The third camp site, too, showed little change. Not even the nearby "flowage" area was much changed. The trees drowned by damming looked as ugly as they had looked twenty years ago.

There was, along these lakes, little new construction, and several "For Sale" signs. Local residents explained that the reason these shores were not teeming with new cottages lay in the shortness of the season, and the coldness of the water for water sports, coupled with the flatness of the terrain which offered no good skiing.

"For fishermen it's great, be sure you take a look at that record-breaker of a muskie on display in that store window down the street," a garage attendant told us.

We came to the fourth camp site perched high on its bluff above the Trout River, overlooking a sea of wild rice. It had changes. We could see the marks of the drainage-ditching around four evidently large tents; and much evidence of fire-building; and gouging by many feet climbing up over the bluff. The yew was gone, as was the hemlock and the arborvitae. There was a little arbutus, and bearberry, but the forest floor wore chiefly bracken fern. The pileated woodpecker scars still showed on several pines, but they were old scars. The bark

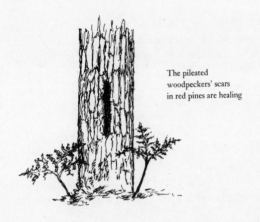

The pileated
woodpeckers' scars
in red pines are healing

was closing in over their edges. This place had become too worn, too trafficked upon, and too reduced in size for that bird of the wilderness. We crossed the area among the pines in a few steps, and were abruptly in a quite different area—not a forest, not layered with light and shade, not canopied and carpeted, no. It was a seemingly endless stand of sameness, for the swift raising of pulpwood. Big-toothed poplar, it was for the most part, with some trembling aspen.

"For the paper mill," explained an Indian official at the Bureau of Indian Affairs in the town of Lac du Flambeau.

"Don't you get any hard maple?"

"Maple?—no more. That is all gone. The popples grow fast. We don't want other trees among them—only popples. We need the work and the money, and the jobs at the mill. There's no time to grow maple."

I asked about the names on mailboxes and beside roads leading to resorts. They were not Indian names.

"The old people sold their land. They sold it cheap. They didn't know what it was worth. Then the government stepped in. They said 'No more selling pieces of the reservation.' They stopped it; but they had to give up. What if an old woman had nothing but her piece of land, and was in need, what could they do? So they said, 'O.K., but before you sell we will decide if the price is enough.' Now the lake edges are all sold off."

What I did not ask about was the hunting. Some of the non-Indian residents of the town had told of new hunting practices that, they said, have come to the reservation with the building of the highway.

"They drive down the highway at night with a spotlight turned on the edge of the woods. The spotlight catches the two gleaming eyes of a deer. It freezes, startled, for a second. The hunters have their rifles ready, in the window of the car, aimed at the edge of the woods. They get the deer."

It is their reservation, where they have a right to hunt whenever they wish. They had the right long before they had a highway, and automobiles, and spotlights.

Not far from what is left of the camp site on the bluff, a new road runs into the woods, with a big sign for a new real estate development.

BIBLIOGRAPHICAL NOTES

"Woods of Wisconsin" by Increase A. Lapham. *Transactions of Wisconsin State Agricultural Society* (1852).

"Native Vegetation" by T. C. Chamberlain. *Geology of Wisconsin, Wisconsin Geological and Natural History Survey* (1877).

Report on the Forests of North America, Exclusive of Mexico by Charles Sprague Sargent. (U.S. Department of Interior, Census Office Report.) Government Printing Office, Washington, 1884.

"The Hemlock-White Pine-Northern Hardwoods Region of Eastern N. America" by G. E. Nichols. *Ecology* (July, 1955).

A *Sand County Almanac and Sketches Here and There* by Aldo Leopold. Oxford, New York, 1949.

"The Forests of Itasca in the Nineteenth Century as Related to Fire" by Stephen H. Spurr. *Ecology*, 35 (January, 1954), 21–25.

Listening Point by Sigurd F. Olson. Alfred A. Knopf, New York, 1958.

The Subversive Science edited by Paul Shepard and Daniel McKinley. Houghton Mifflin, Boston, 1969. Part 3—"Men and Other Organisms," by Erich Isaac. Part 4—"Men in Ecosystems," by F. Fraser Darling.

"Openings in the Woods" by Alfred Etter. *The Morton Arboretum Quarterly* (Autumn, 1972).

11

Looking Down on Improved Property

OR

AN AIRPLANE VIEW OF MAN AND LAND

THE two men with briefcases, waiting beside me at Gate 5, were bragging to each other, in a refined way, about their evergreens.

The man with the hand-painted tie, who had left the hose running on his best specimens and hoped his wife would remember to move it, owned an even fifty of them—seventy-five, if you counted the two-year-old transplants he was raising in the nursery row.

The man with the long cigarette holder had only twenty-six, but they were big and dense, having been kept on a rigid pruning schedule; and they included two specimens of Carolina hemlock, and two gold-tipped, ball-shaped arborvitae. It sounded as if, on a quality basis, or a cubic-foot basis, or a tonsorial basis, he might be ahead.

Eventually, perhaps, Dun and Bradstreet may list a man's evergreen status. As a criterion of success, it seems to be finding popular acceptance, especially in landscapes from which Nature long ago eliminated the evergreen.

The conversation had started with an appraisal of the plantings around that Chicago airport, where the inevitable competition was evident, between man's choice of plant material and Nature's choice. About man's choice there was no question. It was evergreens and tailored lawn. But Nature had other ideas, raggedly informal—such ideas as the native pioneers, cottonwood and box-elder;.or the foreign camp followers, ailanthus trees and dandelions.

How long would it be, I wondered, before that seedling cottonwood would be discovered by the authorities, trespassing there between the Pfitzer junipers and the arborvitae; or that vigorous ailanthus sapling that had pre-empted the angle in the concrete wall as its universally established domain.

Then a woman with an orchid breasted up to the fence just beyond the two conifer-proprietors.

The orchid's dramatic lower petal was extended with a receptive gesture. Flowers certainly offer more decorative landing places than airlines do, I thought, as I looked at that extraordinary threshold that the orchid holds out to insects.

That particular orchid offered a landing place like sculptured purple marble inlaid with lines of gold that converged at the luminous portal to the business section of the flower. But the glamorous structure was not functioning, except as a badge of solvency, like the briefcasers' evergreens.

As I tore my eyes away from the orchid, I saw yet another landing place, a lowly one. There was a dandelion blooming in a crack at the edge of the cement runway. It appeared to be functioning; at least, a fly was on it, apparently drinking. Whether or not he was paying for his drink by delivering pollen, I could not see, and November was hardly the time for maturing seeds, anyhow.

That landing place was as different from the orchid's pastel colored one as the entrance to Coney Island is different from a vaulted portal with a purple wedding carpet laid before it—and as much more likely to lead to vigorous, abundant progeny.

The dandelion was holding its nectar in shallow goblets, not too deep for the tongues of numerous insects. Its presence was advertised by a color visible to the partially color-blind bee, a color conspicuous in the sunlight. Its form was as economical of expenditure for display as the orchid's form was spendthrift. The dandelion was composed of many flowers, a hundred or more, packed tightly into a head, and pooling their expenditure on stem and petal material.

And each of these yellow flowers makes only one seed, while the orchid (if its elaborately specialized pollination mechanism has an opportunity for functioning) makes thousands and thousands of seeds. Here the tables are turned—now the orchid, so spendthrift of advertising and allure, proves niggardly in its seed-packaging. Each little embryo plant starts out with such a meager endowment of food that its chances for survival are slight. But the dandelion's embryo is provisioned with a supply of food adequate to give it a bounding start in life.

The lasting qualities of these two landing places speak, too, of their individual problems. The orchid, poised on a branch in a steamy atmosphere, needs to last a long time while it awaits the languid, fluttering approach of the pollinating visitor that may not come for many days. But the dandelion, pioneering in earth's wounds, has many a bustling visitor hurtling in to drink. It requires no durable substance. No wonder the orchid rides the perfumed pearl-gray lapel and mink, while the dandelion gets the dust of the runway blown across its face.

Then the DC3 was ready. It lifted us, orchid, briefcases, and all, up over backyards and alleys that are the fouled nests of humans, and over the unyielding geometry of the industrial districts, where Nature's only opportunity for shaping curves is the smoke.

From Chicago to Dayton, we looked down on a battle, the battle between man's passion for square corners and Nature's penchant for curves.

Across one stretch of country the grid of lines was so accurate, the lines so straight, that I thought that the terrain down there must be as flat as a billiard table, until I noticed that the shadow of our plane was riding humps down there.

It was not only the roads that made squares. The rivets on the wing of the plane were a geometric pattern riding over that other geometric pattern down below—a pattern made of fields, and fences, corn rows, wood lots, orchard rows, cemetery plots, and lines of plowing and mowing and irrigation, and sidewalks and driveways of city sub-divisions—so uniform that they looked like products of a punch press.

Under this net, Nature was squirming and resisting.

She was scrawling a meandering stream zigzag across the ritual of straight lines. And where a farmer had turned his back for a moment, she was rubbing a thumb across and blurring the precision of impecca-ble fence rows with a welter of hawthorns, wild plums, and wild roses. It was easy to identify the hawthorns from the DC3. There is no mis-taking the gray foam of them. And the rest of the fraternity inevitably comes along when the hawthorn invades the fence row.

In one place the farmer's fence had been shifted slightly by an undermining gully.

It could be seen, from this height, that Nature was tampering even with the over-all pattern of man's wheat and rye fields, by over-laying the flat squares with a dappled marbling that was sheet erosion.

The pattern of the square is a rare one in living things. Flowers are most often five-parted, less often three-parted, and seldom four-parted. It is true, there are some four-parted ones: the mustards, pop-pies, and olives are in fours; and the mints have square stems, as do the blue ash and usually the euonymus. But even these squares are softened by flowing contours.

The spiral appears over and over again: in the center of a sun-flower head; in the outward corkscrewing of a twig; in the downward thrust of a root tip; in the ascent of a vine. The circle and the five-pointed star are often repeated, the triangle, too. But not the square.

Just when it seemed as if man's geometry was everywhere an alien temporary mold that had nothing in common with Nature's lines, just then we noticed paths, footpaths that crossed fields near the edge of town, or made a short cut to a country school or a crossroads commu-nity.

These little paths ambled and sauntered. They swung out into curves for no apparent reason. But there must have been a rise of ground, or a depression at each curve, not visible from the air.

Cow paths, too, followed the contour.

Then we saw a country road, dark-colored, with edges that were blurred probably by elderberry, blackberry, bittersweet. It ambled and curved like the little paths. It wandered through a small town, and then, abruptly, it straightened with a jerk, and cut like a gash across a

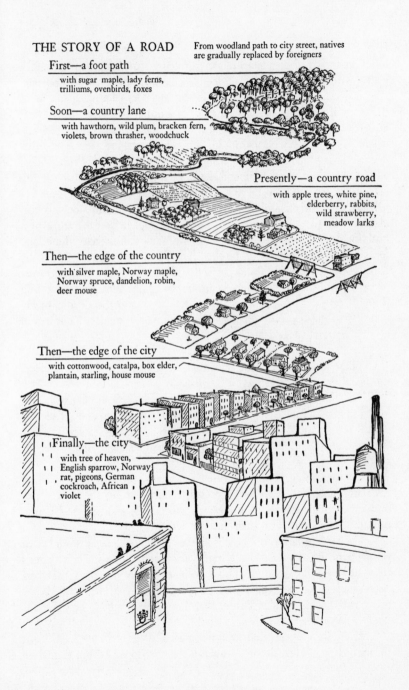

THE STORY OF A ROAD

From woodland path to city street, natives are gradually replaced by foreigners

First—a foot path

with sugar maple, lady ferns, trilliums, ovenbirds, foxes

Soon—a country lane

with hawthorn, wild plum, bracken fern, violets, brown thrasher, woodchuck

Presently—a country road

with apple trees, white pine, elderberry, rabbits, wild strawberry, meadow larks

Then—the edge of the country

with silver maple, Norway maple, Norway spruce, dandelion, robin, deer mouse

Then—the edge of the city

with cottonwood, catalpa, box elder, plantain, starling, house mouse

Finally—the city

with tree of heaven, English sparrow, Norway rat, pigeons, German cockroach, African violet large town. As it entered the outskirts of the large town, it passed close to an area marked by a snarl of exaggeratedly curveting roads and sidewalks, with dark masses of evergreens. That must have been Suburbia.

It occurred to me that there, in the life story of a road, just as in the story of a filling lake, or the story of a dune, or a bog, the vertical and the horizontal successions would be the same. A barefoot boy might follow a deer path through the woods, among lady ferns, trilliums, sugar maples; he might continue on as the path became wider, with a plank laid down here and there; he might find himself presently on a dirt road; and then he might be walking on a cement sidewalk beside a paved street; and finally he might find that the sidewalk ran close beside the pavement on the one side and beside the front of a building on the other, while fireplugs and newsstands grew where lady ferns had been. That would be the "horizontal succession." But, if he had the time, he could stand perfectly still on the deer path, and simply wait until the same changes came to the path. It might take a long time. It might all happen within a lifetime, but if the deer path lay near a growing town the changes would come eventually. That would be the "vertical succession."

There are aspects of the land that are revealed to the air traveler, though they are seldom seen otherwise.

The shame of many a farmer, for example, is laid bare. Gullies, far from the public road, and heretofore hidden from the passer-by, are all too apparent from the air. It will be interesting to see whether the spotlight of public scrutiny will have an effect on these indecent scrawls.

Another thing revealed from the air was bee-hives, long white rows of them. They looked like sugar cubes along the end of an orchard in one place, ambling beside a brook in another, and strung out along the edge of an open field in another.

Then we began to notice differences in the occasional stretches of woods beneath us. There were many woodlands that were transparent right down to the ground. Those were evidently the ones that had been grazed, or perhaps burned over each spring. Probably both, because the same kind of farmer that allows his woods to be grazed is likely to burn them over too.

There were woods that were not grazed. We could not look down through those—even though November had stripped all but the white oaks of their leaves. It was easy to understand that raindrops, dropping from our viewpoint and passing through that layered vegetation, would be broken and broken again, until they sank, captured, into the leaf mold. But on the grazed forest, where seedlings and shrubs and saplings had been eliminated, raindrops would hammer down with a gouging force; the few raspberries and thistles would not break their force enough to matter.

Those grazed forests would be gone, soon, unable to reproduce themselves in the face of the cows.

We looked down on many planted wood lots. Almost all of them were as accurately-squared lots as the rest of the scenery. I wondered how many of those farmers knew about the interesting piece of research on bird population that had been done by the Academy of Sciences in Chicago. If they knew about the evidence that bird population varies directly as the amount of edge on a forest, they would surely feel inclined to work some scallops, bays, peninsulas, onto the edges of those wood lots, and double their bird population.

We landed at South Bend. The evergreens were neat. So was the grass. The dandelions, cottonwood seedlings, and an ailanthus tree were doing their bit toward blurring the man-made straight edges.

At Fort Wayne, Indiana, we made another landing. The evergreens, grass, dandelions, and cottonwoods were there, too—and a few ungainly box-elders.

We left the plane at Dayton, and walked over to the bus, past dandelions, grass, clipped evergreens, and an invading ailanthus tree.

BIBLIOGRAPHICAL NOTES

Nesting Birds and the Vegetation Substrata by William J. Beecher. Chicago Ornithological Society, Chicago, 1942.

Hedgerows by Nicholas Drahos, *Cornell Rural School Leaflet* 40 (Fall, 1946), Number 2.

Pleasant Valley by Louis Bromfield. Harper, New York, 1945.

Bees: Their Vision, Chemical Senses, and Language by Karl von Frisch. Cornell University Press, Ithaca, New York, 1950.

"A Comparison of Reproductive Potential in Two Rat Populations" by David E. Davis. *Ecology* 32 (July, 1951), 469–475.

Airways of America by A. K. Lobeck. The Geographical Press, Columbia University, New York, 1933.

12

Reading the
Headlines Only

OR

*BY SUPER HIGHWAY FROM
CHICAGO TO ATLANTIC CITY*

To EVEN the most abandoned of small-road addicts there can come a
time when need dictates that a trip from here to there be made with all
reasonable speed—no stopping to chew a sassafras twig, or look under
a stone, or listen to a brook, or feel a mullein leaf. No time to read the
landscape—not really read it, not the fine print. Only time to scan the
boldest headlines, which "he who runs may read."

In March, 1973, we (my rock-reading friend and I) had seven
days to drive to Atlantic City and back to Chicago.

On the morning of March fourteenth, early, we started off from
the corner of Michigan Avenue and the Eisenhower Expressway. At
that corner we lingered for a minute (there were not going to be many
places on the highways ahead where lingering would be tolerated) to
look north toward the Art Institute lions, recalling the reminiscences,

given several years ago, of two eighty-year-old aunts who had re-counted the time when their father owned a store situated where the institute now stands. They told that the store was right on the edge of Lake Michigan, and "our father used to dump all trash right out of the back door into the lake." We were paused at the former edge of the lake, before it was pushed back with fill of one kind and another.

Another edge was represented here. The irregular edge, where the tall-grass prairie meets forest, extending its long fingers to entwine with the fingers of forest extending from the east. We were stopped be-side a planted semicircle of native hawthorn trees, the trees that more than any others make up the margins of midwestern forests, and often fill the fence-rows, marking the edges of farms. But something was lacking on those Michigan Avenue hawthorns—their thorny twigs were not lighted by shining red buds. I stepped out to wipe a bud red, and found my fingers sooty. A police car was moving slowly past this suspicious twig-rubbing activity. We didn't wait to be asked to move along.

Yet another edge is an ingredient of Chicago, probably the deci-sive ingredient that inevitably made this a trading-place, by tangling

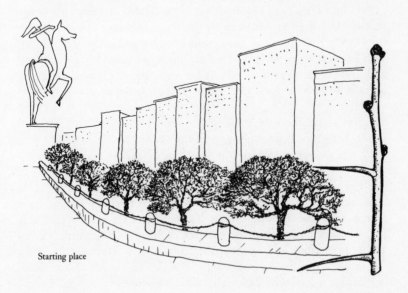

Starting place

men's paths. From canoes to Conestoga wagons to trains and trucks, traffic from east and west has had to dip south here to get around the edge of the lake.

As we turned south, we looked back at the facade of the city. The buildings stood like the tombstones in a cemetery—all facing east, towards their various gods, and towards yesterday's pioneers and Ellis Island; and towards the new day.

Past the stretch of disdained lake front given to a fog-endangered flying field, and to acres of paved parking places, lay neighborhoods of small houses. The eagerness of the Ellis Island immigrants to put up acceptable facades in this new land was expressed by brick cottages with pressed brick on the street front and common brick on the sides; and by the corner store, or saloon, with its inevitable meager round tower. It looked to me like a community originally rye-bread nourished, built by the people of the poor-land countries of Europe where rye grows better than wheat. As we approached the bulk of U.S. Steel, beer signs accumulated. And then we were poured into one of those humanity gutters officially called interstate highways, which are grafted onto the landscape hot off of a drawing board, and bear no relationship to the shapes molded by life and time. We were welcomed by a huge sign: "Main Street of the Midwest." What presumption to elect itself to represent all the thousands of real main streets: busy or sleeping; paved or mud; with hitching-posts or parking places; with butcher shops with sawdust on the floor, or with supermarkets; with general stores selling overalls for work, or with boutiques selling overalls for fashion; with feed stores, or with laundromats. What presumption!

But ahead there were low places loud with the ratchet sound of cricket frogs, and higher places with last year's corn-patches; and then there was a succession of low dunes, where black oaks gestured jerkily.

Suddenly there was a beech tree, standing out pale gray against the dark woods, making a headline that was easy to read even at sixty miles an hour. The presence of the beech was evidence that we were approaching the Atlantic Ocean (though we were only about sixty miles from our starting place); and that we were leaving prairie winters and prairie winds and summer droughts behind, and coming under the influence of the humidity and equability of the Atlantic climate, bolstered, no doubt, by the ameliorating influence of the Great Lakes.

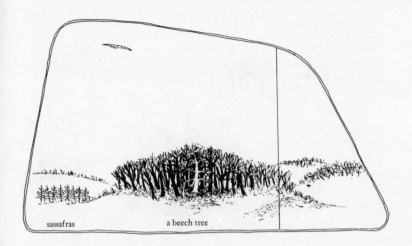

sassafras · · · · · · · · · · a beech tree

In a sunny fence-row appeared a line of small trees that we could not have seen an hour back, where fence-rows were hawthorn domain. The sassafras is recognizable from far off because its side branches reach out and then swerve upward at their tips.

Where the duneland ended stood a service area named for Notre Dame's football coach, Knute Rockne. Around it was tailored landscaping, imported and expensive, all made of bluegrass from Eurasia and Japanese yew, crew-cut.

We entered hilly country, terminal moraine country, where we saw three concentric semicircles of clay with embedded pebbles, each semicircle marking the place where the southern end of a glacial lobe had paused awhile before finally retreating to the north, leaving "Lake Chicago" to shrink down to Lake Michigan.

As the humping hills subsided to a flat plain, it seemed as if we must have backed up. Plainly we were in prairie country again. Bigger farms, more silos, hybrid-corn signs on the fences, an occasional bur oak pushing out its corky elbows, hedge-rows of osage oranges—all these suggested it; and the still-tall bunches of russet prairie grasses in fence-rows and along railroad banks—those confirmed it. We were on an outlying island of the prairie peninsula.

Then the low clay hills started again, and we started across another series of concentric semicircles. This series marked the pauses in the retreat of another lobe of the ice sheet. We crossed them and came

Overnight on former lake bottom

out onto the flatness of the bed of the glacial lake called Maumee, now shrunk to Lake Erie.

All that day, ever since that first beech tree had appeared in the sand dunes of Indiana, we watched beeches become a more and more important ingredient of the forests; and we could detect the many sugar maples by their spray of fine twigs. Even where the woods showed neither of these, but were composed of second growth, we could often detect that the natural succession was starting to reinstate the original beech-maple forest. The clue was in the light tan leafy understory made by the leaves of young beech trees, persistent through the winter.

On the former bottom of Lake Maumee flatness stretched ahead far into Ohio, and we stopped at a motel not far off of the "Main Street of the Midwest." Under a flat roof that had no relation to the climate (the indoor climate belonged to the desert), we looked out past the big lamp in the picture window; past the Pfitzer junipers from the Alps and the clipped Japanese yews, and three ailanthus trees from China, and bluegrass from Europe, and an oval pool, to the old narrow brick farmhouse across the road with its scroll-saw decoration, set in clumps of elms and billboards.

The next day started through a tiresome landscape. The flatness was interrupted by small farms with narrow houses, and was dotted with forests without charm. How could elms crowded between other elms ever make a sightly forest? An elm needs to stand alone, or at least in a row, to show its fountain form.

These forests seemed to stand on the parts of this old lake bottom that were still too wet to plow.

We turned away from the lake bottom and headed southeast. In no time the land started to swell gradually ahead of us, and to be topped with forests of tall oaks. It was easy to pick out the red oaks with their dark trim trunks and upward-slanting branches; and the white oaks with their ashy bark.

Suddenly, in a road cut, we saw bed rock: shale in one cut, thin-bedded limestone in another, thick-bedded in another, undistorted, and almost as horizontal as the ocean laid it down.

Farmhouses were wider here and had big chimneys at both ends. White-fenced pastures were greening, and apple orchard twigs were reddening with spring. We crossed the Cuyahoga River in the deep incision it has made in the upland.

Then came, in rapid succession, two milestones of the landscape: We crossed the divide between the water that flows to the Atlantic and the water that flows to the Mississippi; and we left behind the gridiron of roads that marks the township system, as we crossed its "first principal meridian" at the boundary line of Ohio and started onto roads that follow the contours of the valleys and ridge tops.

There was another change that delighted us. We were now on the Pennsylvania Turnpike, which is older, and not in so much of a

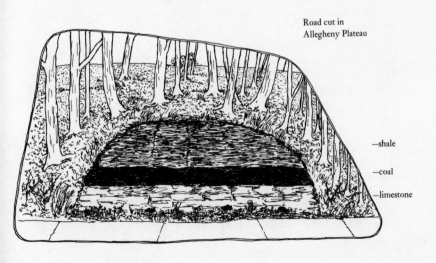

Road cut in
Allegheny Plateau

—shale

—coal

—limestone

hurry for its travelers to be somewhere else. It actually granted us places to pull off to examine the layers of a roadcut, or look down a valley or into a forest. What sudden wealth! (The accumulation of beer cans at such gracious places showed reason enough for not offering motorists a chance to stop.)

We did pull off, after passing strip mines, and brookside pussy willows and roadside daffodils, at a road cut where we could see a foot-thick belt of coal under thin-bedded shale. Soft coal it was, and crumbly, still as horizontal as it was when the trees that grew in the green, warm humidity of the fern forest quietly died and subsided into the swamp at their feet.

We stopped again at a deep stream valley to enjoy banks shining dark green with rhododendrons and laurel and hemlocks. Laurel ran like a ground cover under the forest trees. Tips of hemlock trees and of white pines showed above the forest. Each of these evergreens tops itself with an unmistakable gesture: the hemlock bending with the wind; and white pine spreading with an asymmetrical slant.

We traveled for many miles across this high section, seeing only horizontal layers in the road cuts. Geologists call it the Allegheny Plateau, knowing that it once was a continuous platform before the streams had their way with it. But an average person sees it as hill country, so deeply and irregularly have the rivers cut the formerly flat surface, and the roads wound around the cuts.

We came presently to the Allegheny Front, as the east face of the plateau is called. There was an abrupt drop.

Ahead lay dramatically tilted rock layers. Erosion had left the harder rock layers as ridges, and worn the softer layers into valleys. The ridges, the valleys, and the rivers, and the roads made a parallel pattern, a trellis pattern running northeast to southwest.

This was folded land, the "Folded Appalachians," where the rock

a white pine————————and ——————————three hemlocks

layers had been compressed like heavy drapery. The western part, starting at the Allegheny Front, had been upfolded. Any coal near the surface had been eroded away, washed down the streams. The eastern part had been downfolded, placing some coal layers down where erosion had not reached it. But miners had. There were mines and coal cars in the downfolded part.

The Pennsylvania farmhouses showed wide porches, and dark evergreen hedges, probably boxwood, and proud barns with narrow, round-topped louvered windows, and lightning rods. Some were protected by hex signs.

We stayed at a motel on the highway, at a corner where trucks shifted gears. The Japanese yew and Pfitzer juniper at our foundation were joined by boxwood from Europe.

Soon after our start the next morning we passed through a double tunnel through the final ridge, and emerged into an entirely different landscape. The ridges and valleys and coal of the Folded Appalachians were behind us, and we could see forever down the straight road that lay ahead.

The explanation was in the limestone-strewn soil of the rich farms all around. That soil had been made in place, by the gradual disintegration of the soft limestone that extended from the base of the hard ridges that we had just left, to the still harder ridges that lay ahead. We were in the Great Valley, which several streams, and roads, and railroad lines, and the trails of early settlers and frontiersmen and armies and Conestoga wagons have used for traveling in a northeast-southwest direction.

The white chunks and occasional knobs of limestone looked discouraging for ploughmen. No wonder there were many orchards.

Soon we no longer had a long view down a straight road. As we climbed and turned, the road-cuts revealed rocks that we had not seen before on this trip. So far the roadcuts had shown only rock laid down by a sea, but here was rock that had been hot and had cooled slowly to form crystals, and later had been reheated, as forces within the earth folded and compressed and contorted it to form gneiss.

Presently we had left the tortured rock behind, and were on the section known as the piedmont, or the oldland, where the crystalline rocks had lain so long exposed to erosion that they had been worn

Sycamore branches
above the Schuylkill

down into mere stumps of mountains, and gradually covered themselves with clay. This clay, like the soil of the Great Valley, had been formed in place, from disintegrating rock—"residual soil."

After turning southeast, we got locked into a traffic jam just south of Philadelphia. There we enjoyed a splendid view under the truck bed and between the big wheels of the truck from Los Angeles stalled beside us.

We could look across the Schuylkill Valley, and up past the white arms of the sycamores along its margin, to a big well-settled graveyard, with thick granite monuments and thin marble ones, to spires and mausoleums, and heavy low masses that could be boxwood, or mountain laurel. Surely one could find interesting reading over there. There would be memorials to early Quakers and Germans who came by sailboat up the Delaware River, to work the soil. And there would be the mechanics and engineers who brought waterpower from the falls of the Schuylkill to the city so long ago, and those who built a canal and a railroad out to the coalfields and brought fuel to Philadelphia and started its factories. And there would be ship designers, and shipbuilders to send warships down the river to the First World War; and there would be long lines of soldiers from several wars. But the truck was grinding into action, and we had to move on again.

Soon we left the oldest land of our trip to drop down to land that is so new that it is still being born out of the ocean.

We crossed the Delaware River, and headed for the flat horizon.

Ahead spread recently emerged ocean floor, the Coastal Plain, topped by clay, sand, and gravel washed down from the oldland, by streams that once dumped their burden directly into the edge of the ocean.

The highway cut straight across to Atlantic City. We could not resist stopping on a side lane provided for emergencies (with cars, not with botany, surely), but there was a different tree standing in the ditch beside the road. It resembled an arborvitae, but those globular cones marked it as the coast white cedar, *Chamaecyparis*, a tree confined to swamps along the Atlantic coast, and part of the coast of the Gulf of Mexico. Once more it became clear that we should move along. But we could see the crimson showers of the red maple flowers in the swamp, and pitch pine dominating the ragged woods on the sand.

Within Atlantic City we were plunged suddenly into memories of Monopoly games, and checked off the well-known street names: Atlantic Avenue, Ventnor Avenue, and the others. We compared their relative property values, with or without hotels, or mortgages, and finally went to "take a walk on the boardwalk" which seemed to extend for miles up and down the shore. From the boardwalk we looked out across the Atlantic, realizing that this wet edge, with its sand dunes and sandbars enclosing tidal marshes fringed with the grass called saltwater thatch, was no decisive edge at all, but a vacillating uncertain one; and that, if we could walk out from the sloping beach on to the continuing slope underwater, we should arrive abruptly (when we had walked about the same distance as we had come from the hard oldland) at the edge of a precipice where the ocean floor drops off several thousand feet, marking the limit of the continental shelf.

Dark was approaching, and we turned our backs on Atlantic City—perhaps unconsciously we were urged away by memories of the fortunes we had lost in a Monopoly game, when chance had made us spend a night in a hotel held by a rich opponent Monopolist.

We were lucky in finding a motel at the edge of the Pine Barrens. Before we signed up for a room, we asked the proprietor, "May we investigate those woods across the lawn in the morning?" and were warned to wear stout boots.

Perhaps our landlord was really thinking that we might need hip boots, for at least part of our prowl. The land was soggy in part, with many bogs and ditches, with brown tannin-stained water, and thick carpeting of sphagnum moss; and it was sandy in part, with pitch pine dominating and tolerating not only salt spray, but frequent fires. These pitch pines seem to have been divided by fire into two races, different in only one feature: in one race the cones open and release their seeds when they ripen—then they drop; in the other race the scales of the cones are firmly locked and the cones hold firmly to their places on the tree, unless they are pushed off by new cones. When fire comes, it opens them and reseeds the area. Fire must have selected out these chance freak cones with the ability to wait. Their place seems to be within the areas of most frequent fires. But the pitch pine seldom needs to start over again with a seedling; mature individuals often get a second chance after the passing of a fire, or several fires. Underneath the bark of the trunk and branches are many dormant buds. When the fire has killed small branches, these buds become active, and beard the tree with the crowded needles of new growth. In an area where the trunks were blackened by fire, the trees were thriving. Underneath them were masses of last year's bracken fronds, now brown, and laurel.

At another stop along an indistinct side road we came to blueberry plots, and a neat, square, flat cranberry bog. At another we were among truck gardener plots, and bare plots which would soon be planted with the watery crops that thrive on this watery soil—muskmelons, watermelons, and tomatoes, and many others.

As we drove west we passed forests that were on drier ground, and filled with more kinds of trees, especially oaks. We were lingering here (allowing ourselves one sneak look at the fine print) because it seemed that the highway was a permissive one, and we wanted to take advantage of its temporary tolerance of our weakness for prowling.

Actually the permissiveness was not temporary at all, but a dependable quality of the route we were following since leaving Atlantic City. It was Route 40, bless it!

At the west edge of the Coastal Plain, the piedmont rose in a long gray ridge. At that long ridge, rivers from Georgia to Maine have long tumbled down, at first into the ocean and later on to the new Coastal

Plain, and many wheels in many factories have turned with the power of those falling rivers.

We came to the bridge across the Delaware River, and made a bitter decision. We would not take that road that slanted off southwestward to the river, even though we knew that Route 40 had gone that way originally, crossing by ferry to New Castle in Delaware; positively we would not.

But after we crossed the bridge our controls weakened.

We had caught a glimpse and turned south to see more. To make our detour excusable we drove to the end of Chestnut Street, where "travelers" following the former route would have "left" the ferryboat. Then we turned around and started to savor our detour back into time. To symbolize all the architecture of that town of another time, I would choose, from the road, a small piece that belonged to the road—an imposing drinking fountain offering water to humans, on the sidewalk side; to horses at the road side; and to dogs down at their level. It stood at the edge of the Old Market Place, laid out by Peter Stuyvesant.

From the place where Route 40 crossed the Delaware to the place

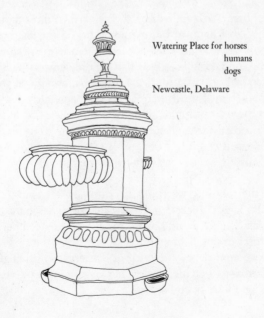

Watering Place for horses
humans
dogs

Newcastle, Delaware

where it crossed the Susquehanna at the head of Chesapeake Bay and on into Baltimore, we had frequent views of the two great estuaries. It seemed as if frantic traffic, pushing south or north, was crowding that edge. It was like riding the prongs of a row of forks of water. Close beside us, a new multilaned highway bestrode the forks.

Two rivers, the Delaware and the Susquehanna, started all those watery intrusions into the land.

The Susquehanna River at a time long past flowed in an unimposing valley across the oldland area and across the Coastal Plain to the ocean. As the level of the Coastal Plain was gradually elevated, the river cut into it more and more deeply. Then came a slight lowering of that coast, allowing the ocean to extend itself further into the land up the river valley and its tributaries. The lower reaches of the Susquehanna became Chesapeake Bay. Meanwhile the same changes had turned the lower reaches of the Delaware River (after it accumulated the waters of the Schuylkill River) into Delaware Bay.

Baltimore sits on the very edge of the piedmont, but its face is turned toward the Coastal Plain for vegetables to can, and toward Chesapeake Bay for the oyster beds and shipping. Route 40 did not by-pass Baltimore. It showed us the famous "row houses," blocks and blocks of them, so much alike, always narrow, three-and-a-half stories high but all of them of warm-colored brick, and many of them with scrubbed marble front stairs. None of them had any space between its stiff facade and the sidewalk. When we did come to such a space, in it there stood a broad dark southern magnolia, ever green and full of buds that would soon spread their waxy whiteness and send fragrance in through the open windows of many row houses.

We turned west and suddenly there were lawns, with beech trees and then open country. The light lasted long enough for us to read a "Deer Crossing" sign. It was late when we found a motel, on the piedmont.

In the morning we could see our view—a low hill with junked cars and a ragged thicket, and a few shacks and ailanthus trees—and a water tank. But all around rolled the pleasant fenced fields and greening pastures of the piedmont.

As we approached the town of Frederick, we thought, of course, about Barbara Frietchie waving her flag from her second-story window. We quoted, of course,

"Shoot, if you must, this old grey head,
but spare your country's flag," she said.

But we remembered a few other of Whittier's lines about that
morning. These were about the piedmont which we were crossing:

Up from the meadows rich with corn,
Clear in the cool September morn,
The clustered spires of Frederick stand,
Green-walled by the hills of Maryland.
Round about them orchards sweep,
Apple and peach-tree fruited deep,
Fair as the garden of the Lord
To the eyes of the famished rebel horde.

All the little streams were running brown with clay. Since Whittier wrote his verse they must have carried away some tremendous ton-
nage from the ploughed fields of the piedmont to become part of the
Coastal Plain. If the rains are allowed to take the soil much longer, no
one will ever again compare this land to Eden. The apple and peach
trees are a much better idea for this well-drained surface. It would
require slow ages for the rock to disintegrate and replace the thin soil
that remains.

Beyond Frederick we crossed the two ridges that make up the
Blue Ridge at that point. Road cuts gave us glimpses of the ancient
folded rocks. We saw gneiss and schist and slate, and then we came
down to the Great Valley again, with its limestone soil.

History was very present in this part of the Great Valley. The
Confederate army advanced north by way of this broad corridor; and
the Union army advanced south. The decisive battle of Antietam was
fought here. The town of Winchester, in the Virginia part of the
valley, was captured in turn by the Union army and the Confederate
army seventy-two times. Early settlers, wanting to move west but prevented by Indians from crossing New York State, used the Great
Valley. As many as twenty wagons a day went through towards the
Cumberland Gap and Kentucky.

Masonry arches of old bridges, and silos, and big barns, and pastures dotted with cow-pruned red cedars, and frequent signs about
caves to be visited, and springs, told of the limestone bedrock in the

valley. Wide porches, sometimes two-storied, with pillars, and lawns set with holly trees, or wide-topped mimosas, reminded us that we were in the South.

A long flat horizon up against the sky ahead, would have convinced us that we were about to mount to an unbroken plateau, but we knew better, having traveled eastward over that ridge and valley province in Pennsylvania three days ago. We knew there would only be narrow pieces of the once-continuous plain left on the tops of the ridges between the stream valleys.

As we climbed out of the Great Valley, road cuts showed us sandstone, shale, and limestone. Signs of prosperity dwindled up there, but forests were more abundant. They had been lumbered off from the flat ridge-tops, where second-growth forests of oaks were coming in. But the steep ridge sides had been protected by their inaccessibility. Down the slopes we could detect the presence of a rich variety of trees that reminded us of the forests of the coves in the Smokies. Actually we were within the boudaries of that rich mixture that has proved too assorted to be assigned such a name as "oak-hickory forest" or "beech-maple forest," and has been given the name "Mixed-Mesophytic Association."

But we were on a highway, and in a windy snowstorm, and must try to move along.

We could see the dark masses of evergreens under the trees; and we could see an antique toll station; but we crossed the once-important Mason and Dixon Line without noticing it.

The snow wrapped up most of the Allegheny Plateau, but lifted its curtain on a scene of a coal-mining wreckage, where forests and pasture and farmhouses had been swept out of the way.

After about 150 miles of coal-mining country, we crossed the broad Ohio River into a short piece of West Virginia.

That day we had been traveling much with reminders of famous men: the grave of General Braddock; the birthplace of Francis Scott Key; the little Fort Necessity of George Washington built between two high ridges, Chestnut Ridge and Laurel Ridge. It made a pleasant contrast to come to a town celebrating itself as the birthplace of the man who wrote the famous *Ray's Arithmetic*.

In Ohio we stopped at a motel on the very top of a high hill, with placid farming country rolling off in all directions.

When we spoke appreciation of the views, the room clerk and the bookkeeper sighed.

"Better look quick at the country here if you like it," said one. "Big Muskie is chewing its way up here. Only a few miles to go and then this place will start being gnawed off and vomited out."

"I live south of here," said the other. "Our farm and barn and house are going soon. You should go down and see Big Muskie— everyone does. It is twenty stories high and removes over 300 tons of overburden with every scoop. Overburden means farms and pastures and cemeteries, and woods that have to be peeled off of the coal."

We chose not to go to see Big Muskie. Instead we started west again, enjoying the lovely overburden along the way.

But not for long. Vast areas of strip mining humped along the road, first on one side, then on another. The refuse that had been overburden was indiscriminately mixed. In Britain, the National Coal Board would have required that the topsoil be carefully stripped off and piled up, and then each layer of rock be carefully lifted out and kept separately. Afterwards the stuff of the former layers would be returned in their original order. Then the land would be modeled back to its former contours (as far as possible) and the top soil would be spread, and compacted, and planted with grass and trees.

Our stripped landscape now amounts to twice the entire surface of Connecticut. Half of Iowa has temptingly thin overburden, as does four-tenths of Illinois. The Big Muskies are drooling.

For a long stretch our Route 40 was incarcerated (because of roadwork) in the vacuum of Interstate 70. An abandoned one-room school stood below road level, and a farmhouse with empty windows stood on the ridiculously narrow strip between the two highways.

I was glad for this exposure to Interstate 70, as well as the several other exposures that we had been subjected to, when Route 40 had been denied to us for one reason and another. It served to crystallize my project for utilizing the vacant, characterless length of some interstate highway by allowing its whole length to become a "Strip of Reality." The procedure would be simply to do nothing: no mowing; no application of weedkillers; no shaping to channel the rain off before it soaks in—nothing. Then we could all watch as the potential vegetation returned, to this nationwide strip, changing from east to west as conditions changed: from pitch pine on the Atlantic coast, to oak woods, to mixed-mesophytic forest, to beech-maple forest, to tallgrass prairie, to shortgrass prairie, to plains, to sagebrush, to mountain evergreens, to redwoods on the Pacific coast.

In a wooded area, spaces would need to be cleared around crossroads, and converted into meadows, either grazed, or mown once a year in late fall.

I wrote up this plan, in greater detail, and submitted it to a leading conservation-minded magazine. They pondered, and then asked for more pondering time. Then they wrote, expressing enthusiasm for the project, but explaining that as much as they would like to print it, that would not be feasible because "we would have the highway men at our necks." How far that little lobby throws its beams!

Interstate 70, which we had observed for many unwilling miles, seems a good candidate for that strip of reality, extending from the Atlantic to the Pacific and letting the rain soak in.

When we were released from the cold embrace of Interstate 70, we came down to cows and an orchard, and a roadcut showing shale above thick-bedded limestone above a soft, disintegrating shale. We were still up on the Allegheny Plateau. But, soon after Zanesville, we came to the last of it. Flint Ridge is named for the hard nodules in limestone, which have lost their importance, since Indian flint-chippers are gone; but now have a new importance, since being designated the official gemstone of Ohio.

No sooner had we come down off of Flint Ridge than we saw a lawn with two big boulders at the end of its drive, and realized that we were back again in glaciated land. We crossed the moraine marking the furthest advance of the last glaciation, and then realized that we were back in a landscape cut into squares by the township system of roads.

That checkerboard rolled out before us, passing fields where corn or soy beans would be planted; and a scattering of forests that had not yet been cleared off to provide room for more corn or soy beans, and farmsteads that usually included an orchard; and a woodlot thick with black locust or catalpa for fenceposts; and some cows, and pigs, and a chickenhouse. At two places we actually saw chickens running free on the ground. (I was reminded of the roadside signs in England that advertised "Brown eggs from free-ranging hens.")

The same landscapes continued across Indiana, except for a glimpse of a covered bridge with its usual attendant sycamores; and signs for fresh maple syrup, and sorghum molasses, and more Baptist churches, and a bur oak, now and then, standing alone. It was reassuring to see, above a movie house in one small town, a sign offering "The Darwin Story, rated G." There have evidently been other changes beside physical ones.

We crossed the Wabash River, and saw a sign that said "catfish." And then stopped on the edge of Illinois at a motel with clipped Japanese yews and lamps in the windows.

I hurried to look at the Gideon Bible. It failed me. It was closed. For four successive nights of our trip the Gideon Bible had been carefully placed in the middle of the dresser, opened—each time at the Psalms, three of the times at Psalm 23, the other time at Psalm 100. Someone must have planned these openings, and managed to arrange to have them carried out day after day.

Who? and how? Someone who realized that a traveler would be more likely to read a short familiar piece, and would feel warmed by this evidence of concern that had no pricemark, and might even sit down to read a bit more. I did.

We left Route 40 to turn north and follow lesser highways. We left beech trees behind in the Wabash Valley and started across prairie country, with trees mostly confined to the moraines or river bottoms or fencerows or plantings around houses. The general farms, the family farms, that had come west with early settlers were changing to specialist farms, factory-type farms, specializing in corn and soy beans. The machinery was getting bigger, and so, plainly, were the farms.

The farms that had been brought up and absorbed into the wide fields that fitted the new machinery had usually left something to tell of their existence. Sometimes the foundation of the farmhouse and barn were still showing; some farms had only a surviving clump of lilacs or a hearty stand of daylilies beside the road, or a drift of lily of the valley, or a pair of thriving Austrian pines, to show that a farm family had made their homeplace pleasant. Sometimes the new owner had left the pump standing, or the cement stairs that had led up to the front porch. We watched hard for as many of these evidences as we could find, knowing that soon the powerful tractors will rebel at going around relics, and turn it all under and smooth it over for corn or soy beans. A way of life is past.

READING THE LANDSCAPE FROM THE SIGNS

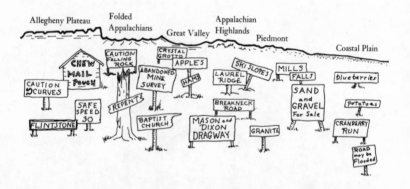

But the long swell and dip of the open prairie was beginning to work its slow charisma on us, and we were glad to be home again, even though home is on a straight street in a flat town, and neither beech trees nor rhododendrons like it here.

BIBLIOGRAPHICAL NOTES

Guidebook to the Geology of the Pennsylvania Turnpike by Arthur B. Cleaves and Robert C. Stephenson. Commonwealth of Pennsylvania, Department of Internal Affairs Topographic and Geologic Survey, Bulletin G 24, 1949.

Things Maps Don't Tell Us by Armin K. Lobeck. Macmillan, New York, 1956.

Airways of America by Armin K. Lobeck. The Geographical Press, Columbia University, New York, 1933.

A Traveler's Guide to Historic Western Pennsylvania by Lois Mulkearn and Edwin V. Pugh. University of Pittsburgh Press, 1954.

U.S. 40, by George R. Stewart. Houghton Mifflin, Boston, 1953.

13

Botanizing from
a Lower Berth

OR

WINTER NIGHTS SILHOUETTES–
CHICAGO TO DENVER
JANUARY, 1954

"THIS story is going to be read backward," I told myself, as the City of Denver made its imperceptible start. "Backward for a textbook account, at any rate, or a history book, where stories are usually told in chronological order. But it is good form for a mystery story, where clues start right off pointing to the villain who isn't going to be revealed until the last page."

In addition to being read backward, the story was going to be read, of necessity, chiefly from silhouettes, because the City of Denver leaves Chicago at five o'clock, which means twilight on New Year's Day.

The first visible bit of botany was a Tree of Heaven, growing, true to form, in a place that looked like Hell. It spread bony fingers before a street light at the end of a factory alley, where windows were dark for the holiday.

222

In a minute or two we were passing lower roof lines, all flat against the gray sky. In another minute the roofs were low enough for irregular scallops of tree tops to show above them—cottonwoods, evidently.

Then the Christmas tree lights began to show. Three-deep they were, under blocks of flat roofs, fringed with scallops of elm tops. But soon they were two-deep only, and the flat tops were lowered enough so that the elm tops showed fan-like.

By the time we were rolling past roofs that sloped over single Christmas trees, the elms showed feather-duster shapes. Then came a stretch of huddled, one-chimney-and-a-television-aerial houses, with haphazard and tired roof lines, where trees reared unkempt heads— evidently cottonwoods and box elders.

And then we rumbled over a bridge, and the long-haired gestures of willows and silver maples outlined a frozen river. But suddenly those lowland brooms of whip-like, swift-growing twigs gave way to a quite different twig formation.

We were in a cut between hills, and the twigs were higher above our heads, and made a tighter, tangled, twisted mass against the sky. It was plain that these were the gestures of the slow-growing hardwoods: the oaks, hickories, and sugar maples.

The sudden change in twigs came at the point where we left the bottom of the "Lake Chicago" of glacial times—the flat land where the city of Chicago sits, and the men who do her hog-butchering live.

Now, when we passed openings in the upland woods, it was plain that we were up on the moraines that encircle the city, out in the higher suburbs where live the men who package and sell the butchered hogs, and have white collars and briefcases, and twin beds and coffee tables. Here were wider, two-chimney houses, that drew apart from one another. Outdoor Christmas trees were dazzling here, but the indoor trees were dimmed. This, no doubt, because of Venetian blinds.

Then the house-tops became abruptly lower, much lower, and farther apart, and indoor Christmas trees shone bigger and brighter. We had reached the ranch-house suburbs, where live the men who advertise the packaged hogs, and have tweed suits, and cocker spaniels, and Colorado blue spruce trees. We were seeing those bright trees through their picture windows.

Between the suburban areas, and beyond them, the oak groves went flashing past. They covered all the moraine where man had not removed them. And they had something definite to contribute to the story we were reading from end to beginning; from effect to cause; from Chicago to Denver.

Their high growth spoke of deep roots. And the deep roots spoke of rainfall of thirty-three to thirty-four inches a year.

A light flashing beside a ringing bell tinted the snow pink, piled car-high on both sides of the highway, proof of this abundant precipitation. Then a line of willows, evidently along a stream, added another comment, as important as any. All their branches leaned toward the east, and spoke of the prevailing west wind.

As the oak groves were more and more scattered, the shape of silos stood often against the sky. They told of the corn fields we were passing but could not see.

Then there was a different set of lights to watch. Christmas trees were no longer in evidence, except in the cluster of a town, but, beside a silo, there was an occasional long row of square, lighted windows. They told of a farmer who was milking, and they told of pastureland that we were passing but could not see.

It was interesting to notice that, when barn lights showed it was milking time, the only light in the farmhouse was usually low, at the back of the house. The farmer's wife was in the kitchen, getting supper, probably.

It was time for supper in the diner, too.

But the diner lights were too bright to permit seeing silhouettes outdoors. At one station a bright light shone full on a large "Ful-o-Pep" chicken feed sign, and gave some clue to what we were passing. Otherwise the windows reflected only lights and people, chiefly boys and girls on their way back from Christmas vacation to the University of Colorado at Boulder. They talked of how sleepy they had been at home because of the heavy air, and of how anxious they were to get back to the skiing.

Back in the sleeper I had the berth made up early, so that I could have complete freedom from reflected lights; for watching the landscape unroll.

The darkness helped a lot. The knobby tops of occasional orchards were visible, and even corn shocks once in a while.

The farm lights had shifted since I left for the diner. The barns were all dark now. And there was a light at the front end of some farmhouses where the light in the kitchen still burned. The farmer was, probably, listening to the radio while his wife did the dishes.

Trees were farther and farther apart, and seemed to be chiefly gathered into the hollows of river valleys. An occasional row of willows still waved airy finger tips toward the east.

We had long since left the oak-hickory forests, and the "oak-openings," and entered the prairie, where grasses dominate the cover that Nature inevitably establishes. The grasses were invisible from the train because they did not stand against the sky as the trees in the oak-hickory climax had done. But, although they were low in comparison with trees, I knew that the native ones, which had greeted the pioneers in covered wagons, were tall in comparison with most grasses. We were crossing the area of the "Tall Grass Prairie." And I knew, too, that they were often not so tall as their roots were deep.

These tall, deep-rooted grasses told of abundant rainfall—thirty to thirty-two inches. But the way that the woods nestled into the hollows suggested that the wind was taking away a considerable part of this rainfall. Not enough to matter to crops, evidently, because there was usually a serrated silhouette of a windbreak beside a farm house, but no windbreaks in the open country to protect the crops.

Another serrated silhouette closer to the tracks, were the tops of the round, metal corn cribs in long rows. Practically every farm seemed to have a conspicuous wind-mill. And every town had a grain elevator.

The gradual coming in of the grain elevators told of rainfall that had dropped to twenty-eight inches here, and showed that farmers were having to take advantage of the fact that wheat crops can use the winter. The decision between corn and wheat is difficult on these deep loess beds that make corn production so tempting, even while drier summers make it so uncertain.

I wished for moonlight so that I could see the white-faced cattle that must be feeding out there on that flat land. But there was no moonlight, and all that I saw by straining and peering were black hulks that must have been either the ghosts of buffalo herds—which would have every right to haunt these ranges—or imagination, or sleepiness.

By the time that sleepiness began to get the upper hand, there was practically nothing at all to be seen. No trees. Only telephone poles, and an occasional wind-mill standing alone, far from any farm-house. This must be pumping water for cattle, and that must mean land too dry for wheat, too sandy for any other crops except forage, and stream beds that are dry most of the year.

There was one new silhouette. It was a broad windbreak, built of several rows of trees and shrubs. These broad windbreaks were not sheltering farmsteads. They were sheltering fields.

I thought how the west wind had seemed to gain importance steadily ever since we left Chicago. First, there had been just willows bent toward the east. Then there had been the willows bent east *and* windbreaks at farmsteads. Then there had been the willows bent east, and thicker windbreaks, and many windmills, and grain elevators at every town. Then there had been no willows to be seen, no trees at all, windmills standing alone in fields, thick shelter belts around fields, and few grain elevators.

When I woke up it was still dark. But I saw light in a tiny house under a cottonwood and a tall windmill.

Then there was another light in another tiny house under another cottonwood and another tall windmill. The oatmeal was being warmed up again.

Then there was a new silhouette. It was a man. There was a yard light on in a ranch, and he stood in front of it, either facing the train or turning his back to it. I could not see which. But I could see that his silhouette was different from the silhouettes that I had seen in suburbs and towns west of Chicago. His hat was wider, and his waist and hips were much narrower.

And then I could see the cattle on the gray sand hills. They had a different silhouette, too, from the dairy cattle around Chicago.

There was a new outline to the stores in the tiny towns that lay along the railroad, far apart. It was due to the false fronts on one-story buildings. I saw hitching posts in front of one of them. It was no longer dark.

How straight the lines of the landscape had become! In one place I could see two lines of highway and two lines of telephone poles, and four lines of railroad tracks, all converging to meet at the horizon—just like an illustration in an art instruction book, in a lesson on perspective.

Soon I noticed some new straight lines added to these others. The new ones were the lines of the irrigation ditches. I saw clumps of sagebrush. Their gray-green color is the characteristic color of plants with a thick hairy covering that helps them to hold on to their water.

As the train headed southwest, after North Platte, the grass was short, in clumps and patches, and the houses were farther and farther apart. Each house had its tree, and the tree was a cottonwood.

We were crossing the area with an annual rainfall of less than twenty inches. We crossed a river bed with no river in it; then another, just like it.

Everything spoke of a need for water.

Suddenly, to the west, we could see the force that had shaped the changing silhouettes; the villain that had picked the west wind's pockets. There were the Rocky Mountains, and on their peaks lay abundant snow.

And then we were in Denver.

In the railroad station in Denver, the train passengers soon mingled with the waiting crowds. But the people from Chicago were still easy to identify. They were the ones who wore galoshes.

14
Running away from Spring

OR

FROM PLAINS TO TIMBERLINE
IN THE ROCKIES

RIDING the ski tow at Berthoud Pass, in March, is fun for anyone.

Whether it is more fun for the supple and besweatered, who ride up in order to come winging down, or for the slightly brittle, who ride up just for the ride, is debatable.

Anyhow, we were glad indeed to be riding up in the company of glinting skis and gay voices (and only a few set jaws, and perhaps a leg or two that might, by nightfall, need to be set) and just a little glad that our brittleness and years excused us from speeding down in that exuberant company.

"Spring! It's O.K. with me if it never comes," the young voice floated up from the chair behind mine.

It certainly looked from where we sat as if that young skier might have her wish. With every soundless, effortless foot of that soaring rise

233

we were retreating farther back into winter, running farther away from spring.

But that was what we had been doing all day, ever since we left the foothills by car, to drive up to the foot of the ski lift.

Down there in the foothills (to start the story of our day at its beginning) the pasque flowers had definitely said it was spring. They said it in several different ways: by wearing the Easter finery that befits their names, while pessimistically keeping on their silk-wool underwear; by displaying the pattern of the primitive Buttercup family (see Chapter 1) and reminding us that spring is a time of primitive floral patterns; by blooming close to the earth, where competition for sunlight would be much too great after the season advances; and by being soft to the touch, with a softness that would be much too vulnerable in the parched summer of the east face of the Rockies.

In the foothills the pasque flower said it was Spring

The rest of the foothills population offered only a few hints of spring. The south-facing grazed slopes wore snow only in the form of neatly tapered streaks—a streak to the north of every yucca and juniper and mountain mahogany. In the open groves of ponderosa pine, the snow blanket had become so patchy that dark masses of kinnikinnick showed through, and squaw currant bushes, and rusty clumps of mahonia. There were tight knobs of flower buds hidden among the ruddy leaves of the mahonia.

The river bottoms in the foothills said it was spring, but river bottoms are addicted to misstatements (if failure to agree with the stated

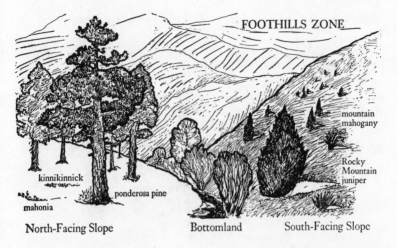

mountain mahogany

Rocky Mountain juniper

kinnikinnick

ponderosa pine

mahonia

North-Facing Slope   Bottomland   South-Facing Slope

opinion of the mass is a misstatement). River bottoms everywhere have a way of extending a finger of one type of vegetation into the mass of another type. Into the Foothills zone (usually extending from altitude 6,000 to 8,000 feet) they were inserting fingers composed of plant representatives from the Plains zone (4,000 to 6,000 feet).

The river bottoms said it was spring by showing color in twigs, the same colors that had marked the twigs all winter, but deeper, brighter, more alive. The osier dogwood was redder, the willows were yellower, or more russet, according to their kind. The narrow-leaved cottonwood was whiter, and the thimbleberry more orange. On aspens and cottonwoods the catkins bulged under the scales of the winter buds, showing gray on the aspens and brick-red on the cottonwoods.

The prevailing barrenness of those colorful twigs told something about the length of summer down there in the Plains zone. Evidently spring comes early enough so that there is plenty of time for growing a new set of leaves and getting full use out of them before frost calls a halt.

Perhaps there was a hint of spring in the footprints we saw at one stop in the foothills, big cat footprints looped around a mountain mahogany bush. Their size, their reach, the way each paw, and evidently the tail too, dragged the snow, made us believe (or perhaps we wanted to believe) that a mountain lion had passed there rather than a lynx or a bobcat. It was easy to visualize his low-slung prowl against moonlit

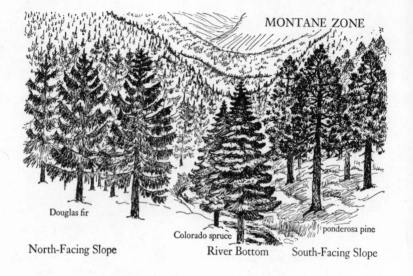

Douglas fir

Colorado spruce

ponderosa pine

North-Facing Slope   River Bottom   South-Facing Slope

snow, as he hunted such small creatures as might venture out in the milder nights of March.

Back in the car again, we started to climb steadily. At about 8,000 feet we were leaving the Foothills zone behind and entering the Montane zone.

There was no abrupt change in vegetation. Open groves of ponderosa pine were no longer as extensive as they had been in the foothills, but they were still abundant, especially on south-facing slopes. The snow lay in patches there.

Then the north-facing slopes began to present solid black-green stands of Douglas fir rising from deep, unbroken snow.

The river bottoms no longer offered a hint of spring, except possibly in those holes in the ice where black water tumbled past. The bare-twigged trees of the river bottoms were replaced by Colorado spruce.

As we continued to climb through the Montane zone, the ponderosa pine was left behind. Its place was filled by the Douglas fir that had first appeared only on north-facing slopes or in sheltered ravines. The forest, without ponderosa pine, looked different—more compact, with more conical trees.

As we climbed we began to see trees that were narrow spires, growing close together. Those were Engelmann spruces. The first ones we saw were in sheltered ravines and on north-facing slopes.

At 10,000 feet we left the Montane zone and entered the Sub-alpine zone. The Engelmann spruces were no longer confined to sheltered places. They filled the mountainsides. Douglas firs persisted for a time, but their ranks dwindled fast, and Engelmann spruce and its companion, the alpine fir, took their place.

Places where the spruce-fir forest had been burned were filled with groves of aspen, or with the close-packed match-sticks of lodge pole pine. Incidentally, those lodge-pole pine stands were marking not only the places where forests had been burned, but also places where forests would probably be burned again, soon. Their dead and leaning wood offered ready tinder to any spark. We could see the many tightly-closed cones that open at the touch of fire, and thus re-seed a burned area. The same fire that consumes a forest may thus be a factor in reseeding it (compare pitch pine and jack pine).

Occasionally, on some wind-battered knob, we saw a limber pine, bent and beaten, but uncrowded (hazards and blessings of a non-conformist?).

The car skidded, and we had to stop climbing to put on chains. It seemed as if we had turned the calendar back to winter; or as if we had been traveling north at a great rate. By climbing the last 2,000 feet we had seen many of the same changes we might have seen by traveling north through Canada up to the Hudson Bay area at latitude 60 to 66 degrees.

Then we saw timber line, up above us.

A snow plume waved from the mountain ahead and snow cornices stood out all along the ledge. That was where we first saw skiers come winging down, and where we decided to put on, not skis, but snowshoes. How glad we were that we had brought those snowshoes. The snow was much too deep for walking on without them.

The dark forest of Engelmann spruce was inviting, and we wove our way around the trees' neat narrow spires.

Two features of this forest surprised me. In the Engelmann spruce forests that we had been seeing from the road, on our way up the mountain, the trees had seemed to stand closer together. They had seemed taller, too. The difference was made clear when we talked to the man who was operating the chair-lift. He told us that in the area where we had been walking the official measurement of the snow depth was twenty feet.

We had been walking almost up among the tree tops. After hearing that, we went back and walked again among those trees, just to savor the feeling of twenty feet of snow underfoot.

No wonder that the alpine fir and Engelmann spruce from those close-ranked forests of the Subalpine zone, with their superabundance of water, refuse to grow in our landscape plantings and forestry projects back home in the dry midwest; while limber pine, which, in the Subalpine zone, usually inhabits some wind-swept knob, will succeed for us; and members of the drier, lower altitude forests—ponderosa pine, Douglas fir, junipers—thrive for us.

Several chickadees and a golden-crowned kinglet moved among those treetops where we walked. Were they, at this altitude, a sign of spring, or simply an evidence of the shelter that is offered by such close-packed spires?

SUB-ALPINE ZONE

limber pine

Engelmann spruce

Alpine fir and Engelmann spruce

If they were a sign of spring, they were doubtless the last sign we would see on that mountaintop, we decided, as we took off our snowshoes and walked over to the ski tow.

That was where we were mistaken.

But it certainly looked as if winter was eternal there, as we sat and soared, up over the gradually shortening spears of Engelmann spruce, up past timber line, up over unbroken fields of snow, to the continental divide.

We got off at the top and walked, with plenty of panting pauses.

We spoke of how we had left spring behind, and of the pasque flower buds that might possibly be huddled under the snow beneath our feet, buds that would probably bloom in July, long after those that we had seen in the foothills had turned into the tousled heads that win them the name "prairie smoke."

As we looked toward mountain ranges hunching to the horizon, with black forests on their shoulders and hips and knees, and their feet somewhere down there in the white mist, we realized that some of those shawled huddles were named the "Never Summer Range."

Was summer never coming there above Berthoud Pass? we wondered.

The answer came speedily, but we did not recognize it at once. It came as I walked, looking far off to the Never Summer Range.

One of my feet sank deep into the snow with a suddenness that toppled me over. I pulled it out, and went on, and sank through again. This time it was not so easy to pull out. I looked down into a surprisingly big cavity, and found that I had one foot tangled in greenness, vivid, alive greenness.

Just then my companion went down sideways. As she struggled to get up, she called out, "I'm in a treetop, it seems."

We were not above timber line at all. But we had reached the height at which no tree, or no part of a tree, can endure the winter, except by hiding. We had broken through, down into the hiding place.

As we peered down into these treetops we noticed that they did not terminate in an upright leader shoot, but bore, instead, a tuft of shoots at the tip. Some of the trees had one shoot that did actually extend a few inches above the snow, but that shoot was inevitably dead and dry. The sun and wind and cold had finished it off long before this last week of March.

Suddenly the reason for these strangely shaped trees, the "elfin timber" of timber line, became apparent. Here is the story as it might be told by one of these snow-covered trees:

1. A seed falls and takes root.

   A young shoot starts upward.

   There is plenty of water and sunshine in summer, but summer is only two months long.

2. Winter covers the young spruce deeply with snow.

3. Each summer the little tree grows, both upward and outward.

4. Each winter the snow covers it, completely but less and less deeply.

5. One winter the snow barely covers the little tree.

6. In the following summer the tree's leader grows upward as usual.

7. Next winter the snow does not cover the new growth of the leader. The wind dries it; the winter sun reflected from the gleaming snow surface helps to dry it; the cold freezes it. Ice blizzards and hail help to kill it.

8. The following summer another side shoot rises to take the place of the brown, dead leader. It grows, during the summer, just about as high as the first leader had grown.

9. Next winter sun and cold and wind and ice and blizzards and hail kill the new leader.

10. Summer after summer the tree continues its outward growth from the tips of its branches. On the windward side, these branches are dwarfed, or shorn. On the leeward side they elongate steadily. Summer after summer the trunk lays on a new layer of growth.

11. Winter after winter the new leader that rises above snow level is killed. Winter after winter the deep snow lies on the elongated side branches and flattens them.

12. This little tree may grow to be hundreds of years old. Its

ELFIN TIMBER tells this story over and over

1 A young Engelmann spruce grows in the brief summer of timberline
2 Snow covers it deeply through the long winter

3 Each summer the tree gains a little height, a little girth
4 Each winter the snow covers it less and less deeply

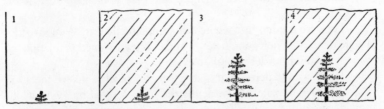

5 One winter the snow barely covers the small spruce
6 In the following summer, the tree's leader grows as usual

7 Next winter the snow does not cover the leader, wind and sun dry it, blizzards, hail, and cold help to kill it

8 Next summer a side shoot rises in place of the dead leader

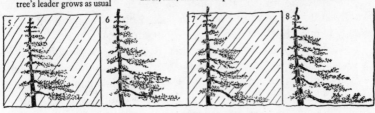

9 Next winter, cold and sun and wind and blizzards and hail kill the new leader

10 Summer after summer the branches grow longer, the trunk grows thicker, the windward side is shorn, and a new leader is lifted up

11 Winter after winter the leader is killed, and the weight of snow flattens the branches

12 The tree may grow to be hundreds of years old, but it will never be taller than the depth of the snow

Such trees often grow close together, forming a continuous mat

trunk may be stout with many annual rings. It will not grow any taller.

The story of this tree is repeated again and again just below timber line.

Then we tried to find where timber line really was. We looked for an area that was not punctuated by dead brown spruce or fir tips, an area that would not let us sink through.

There were patches like that, up there, patches where the snow was thin—windy patches. Evidently the full sweep of the wind would not let snow accumulate. Here was no hiding place for firs. They could never have grown more than three or four inches high.

I knelt and pushed away the snow to see if I might uncover the woolly button of an alpine forget-me-not. I brushed against a twig. A woody twig! A line of them! I picked one and looked at it.

Well, a willow twig is a willow twig the wide world over. Its winter buds, with their single foolscap scale, are unmistakable. Those winter buds on that low-growing twig held undeniable promise of spring. This twig was only two inches long. But it sprang, I knew, from a branch that was lying down, in the frozen soil. The trunks of this willow tree were lying down too. Here was the ultimate in tree reduction—a willow that was lying down, the creeping willow, *Salix petrophila*.

We strode across those willows, recalling the regions where we could stride across that same willow, or other similarly recumbent ones, in widely separated parts of the earth: Mt. Katahdin, in Maine; Greenland; the barrens about Hudson Bay; Siberia; the Torngat Mountains in Labrador; Gaspé Peninsula; and arctic northwestern America.

Then we headed down the mountains, down towards tree-sized willows—and spring.

In August we came back up the mountainside. We wanted to see the whole of the little trees in whose tops we had been standing in March.

On this trip to Berthoud Pass we could see more than trees and snow. We could see what grew under the trees; and, especially, we could see what replacements for itself each forest was providing.

Down under the ponderosa pines of the foothills there was much grass, most of it brown and dry. Young pines were few, and the ones that were present represented a few distinct ages, not all ages. Probably each group of a uniform size had developed from seedlings that had germinated in a year that was the first in a series of years without fires—enough years for the young trees to develop the ponderosa pine's characteristic thick fire-resistant bark. Many of the old pines wore fire scars.

We found some very young seedlings. As we listened to the grass crunching under our feet, we wondered whether those seedlings were not destined to be wiped out soon by fire. On the other hand, the heat of that August sun seemed enough to burn them up without assistance. But we had read that these seedlings had other special equipment for tolerating that dry heat. A ponderosa pine seedling puts down a deep root with outstanding speed. There is no accumulation of duff for it to penetrate, and the porous, well-aerated surface of the foothills favors deep penetration. The fingers of ponderosa forest that extend farthest toward the Plains zone inhabit only the most porous soils.

Farther up the mountain we walked for a while in the dense shade of the Douglas fir forests. No dry grass crumbled under our feet. The duff of fallen needles and twigs was much deeper than it had been under the pines; but evidently it was not too deep for Douglas fir seedlings to penetrate. We found enough young trees to see that this forest was replacing itself.

Our next stop was up among the Engelmann spruces. There the duff lay so thick that we wondered, as we poked down through it, how a seedling had time enough, in the abbreviated growing season of this altitude, to penetrate to soil moist enough to carry it through the summer. We did find spruce seedlings, some that had died, and some that had survived. Some of the surviving ones were growing in rotting logs. This had probably favored a more rapid root penetration.

Alpine fir seedlings we did not succeed in finding in that forest. We did locate some small trees, but they were not seedlings apparently. They seemed to be growing where branches had been layered firmly into the ground by the weight of snow.

Seedlings of Engelmann spruce and alpine fir, so difficult to find in the forest solidly composed of their own kind, were easy to find in some other types of forest—three other types.

The first place where we found them was in a sunlit aspen grove.

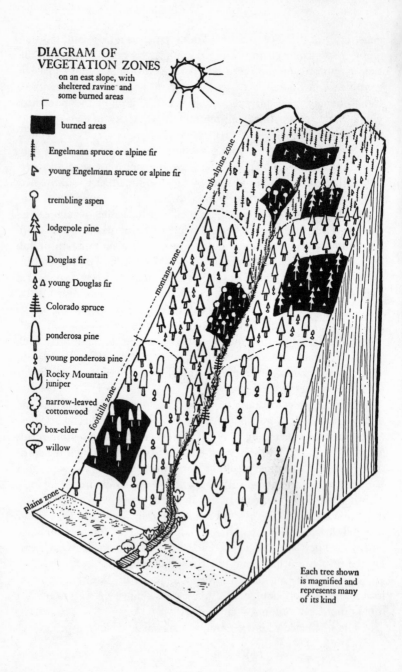

DIAGRAM OF VEGETATION ZONES

on an east slope, with sheltered ravine and some burned areas

- burned areas
- Engelmann spruce or alpine fir
- young Engelmann spruce or alpine fir
- trembling aspen
- lodgepole pine
- Douglas fir
- young Douglas fir
- Colorado spruce
- ponderosa pine
- young ponderosa pine
- Rocky Mountain juniper
- narrow-leaved cottonwood
- box-elder
- willow

sub-alpine zone

montane zone

foothills zone

plains zone

Each tree shown is magnified and represents many of its kind

Those aspens wore a memory of winter, in the black scars that marked the places where their bark had been nibbled by elk and mule deer when snow covered their usual browse; and in strange stumps that remained from trees the beavers had gnawed off for winter food. One aspen grove held a record of the past, in the form of charred trees, remains of the forest fire that had given the aspens the place in the sun that they require. Another aspen site held a record of more than one fire. The young aspens were root sprouts from the base of an older stand of aspens that had burned. But whatever an aspen stand might have to say about the past it usually predicted a spruce-fir future. In the flower-filled, grassy forest floor, the blue green of Engelmann spruce or alpine fir was conspicuous. (At lower altitudes Douglas fir took their place.)

The second place where we found seedlings of Engelmann spruce and alpine fir was under lodgepole pines, standing so packed on dry slopes (drier than the slopes covered by aspens) that a dead tree could not fall down. The dry tinder of dead lower branches worn by each tree (unless it stood at the edge of a clearing) cracked as we poked our way into the deep shade. These branches indicated that this was not a shade-tolerant tree but, like the aspen, a pioneer that had seized a fire-made place in the sun. Like the aspen, too, it would not be able to replace itself in its own shade. But the seedlings of the shade-tolerant Engelmann spruce and alpine fir were present, predicting a future spruce-fir forest, if fire stayed away from the tinder-box that was their nursery.

The third place where we found young seedlings of spruce was not in the shade of nurse trees. It was up near timber line where a forest had burned many years ago. There the altitude was too great for aspen and lodgepole pine. But out in the sun and wind, seedling spruces were appearing here and there among the old whitened skeletons of the forest. Slowly, so slowly, the Engelmann spruce was replacing itself, without benefit of pioneers.

Willow
seven years of growth

At the upper limits of the spruce-fir forest we took to the ski lift again.

This trip we rode behind a flamingoed sport shirt, and a pair of waving open-toed shoes, instead of the Norwegian sweaters and skis that we had ridden behind in March. We were anxious to see the pygmy-sized willows that we had found up there under the snow, and the little spruce trees in whose tops we had stood.

Not far from the place where we alighted from the ski lift we found, in an open meadow, a ground cover of glistening willow leaves, with seed heads formed among them. On a small twig separated from the mass, the record of the last seven years of growth was easily read.

Then we walked over to the compact mats of "elfin timber." The tree-tops that we had broken into from above, in March, were about four or five feet from the ground. We inspected the top of one tree. Its story was plainly written. There was the cluster of dead twigs, drooping from the point at which they had once been uplifted, too high. There was the new green upright twig, also uplifted too high, and doomed to death next winter. There beside the green upright one was the brown twig that took the wind above the snow level last winter.

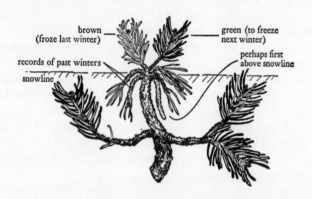

As we crumbled those dry needles between our fingers we realized that, for all the changes we had witnessed from lower timber line to upper timber line, changes in quality of greenness, in root length, in thickness of needles, in tree shapes, in surface cover, in porosity of soil, in temperature, in depth of snow—there was one outstanding feature that was the same at the beginning and at the end of the trip. At the lower tree-line plants were facing a lack of water, an actual lack—a physical drought. At upper tree-line the high wind that takes water from leaves when the intake down below is stopped or slowed by cold, was causing a physiological drought.

In traveling from tree-line to tree-line, we had traveled from drought to drought.

Rockies–Revisited

Tension—it can hold a poem together; make a violin string sing; shape the tides; enable suspenders to hold up pants against the pull of gravity; and is the essence of the resilient, buoyant landscape (not landscaping) where forces ever pull against each other.

But it is usually invisible, as it certainly was to the searchers who went to find change that might have come to the east face of the Rockies in the last twenty years.

No change was detected, either on the way up or on the return trip. But down in the foothills a ranger told about one change that is natural, inevitable, but not acceptable.

"Many people who take long trips to see the mountains in the fall, when the aspens have turned, are going to find the golden display gradually diminishing its glory, unless we interfere with the natural succession of events. Our fire-fighting techniques and fire-prevention measures are efficient. But each aspen grove is gradually raising shade-tolerant evergreens in its shade. That spells extinction to the aspens. If we want the gold of aspens to set our fall hills alight we have to repeat, carefully, selectively, and under complete control, the thing that gives aspens a chance—fire."

This would not be a unique procedure. The Black Forest of Germany would not be an evergreen mass of such deep dark green as to be called black, if foresters had allowed the natural succession to proceed to the inevitable shade-tolerant beech trees. The foresters favored the straight trunks of spruces, and kept the forest floor clean of other trees.

In Scotland the owners of heather moors use fire to keep the forest off their lands and to encourage new growth on the heather that makes grouse pasture. There is good profit in renting the land to the grouse hunters.

The trembling aspen is one of the trees that appear usually as temporary occupants of some sunny place to which they have no tenure. Whether we consider the trees of this group as pioneers, or as temporary scaffolding in the architecture of a forest, or as bandages for wounds on the earth, we cannot miss them as important parts of the landscape; but we cannot find them on forestry maps. A large wall map beside my desk shows the *potential vegetation* of the United States. For the area of our trip from Plains to Tundra in the Rockies this map shows pine–Douglas fir forests giving way, as altitude increases, to western spruce–fir forest, and then to alpine meadows—barrens. No mention of the trembling aspen that attracts so many visitors in the autumn. That omission is no oversight. Such a map can only cover the eventual plant cover of the land—the hereditary dynasty. It would take too-complicated a lot of tissue overlays, as well as prophetic vision, to include all the opportunists of disturbance.

BIBLIOGRAPHICAL NOTES

"Plant Zones in the Rocky Mountains of Colorado" by Frances Ramaley. *Science* **26** (1907), 642–643.

The Life History of Lodgepole Burn Forests by Frederic Edward Clements (U.S. Department of Agriculture, Forest Service Bulletin 79). U.S. Government Printing Office, Washington, D.C., 1910.

Plants of Rocky Mountain National Park by Ruth Ashton. U.S. Government Printing Office, Washington, D.C., 1933.

"Timberlines in the Northern Rocky Mountains" by R. F. Griggs. *Ecology* **19** (1938), 548–564.

Mountains and Moorlands by W. H. Pearsall. William Collins and Sons, London.

"Vegetational Zonation in the Rocky Mountains" by R. F. Daubenmire. *The Botanical Review* **9** (June, 1943), 325–393.

"Fire Damage in the Ponderosa Pine Type in Idaho" by C. A. Connaughton, *Journal of Forestry* **34** (1936), 46–51.

Forest Types in the Central Rocky Mountains as Affected by Temperature and Soil by C. G. Bates (U.S. Department of Agriculture Bulletin 1263). Government Printing Office, Washington, D.C., 1924.

Reading the Landscape of Europe by May Theilgaard Watts. Harper and Row, New York, 1972.

Potential Vegetation of the Conterminous United States A. W. Küchler. With accompanying manual. American Geographical Society, special publication Number 36, New York, 1964.

Rocky Mountain Tree Finder, a pocket manual by Tom Watts. Nature Study Guild, Berkeley, California, 1972.

15

Tundra Hailstorm

OR

ABOVE TIMBERLINE IN
THE ROCKIES

THE HAIL was the last straw.

First of all the radiator had boiled, but none of us had minded that. At the sight of the rusty geyser spraying the dusty hood, against the blue backdrop of Observation Point, we had piled out with one accord, crossed the road, and started to climb.

We hadn't climbed far beyond the dwarf trees of timber line, in the relentless sun, before the wind attacked with such sudden fury that we stood close together for a few minutes, arms locked and heads bowed. Then we found a sheltering tor, where our grandchild and her mother could collect shining bits of quartz, and feldspar, and schist, while they stayed behind, near the cooling car to wait for us. The child's finger pointed out a fairy primrose that had found the same shelter and was growing, an inch high, in a tiny Gothic niche.

Soon the wind let us go on, but the sun had become overcast, and the cold needled each of us into making some adjustment, such as buttoning up a sweater, or putting on mittens, or letting down ear flaps, or pulling up socks, or rolling down jeans.

We started out again. And then the hail found us. We added raincoats and bowed our heads and hugged ourselves to reduce our vulnerable surfaces.

A flash of lightning reminded us that we had been warned "not to make lightning rods of ourselves" on a barren height.

A fairy primrose
grew in a niche

At the thought, I stooped lower and looked down to discover that I was huddled over a group of plants that seemed to be huddling too. Gray-green cushions of plants, they were, there at my knees among the gray-green folds of my raincoat.

Hail-stones lay among the cushion plants

Suddenly we seemed to understand each other, those gray-green cushions and I, because we were meeting the weather in such similar ways. Three of the five cushions at my knees were wearing sweaters, woolly, buttoned up at the neck, with ear muffs pulled down, and socks pulled up. Two of them looked as if they were wearing glistening raincoat material on their tiny leaves. They were crouched much lower than I, but they had to face the full round of the year, and I could leave when conditions grew worse.

My hand lens showed that one of them wore a coat of wax, comparable to the protective coat of face cream that we had used against the elements; and that one of them had sticky globules exuding from its hairlike glands.

They had no shoulders to hunch, or necks to pull in, or heads to bow, but two of them had the edges of their leaves rolled under.

Some leaves of the tundra (much enlarged):

hairy   slick   glandular   edges inrolled

underside

Huddled there, listening to the hailstones spitting, bouncing, rattling, off my raincoat, and watching them bouncing off the gray-green cushion plants, I thought how hard, how stony, how spitting, was the vocabulary of a mountaintop.

"Rock, cirque, tor, peak, scree, tarn, tundra, alp, scarp, crevasse, bluff, cliff, crag." I said them aloud to hear how hard they sounded; and when I explained, the others considered for a minute, and then added other pebbly words of the mountaintop.

"Granite, quartz, gneiss, schist, mica."

"Goat, elk, and coney."

"Finch, hawk, pipit."

Stony words—

What a lot of blunt hard rubble those words are that have attached themselves to the tundra, where almost everything seems to be shaped like a stone, or colored like a stone, or to have a name like a stone, or to be a stone. No words here for lullabies.

The sun came out, and immediately we were down on our knees, looking at all the flowers that glistened white, yellow, pink, blue, among the melting moth balls of hail.

I was examining a plant about the size and shape of a winter coat button, that was almost covered with flowers, twenty-one of them, as icy white as the hailstones, when suddenly a bee appeared above those white faces—a bee whose body covered five flowers at a time.

Watching the bee in the sun, I realized that the rigors of climate, tempered for me by raincoat, sweater, face cream, and huddling, were only a fraction of the plants' problems on the mountaintop.

A bee on a
tundra cushion

They have the problem of keeping their pollen dry; the problem of a scarcity of pollinators; the problem of ice blizzards and winter winds that give little rest to snow; the problem of holding on to rock in the face of sliding snow and gouging rains; the problem of holding on to bits of soil and decayed leaves, and moisture, against ice and torrents, parching sun, and drying winds; and the problem of ten months of winter followed by summer days that run the gamut, every twelve hours, of all the season's changes.

We started examining plant after plant to see what features they had in common, what features seemed to make survival possible.

The leaves, certainly, had several characteristics in common.

They were small. Their size brought the memory of other small leaves: those of fir and spruce in the north; of aromatic sumac in the Bad Lands of South Dakota; of heather on windswept dunes in Denmark; of cranberries in a cold and acid bog; of hudsonia in sand dunes; of creeping snowberry on the edge of a northern bog; of cactus in the desert. It was easy to understand that leaves of the mountaintop should be small.

Some of the leaves were smooth with a waxy finish that reminded my fingertips of the feel of wintergreen and balsam fir of the north; of the waxy coat of the century plant; and of the resinous covering of the creosote bush of the desert.

Many of the leaves were woolly, with dense hairiness. Feeling them, I recalled lead plant in the Illinois prairie; mullein in sun-beaten pastures; Russian olive in the windbreaks of Nebraska; sagebrush on the Great Plains; the underside of the leaves of Labrador tea; the hairy lip fern of dry, rocky ledges; and the edelweiss of the Alps.

Many, many of the leaves were fat, thick, or succulent. They reminded me of the many fat-leaved plants that face the wind on the bare bluffs of the Pacific coast south of Monterey; and the crassula that went on growing, even blooming, when we were trying to dry it in a plant press at the university; and the balloon-shaped leaves on a specimen from a salt marsh; and the fatness of the bryophyllum leaf that tourists send home from Florida so that their friends may pin it on a curtain and watch it develop new plants; and the Russian thistle of Minnesota roadsides; and the purslane of every hoof-beaten farmyard; and the little succulents that grow in the backs of china elephants in the desert air of Chicago apartments, needing only to be dusted off with the rest of the furniture. It was not surprising to meet fleshy leaves with water storage facing the summer sun of the mountaintop.

Many had stems or leaves or leaf margins set with glands that were tipped with a sticky knob. Through the hand lens those sticky knobs, reflecting the sharp sun, reminded me of the abundant glands on a catchfly on sun-beaten sand, and the amber globules on bayberry leaves along the Maine coast, and the glands on rose geranium and peppermint and sweetbrier rose.

Many of the leaves were inrolled at the margin, toward the underside. This inrolled, or revolute, leaf margin marks northern firs, bog rosemary, swamp laurel of high cold ponds, Labrador tea of the arctic tundra, sweetfern of stony New England pastures. Some grasses roll up in a drought, and some mosses fold up and roll up into dead-looking brown hairs. When one remembers that the microscopic openings into the moist inner parts of the leaves are situated on those protected under surfaces, it is not hard to understand that there should be some revolute margins on the mountaintop.

There was one feature of the leaves that might have been surprising if we had read about it in a book instead of seeing it on these plants. They had "entire," or evenly continuous, margins, almost all of them—margins without saw teeth or lobes. In view of the consistently deeply divided leaves on the plants of roadsides, prairies, and pastures, these entire leaves might have seemed out of place, except for the obvious fact that they were already so drastically reduced in size that any further reduction seemed almost impossible.

Next we inspected the flowers.

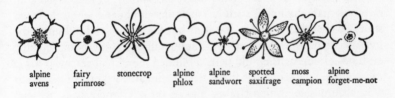

| alpine avens | fairy primrose | stonecrop | alpine phlox | alpine sandwort | spotted saxifrage | moss campion | alpine forget-me-not |

Their pattern had a conspicuous sameness. They were flat-faced, circular, five-parted, small (though their smallness was not in proportion to the smallness of their leaves); they were held side by side, almost overlapping, but not quite; and they were short-stemmed or stemless. In color they were white or yellow or pale pink, for the most part. Many had hairs in their throats.

As the hailstones melted, it was understandable that these flowers could profit by hairs or scales obstructing their throats, helping to keep the pollen dry and the nectar undiluted by the sudden rain, hail, or snow of the brief mountaintop summer.

The massed formation of those minute flowers was akin to the compact community of a sunflower head, where each floret cooperates with many others in achieving a massed showiness that will attract an insect. The flowers of a mountaintop need to be small to endure the weight of the weather, and, being small, they need to pool their showiness.

Since flower stems are a hazard in the gales, the round disk pattern is best for the flower. Side-entranced, or irregular, flowers fit best on a spike. What few flower spikes were found on the tundra were short, short ones, and compact.

We looked then at the plant form—the whole plant.

Cushions, cushions, cushions.

When we dug up one cushion to inspect it, we found that it consisted not only of matted gray-green leaves and short stems, but also of all the precious old organic material of its own manufacture that it had hoarded to itself. Down below, enmeshed in the matted growth, were old brown leaves, old seed capsules emptied of their contents, and old dead stalks, with a few crumbs of soil.

Here was no spendthrift economy.

Because we had so recently taken precautions to make secure all our loose paraphernalia, such as bandannas and caps, when the wind struck, we could visualize what it meant for a plant to hold on to the treasure of humus, there on the mountaintop. Those compact little cushions clutching their old parts reminded me of pioneers who made rugs of their rags, of frogs that eat their discarded skins, of gardeners who accumulate compost piles, and of those Chinese peasants who hoard the family excrement to enrich the garden where the family food is grown.

This cushion plant with its hoarded dry parts makes an efficient sponge for soaking up water. It is efficient, too, in covering the ground beneath it so closely that water can hardly evaporate. This use of the hemispherical form, which exposes as little surface as possible to the thirsty sun and wind, is not unlike other uses of the sphere and half-sphere, in places where it is essential to have as much volume as possible with a minimum of surface—spheroidal gas tanks, and certain echinoderms, and cushion cactus, for example.

We dug up other cushions to see what sort of roots they had. Thick, distorted, ancient-looking taproots they were. A botanist in Switzerland, who counted the annual rings of growth on such heavy old roots of alpine forget-me-not, told of finding plants that were more than thirty years old. Others have told of counting more than a

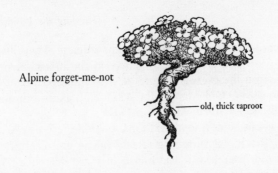

Alpine forget-me-not

old, thick taproot

hundred rings. And the thickness of the rings has sometimes been found to measure one thirty-four-thousandth of a millimeter.

These plants inherit dwarfness; they are not simply dwarfed forms of plants from lower altitudes. Experiments in transplanting them have proved this fact.

But it was not only the possession of certain features in common that marked these tundra plants. It was also the absence of certain other features.

There were, of course, no trees, unless the creeping willow was to be called a tree because of the stature of its relatives. No living thing could stand tall and live through the buffeting and gouging of winter. We had left the trees behind down where they were ancient stunted forms without hope of growing higher than the depth of winter snows.

A thought-provoking absence was that of the dependents. There were apparently no saprophytes, no parasites, no epiphytes, no climbers even. That absent company was composed of plants that flourish where the living is soft, food abundant, and growth flaccid. There were hangers-on at the Roman banquets; and Lazarus lay under the rich man's table, but Saint John the Baptist ate his locusts and wild honey alone.

There was an absence of bulbs and of fleshy rhizomes—absence, in short, of all sorts of vulnerable softness.

Annuals were almost entirely absent. It would be too much to expect of any plant that it should germinate, grow, flower, and mature seeds in that brief summer with so much of winter mixed in it. The wind had abated and the sun had grown hot. We took off coats and sweaters and sat down to rest, and to hunt up some of these strangers in our flower books.

Their common names were of some interest. They showed that hail and wind and cold had not shriveled the imagination of those who had given the everyday names to these flowers. There were Sky Pilot, Snowlover, Old Man of the Mountain, Fairy Primrose, Gem Carpet, Skyland Willow, Mountain Dryad.

The genus names, too, held some interest, for they revealed relationships. It was not surprising to find Silene and Lychnis, Sedum, Primula, and Artemisia, nor to find Betula and Potentilla, Aster, and Solidago, because a botanist expects to find those genera inhabiting the world's open, sun-beaten places. Nor was it surprising to find Saxifraga, Campanula, and Aquilegia, because a botanist is used to seeing those genera sitting on rock. The very name Saxifraga means "rock breaker."

But it was the species names that were most revealing, because, while genus names carry a picture of the floral structure, a species name often has something to tell of the way in which a particular member of the genus has had its stature, its texture, its character selected by adversity, opportunity, and time.

Whenever a list of flowers contains a preponderance of the following species names, one may assume that that company has faced sun and wind, cold and heat, hail and gouging rains, drought and blizzards.

Some of the species names have alp and mountain in them:
  alpestris
  montana
  saximontana (rock mountain)
  austromontana (southern mountains)
  monticola (a small mountain)
  scopulorum (of the rocks)
  oreophilum (mountain-loving)

Some have the north, and cold, and snow, in them:
  boreale
  hyperboreale
  groenlandica
  frigida
  nivea (snow)

Some tell of protection:

   glaucophylla (smooth blue-gray-green leaf; a re-
      minder of our raincoats)
   hirsutissima (extremely hairy; a reminder of our
      sweaters)
   glandulosa (covered with the sticky knobs of glands;
      a reminder of our face cream)

Some tell of pulling in their necks:

   nanum (dwarf)
   pygmaea
   condensata
   repens (creeping)
   reptans (crawling)
   procumbens
   prostrata
   humilis (low or slight)
   acaulis (stemless)
   caespitosa (tufted)

Some of them have names that are filled with human interest because they are the names of the botanists and naturalists and explorers who first found these alpine plants. As we read their names we saw an adventuresome band, wearing ear muffs and carrying green vasculums and plant presses, and peering through microscopes with eyes accustomed to looking at far-off big things such as mountain passes and portages and Indian fires, as well as nearby small things, such as stamens and pistils. It was a goodly company:

   Parryi (for Charles Christopher Parry, 19th century botanist who
      explored remote places, and discovered hundreds of new
      species, of which fifty bear his name)
   Rydbergii (for Per Axel Rydberg, western botanical explorer who,
      in 1900, compiled a flora of Montana and Yellowstone Park)
   Coulteri (for John Merle Coulter, world-renowned botanist of the
      University of Chicago, who compiled a Rocky Mountain
      flora)

Douglasi (for David Douglas, Scottish botanist who in the early 1800s collected plants from America's Northwest for the Horticultural Society of London)

Engelmannii (for George Engelmann, 19th century botanical explorer and writer)

Some of them have species names that are of geographical interest, and so started us off on the old line of speculation about plants called "disjuncts." (In this book we have met disjuncts in several chapters: Bog, Dunes, Canyon, Smokies.) Two such species names were:

sajanensis (from Saiansk mountains, Siberia)
beeringianum (from the region of the Bering Sea)

Some of the species that are disjuncts, because they grow in the Rockies, and in several faraway places, from which this colony is widely separated, are the moss campion, the mountain dryad, and the alpine forget-me-not.

The mountain dryad, a shrub that is lying down, forming dwarf creeping mats, grows also in the White Mountains, in Greenland, in Alaska, and in alpine and arctic Europe and Asia. It is perhaps as typical a mountaintop shrub as one could find.

The moss campion grows also in Greenland, in the Alps, in Asia, in New Hampshire, and in alpine to arctic situations from New Mexico to Alaska. The alpine forget-me-not grows also in the Alps.

Mountain dryad, Dryas octopetala — a shrub that is lying down

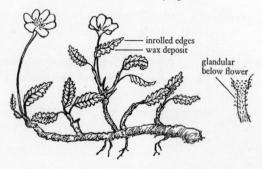

also found in:
White Mountains,
Alaska,
Greenland,
arctic and
alpine Europe,
and Asia

—— inrolled edges
—— wax deposit

glandular
below flower

These widely separated patches of a species have sometimes been considered to be the result of bird distribution of seeds. But we know now that seeds do not travel great distances in the digestive systems of birds.

Such plants, that seem to hop from mountaintop to mountaintop and from arctic tundra to the mountaintops, leaping plains, and lakes, and deserts, and forests, and oceans, are usually recording cold rather than birds.

During the glacial periods, northern vegetation was pushed southward. The glacial cold, added to the cold of altitude, must have clothed some mountains with tundra that extended much further down the mountainside than it now does. Thus, that tundra was often continuous from mountaintop to mountaintop across intervening valleys.

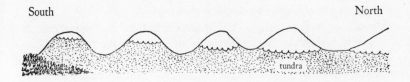

When the ice and cold retreated gradually to the north, the evergreen trees advanced up the mountainsides, crowding the tundra plants into the less favorable places, the places where living conditions were still too rugged for evergreens.

Islands of tundra were left behind on the mountaintops.

Deciduous forests began to push up from the south, invading the foothills and the mountain valleys. Meanwhile erosion was helping to cut the islands of tundra apart.

deciduous forest

In the arctic region, as the ice sheet retreated, there was tundra encircling the globe, with peninsulas of tundra running south along the nearest mountains. Then oceans cut the arctic tundra apart.

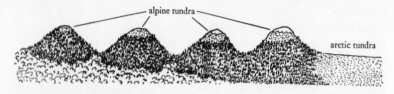

alpine tundra

arctic tundra

Gradually, then, isolated patches of plants were left, far from their kind, until today, a mountaineer may meet a flower which he has learned to know in the Rockies, growing also in the Alps, in Scandinavia, in the Pyrenees, in the Himalayas, in the Altai Mountains, as well as in Greenland, in Spitzbergen, and in arctic Russia.

During the long years of separation, some of these isolated communities have produced members that show differences from their ancestral kind, differences that have survived because they made those plants better fitted to endure the hardships of their mountaintop.

These remote members of some mountaintop species may meet each other some day, if cold again comes creeping down from the north. Then, if Edgar Anderson is right about the areas in which the greatest number of variations occur in plants, a great number of variations should crop up.

The hail started again. We left the gray cushions to face the pelting and the freezing night temperature that threatened, and we retreated down the mountain to conditions that encourage parasites and climbers and vulnerable softness.

Tundra–Revisited

Boiling rusty radiators have decreased as a feature of the overlook stops along Trail Ridge Road. But the last twenty years have brought increases in other features: the number of automobiles stopping for the view; the number of children, and adults, who scramble up onto the tundra; the number of paths across the tundra, and the number of short-cuts made between those paths; and, finally, the recent arrivals, the off-the-road vehicles: trail bikes, four-wheel drives, snowmobiles.

Already, before these increases in wear, the tundra plants were stretching the probability of survival to its very limits. A cushion plant takes many years to build, a moment to destroy, and decades of brief summers to restore.

That moment of destruction might come to an alpine forget-me-not cushion bulging with buds, from a stout hiking boot (no human could ever bear to grind a heel into the porcelain of its full bloom); it might come to a pink perfection of a moss campion from a discarded cigarette pack that cut off its entire short summer of sunshine; or to a pygmy buttercup, from a bottlecap.

ECLIPSE

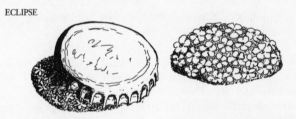

Destruction can come to entire communities of plants, if towns in the dry foothills, appreciating the slow release of tundra snowbank meltwater down the mountainside, should extend their plans for holding more snowbanks for summer release by building snow fences on the tundra. Tundra plants would be destroyed, and their slowly accumulated soil would be washed away.

In the book *Land Above the Trees*, Beatrice Willard and Ann Zwinger give examples of the slow return of the tundra after destruction.

In 1958, in cooperation with the Park Service, an area was chosen to be left exposed to traffic for a time, and then to be closed off. In eight weeks the cushion plants were found to be worn off down to the soil. During the following two weeks the soil began to erode. Then human feet were excluded from the area. Recovery started within a month. Under protection the restoration would not be complete, the observers estimated, for twenty years.

Another example given came from the slopes of Mount Rainier. Paths there were abundant. But hikers seemed to disdain them in favor of shortcuts. The Park Service expects that it will cost about $250,000 to restore the area, eliminating the slightest trace of the existence of a shortcut, lest it encourage a hiker to use it again. Much power, water, and reseeding, as well as burlap and mesh, have proven necessary.

The old Fall River Road, which once crossed the tundra, was blocked off when the Trail Ridge Road was built, and traces of its existence were made as inconspicuous as possible. That was forty years ago, but the old route can still be traced across the tundra.

Dr. Willard, after telling these and other examples of the fragility of the tundra, writes, "Fifty to one hundred years of plant growth can be snuffed out by a beer can."

A layman's account came to me from Peggy Parker, who lives in Denver and takes frequent trips with her family along Trail Ridge Road. She writes:

I've never seen anyone running over the hills, probably because of cold wind and shortness of breath. At one pull-off there is a "Tundra Trail," about ¼-mile long. There is a box of brochures, with pictures and information about the tundra, available for ten cents. It is good. Only a few people negotiate this trail. Probably because of the weather, and the lack of a "view" to photograph. The best friend the tundra has is probably the bad weather. But if that improved wouldn't the trees take over?

Probably.

BIBLIOGRAPHICAL NOTES

Mountains in Flower by Volkmar Vareschi and Ernst Krause. Macmillan, New York, 1940.

"The Vegetation of Alpine Region of the Rocky Mountains in Colorado" by Theodore Holm. Memoir *National Academy of Science* 19, Number 3 (1923), 5–45.

Historical Plant Geography by E. V. Wulff (of U.S.S.R. Institute of Plant Industry, Leningrad). Chronica Botanica, Waltham, Massachusetts, 1943.

Colorado Plant Life by Francis Ramaley. University of Colorado, Boulder, 1927.

Natural Regions of the U.S.S.R. by L. S. Berg. Chapter X, *Mountains of the Caucasus. Macmillan, New York, 1950.*

The Geography of the Flowering Plants by Ronald Good. Chapters 8–11, Distribution of Species. Longmans, Green, London & New York, 1947.

"Alpine Vegetation in the Vicinity of Long's Peak, Colorado" by W. S. Cooper. *Botanical Gazette* **45** (1908), 319–337.

"The Causes of Dwarfing in Alpine Plants" by F. E. Clements. *Science* **25** (1908), 287.

"The Alpine Zone, in Vegetational Zonation in the Rocky Mountains," by R. F. Daubenmire. *The Botanical Review* **9** (June, 1943).

"Adventures in Mountain Botany" by Hugh M. Raup in *The Friendly Mountains: Green, White and Adirondacks* edited by Roderick Peattie. Vanguard, New York, 1942.

The Ecology of Arctic and Alpine Plants by W. D. Billings and H. A. Mooney. Biological Review **43** (1968), 481–529.

"North to the Tundra," *National Geographic Magazine,* **141,** No. 3 (March, 1972) 293–337.

The Effect of Environmental Factors on the Standing Crop and Productivity of an Alpine Tundra by D. Scott and W. D. Billings. Ecological Monographs, **34** (1964), 243–270.

Land Above the Trees, A Guide to American Alpine Tundra by Ann H. Zwinger and Beatrice E. Willard. Harper and Row, New York, 1972.

16

Reading the Records in Old Adobe Walls

OR

The Spanish Conquest
of the Grass Hills

And the same day Pharaoh commanded the taskmasters of the people, and their officers, saying:
"Ye shall no more give the people straw to make brick, as heretofore: let them go and gather straw for themselves. . . ."

So the people were scattered abroad throughout all the land of Egypt to gather stubble instead of straw.
And the taskmasters hasted them, saying, "Fulfil your works, your daily tasks, as when there was straw."

—*Exodus 5:6–7, 12–13.*

WHAT stubble the enslaved followers of Moses and Aaron could gather was rushed to the places where the clay was waiting, having been mixed with water and let stand for a day or two. Then the mass was trodden by bare feet before it was shaped into bricks. The straw, or stubble, was used for keeping the bricks from cracking as they dried in the sun. The Arabs called the sun-dried bricks *atob*.

That word has become *adobe* on Spanish lips. It traveled to Mexico on the lips of Cortez and his men. In Mexico they found adobe bricks already in use; ancient adobe bricks raised into cities and pyramids. It was as if the slaves of the pharaohs had preceded the Spanish explorers.

And so they had (it is now beginning to be believed), arriving several thousand years before tall sailing ships brought the Spaniards to the eastern coast. How else can be explained the natives who greeted Cortez; their finely wrought gold and silver, woven cotton garments, a knowledge of stars and planets and advanced cranial surgery, and possession of a calendar more accurate than any that Europe had achieved? How else could the tradition that white men with beards had come in a boat and might come again, have been told and retold down the generations, making the landing of Cortez a long-prophesized event?

Thor Heyerdahl's reed boat adventure was undertaken to test the possibility of such an explanation for the arrival of skills full-blown and evidently Egypt-linked.

Cortez brought with him a new religion, different from that of the pharaohs and of the natives; a religion that demanded converts to Christ and Mary. In Cortez's wake came the missionary monks. When the time came for them to extend the line of missions northward along the coast into California, they were gradually acquiring a band of converts (the neophytes) who worked at making adobe bricks for the buildings.

Those monks, coming from a long tradition of keeping records—of plant life in their herbals; of history in their diaries and letters and manuscripts—would hardly have foreseen that their own white hands would have assisted the dark, muddy hands of the natives in the new world; nor could they have suspected that some of those natives might have a heritage from skilled, bearded white men who had come to

Mexico in a reed boat many thousands of years ago. Certainly the monks would not have realized that their own hands were actually engaged in making records, without benefit of gold-leaf embellishments, or quill pens, or flourishing calligraphy; their muddied hands were making records of history as it happened.

A complex history it was that they recorded, an account of invasion and conquest by foreign plants, of the green natives of a thousand hills; a record not to be discovered for many years:

This record was not to be read by turning pages of old parchment, but by taking apart the bricks that the monks and the Indians had put together. George W. Hendry, of the Agronomy Department of the University of California at Berkeley, decided to try to find out the stories of the varieties of wheat that had been sown in California by the Spanish ranchers. He suspected that the varieties might be found in the adobe of missions and ranch buildings. They were. *And so were many other plants.*

Hendry and M. K. Bellue, weed and seed biologist of the California Department of Agriculture, went to work on bricks selected from sixty-five buildings in California, Arizona, and northern Mexico. They carefully avoided any restored walls.

First a brick was brushed, scraped, and washed (they weren't interested in a seed that a swallow coming back to Capistrano might have dropped yesterday). Then the brick was immersed in water for twelve hours. There the brick broke down, as it might have done long ago in the wet season had not the wall been seated on a stone base, and roofed with overhanging tile.

The plant remains, now released from the clay, were still mixed with thin mud. Water was added and gently agitated. Gradually the fine clay settled, and the plant parts floated. All the floating matter was skimmed off and then washed through screen after screen until it was clean. Separately, the silt at the bottom was washed and screened for any small particle that might have been missed. Then all the washed and screened material was placed in a screen-bottomed dishpan and sprayed gently for a final cleaning. Finally the salvaged material was spread out on screens raised a few inches above paper-covered tables where warm air dried it out, to prevent development of mold.

The plant remains were then ready for identification, which of

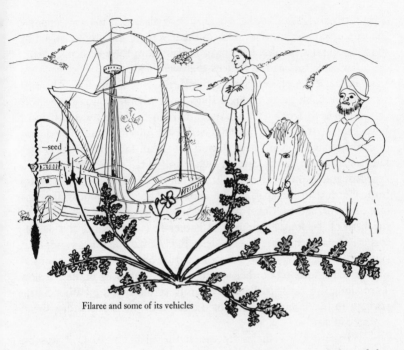

seed

Filaree and some of its vehicles

course could only be historically revealing if the age of the adobe structure were known.

That part was not difficult. The dates of the founding of the missions were located in transcripts of mission records; and the ranch buildings could have been easily dated by land-grant records in the Spanish and Mexican archives of California. However those archives were destroyed in the San Francisco fire. But certified copies were found in land claim cases, and in court records of lawsuits.

Remains of the little plant called filaree were found, and dated as having arrived before 1769. It appeared in bricks of the mission San Antonio de Padua, dated 1771, and in the mission San Juan Bautista, 1797, and in the Rancho Vallejo, 1834, and several others. It must have been one of the first of the foreigners to invade the open places between the high clumps of the native perennial bunchgrasses that dominated the hills at that time. Did this new taste please the prong-horn antelope and the tule elk and the jackrabbit who grazed on the nutritious grasses?—one wonders. It is clear that the ants approve the imported taste, for their nests in the desert are sometimes ringed by the long spiral awns that they have husked from the seeds.

The ancestors of the filarees that were added to the adobe must have had a series of rides before they arrived in California. The first ancestor probably came by Spanish galleon, whether it was a stowaway in a feedbag or tangled in a horse's mane or a sheep's wool. It must have landed, still viable, and screwed itself into the ground and produced a sprawling plant with flowers too small to attract attention. A later ancestor may have traveled awhile in the tail of the big horse of a bearded and gauntleted conquistador; or may have been picked up from the dust of the road by the shuffling robes of a monk. Perhaps one ancestor had the most distinguished conveyance of all, riding at the hem of the long black robe of Father Francisco Kino, the dauntless missionary explorer, as he rode to Baja California, discovering that California was not an island, as reported by others. A still later ancestor may have traveled north along the rough beginnings of the Mission Trail along the coast, perhaps in the robe of the limping Father Serra; perhaps in the stomach of one of the cattle in the four-hundred-head Rivera cattle drive.

Whatever the vehicles by which the filaree arrived, it was on hand to be put into the adobe at an early date. It had become so widely distributed that it was listed as a native by such early observers as Torrey and Fremont. A native? The filaree has the botanical name *Erodium cicutarium,* L'Her., evidencing that it had been named by that famous French botanist, L'Heritier, who taught botany to Pierre Joseph Redoute, court painter to the Empress Josephine!

Filaree ancestors didn't always need to ride; they may have been self-propelled for part of the way. The long awn attached to the tip of a seed twists and untwists, making a tight spiral, then straightens. This can propel it along the ground, and help it, after a rain, to enter the ground, screwlike.

Two other foreigners, like the filaree, were early arrivals—yellow dock and spiny-leaved sow-thistle. But as soon as the cattle started to reduce the height and the spread of the bunchgrass individuals, there were plenty of foreign annuals, and native annuals as well, to take advantage of the sunny places made available.

Three native opportunists were six-weeks fescue, three awns, and love grass. But they were outnumbered, as the grazing pressure increased, by the front ranks of the invading hordes of foreigners: soft chess, ripgut, goatgrass, mustard, and, of course, filaree.

In the adobe of Rancho Vallejo, in the San Francisco area, of twenty-two wild plants that have been identified, sixteen are European.

The most successful, the wild oat, made its conquest after 1800. Hendry's first (1931) report on adobe dating tells of a single damaged kernel, thought to be wild oat, found in the pulpit stair of the Mission San Juan Bautista (1797). A later report (1936) tells that the adobe of the San Francisco Bay area has shown wild oat in abundance after 1800.

During the Spanish Mission period (1769 to 1834), several commoners of many roadsides arrived: Queen Anne's Lace, pigweed, annual bluegrass, lambs quarters, sweet clover, and others.

After the Spaniards and their missionary monks came no more, the wet adobe began to receive bits of plants known as "habitation species," plants carefully brought along for placing close to the house. Some of these would have been handy to the brickmaker, in the rubbish heap at some corner of a ranch. Some of the plant bits, by their nature, hint that workers, free now of the watchful eyes of the monks, were munching beside their work, and spitting out seeds into the wet adobe. A watermelon seed, and an olive pit, both dated as of 1837, were found at Rancho La Natividad, a Mexican grant.

The adobe has yielded other things beside invading plants: cleaned fibers of yucca, strips of woven bark, fragments of tile, a bit of leather. Human bones were found in the walls of a mission in Baja California, probably recording a smallpox epidemic in that area, and a later removal of soil from the site of hasty burials.

And, while some bricks were drying, men, dogs, coyotes, cats, chickens, and birds walked across them, leaving footprints.

Spring has changed. It has become a matter of bursting seeds, instead of a matter of pushing green tips from within the wrappings of the accumulated haystacks of the perennial bunchgrasses: needlegrass, melicgrass, bromes, wild ryes, and others. The bunchgrasses have found retreats, sometimes in the corners of the peach orchards, or vineyards. And the spring wildflowers still find places for survival: blue lupine, cream cup, mariposa lilies, and the California poppies.

But the hills, as the names of many of the towns among them, have become Spanish.

BIBLIOGRAPHICAL NOTES

Man's Role in Changing the Face of the Earth edited by William M. Thompson. Wenner-Gren Foundation, The University of Chicago Press, Chicago, 1956.

"The Adobe Brick as a Historical Source" by George W. Hendry. *Agricultural History 5,* No. 3, (July, 1931).

"An Approach to Southwestern Agricultural History Through Adobe Brick Analysis" by G. W. Hendry and M. K. Bellue. *University of Mexico Bulletin* (Oct. 15, 1936).

An Island Called California by Elna S. Bakker. University of California Press, Berkeley, Cal., 1971.

The Golden Road, The Story of California's Spanish Mission Trail by Felix Riesenberg, Jr. McGraw-Hill, New York, 1962.

Spanish Alta California by Alberta Johnson Denis. Macmillan, New York, 1927.

The Ra Expeditions by Thor Heyerdahl. Doubleday, New York, 1971.

17

The Chaparral

OR

TOLERANCE OF FIRE

AND DROUGHT

CHAPARRAL—the word links the hills with Spaniards on horseback, and with Old Spain, where the name was born. Over there, the tightly-massed shrubs which tore at the horseman's legs (and the horse's legs, too, for that matter) were chiefly composed of a scrubby oak, called *chaparro*. The horseman's legs were protectively encased in *chaparreros*, the word which our tongues have worn down to "chaps," and extended to include riders (and even the drivers, steel-incased, of Pintos and Mustangs).

We wished for body *chaparreros* as we inserted our vulnerable juicy selves into the chaparral on Mount Tamalpais, near San Francisco. We had climbed up there on a late March day, enjoying the rolling view of hill after chaparral-covered hill. From a distance the covering looked like deep but bumpy carpeting; but close up it looked like an embattled resistance force with elbows locked. It exuded charm, nevertheless, in its smell that bore a pinch of sage, a hint of chrysanthemum, and a dash of Worcestershire sauce; in the sound of

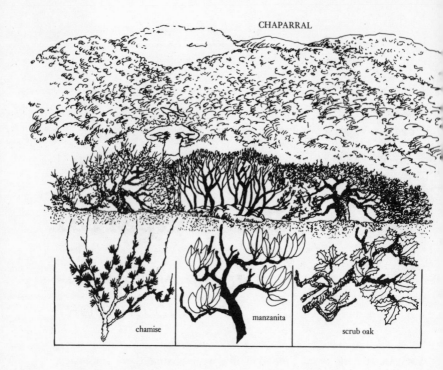

chamise

manzanita

scrub oak

wren-tits; and in the spring green of new shining leaves held above the dark green of the old leaves.

As we pushed through, or crawled to inspect the lumpy burls at the bases of many shrubs, it became apparent that the chaparral, of this area at least, was made up of several kinds of shrubs, but that the dominant one was certainly the shrub with very small, narrow leaves borne in tight clusters, and with shreddy bark. *Chamiso*, or chamise, *Adenostema fasciculatum*, is its name. The name *Chamiso* was conferred in honor of a certain Louis Charles Adelaide Chamisse De Boncourt, "a French nobleman by birth, a Prussian soldier by education, a botanist by choice, a poet by inspiration." He traveled from 1815 to 1818 in the ship "Rurik" on a Russian scientific expedition around the world.

The company included a Dr. Friedrich Eschscholz, who collected seeds from some dry seedpods, standing in the dry sand which

San Francisco now covers. Four years later, after those seeds had shown what glory they could produce, Chamisse, in Madrid, formally gave the plant a scientific name, *Eschscholzia californica*, in honor of "the very skillful, very learned, very amiable Eschscholz, doctor of medicine, and equally expert in botany and entomology." "California poppy" we had called it that morning as we noticed it just beginning to explode along the roadsides.

Europeans had fun giving names, their own and each other's, to the many new plants showing up, unnamed, on the west coast of North America.

Then, in 1954, Edgar Anderson, of the Missouri Botanical Gardens, took a long close look at the chamise, and showed that, in addition to being named by European travelers, it had evidently been shaped, in part, by early European settlers in the New World.

One of its parents, according to Anderson, was a very low-growing shrub living on islands and headlands along the California coast. It had great tolerance for brilliant sunlight, and was able to grow on poor rocky soil. But its coastal home gave it fog and drizzle all year long, even in the rainless summer. The other parent grew in the Sierra foothills, and was a tall shrub resembling a small-leaved tiny-flowered white lilac. It got neither drizzle nor fog, but it needed a deep soil, and did not tolerate intense sunlight.

These two parents never met each other, until man moved into the area. He broke down the barriers between them, with his roads, his cultivation of the soil, his clearings, his animals—who knows what newly-opened route enabled the two to meet? But the offspring of the chance meeting were several hybrids, some of them able to survive on the sunbeaten dry hills, and even to dominate the chaparral. Anderson wrote that the chamise is a "great plastic hybrid swarm" including some that resemble one parent and some the other. In the shade of an oak may grow one that favors its Sierra ancestor; on a rocky foggy ridge may be the island strain. And where man has stirred things up around an old ranch house, and moved on, leaving an open ecological niche, there may be second crosses between hybrid parents.

Next to the chamise, the most prevalent shrubs were a manzanita, and a scrub oak with holly-shaped leaves.

Where a road had recently cut through, a vertical bank showed the length of chaparral roots. We measured one twelve feet long. The cut revealed the way that rock has been fractured on the shaking earth of the California coast. It was plain that this mass could slide easily; and that it needed holding in place by the long roots of the chaparral.

No wonder that householders at the foot of these hills look up to them with fear, knowing that a heavy rain may cause a landslide, and that a long dry season is filled with threat of fire.

When fire comes, as it will, because it is part of the old established rhythm of the chaparral, it will find tinder ready, in the dry twigs with their oils and resins, and in the accumulated debris under the shrubs. In the places where we investigated under the shrubs, there had been a heavy accumulation. In such a place fire can leap across almost explosively, in a northeasterly wind with gusts of 100 miles an hour.

The chaparral can take it, as it has taken it for two million years. Perhaps fire has had a hand in selecting the members of the chaparral. The plants that have a place there now were probably tried by fire, and thus selected out for survival.

After a fire sweeps through, the chamise and the manzanita and the scrub oak and the others all put out new shoots from their burls or roots (unless there has been too long an interval since the last burning and the accumulated debris makes the fire linger). In a place where a fire had recently been, we saw a great lumpy burl that had been apparently reduced to charcoal, but was putting out new shoots around the edges. Such new growth is more resistant to fire and disease than the old.

In soil fertilized by ashes, the annuals and perennials, which otherwise have no place in the chaparral, have their turn. Their seeds are able to wait for years. It takes a fire to crack their thick seed coats, and to destroy chemical substances that some shrubs of the chaparral add to the soil under them—substances that prevent crowding by inhibiting the growth of the shrubs' own seedlings. Again, if fire comes too seldom and finds too much fuel, the rhythm of the chaparral is thrown out of its established order. The seeds are simply cooked.

In time the original inhabitants take over once more. The opportunists are crowded and shaded out. Their hard-coated seeds wait.

Should there be a torrential rain following a fire, before the annual and perennial cover has time to cover and hold the ground, there may be slipping hillsides. But that too is taken care of when vegetation returns.

Even the animal life seems to have become adjusted to periodic fires. Not the individual animal, of course. He may die, while the species survives. But when has Nature shown concern for the individual? It is the race that matters. After the fire there is more food available; the new shoots, the tender seedlings, the seeds, all provide food for some mammal, or bird. And they in turn provide food for a coyote or a hawk.

It all sounds so right, so self-perpetuating, so time-honored. But what about the trim row of ranch houses down there at the foot of the hill, and the new row being started at the foot of the next hill, and the next. . . . The owners have accepted the ever-present threat of earthquakes, but it *does* seem to them that something could be done to protect them from having their houses burned, or buried under a landslide.

The threat is great down in what is called "soft chaparral" as well as up in the "hard chaparral." The soft chaparral is dominated by black sage, *Salvia mellifera,* and a kind of sagebrush, *Artemesia californica.* Their leaves are soft and often fall after a severe drought. This kind of chaparral grows down nearer the coast, where the suburbs also grow, and the schools and playgrounds.

Get rid of chaparral, people plead, and cover the hills with grass or with some low-growing fire-resistant groundcover. Grass was tried, but the cost was prohibitive—the cost of destroying the chaparral, of installing the grass, of keeping the chaparral from returning. And erosion increased.

Controlled burning at regular intervals so that too much fuel could not accumulate—this seems to be the answer, in spite of the fact that any additional smoke pollution is too much along that coast.

One suggestion is for eight wide horizontal strips around a hill, to be burned on successive years, starting at the top. Then the burned top would be a buffer for next year's burning of the strip below, and so on till the base of the hill is reached, and the system starts over at the top. Erosion would be slow, with the burned strip being on the contour.

Another idea is for a green belt at the edge of a residential area—a belt about one hundred feet wide, stripped of chaparral and then landscaped with plants that are not fire hazards. Such a buffer zone must be kept watered by the community; this is *most* important. It must be kept free of debris.

There are many other suggestions. It is not easy for invaders to negotiate peace treaties with the natives.

BIBLIOGRAPHICAL NOTES

"Introgression in Adenostema" by Edgar Anderson. *Annals of the Missouri Botanical Gardens*, **XLI** (1954), 339–350.

"Man as Maker of New Plants and New Plant Communities" by Edgar Anderson. *Man's Role in Changing the Face of the Earth*, University of Chicago Press, Chicago, 1956.

"Brush Fires in Southern California, Their Ecology and Relation to Man" by Kenneth R. Montgomery. *Lasca Leaves*, quarterly publication of the California Arboretum Foundation (June, 1972).

18

The Redwood Valleys of the Pacific Slopes

OR

ANTIQUES IN AN ANTIQUE CLIMATE

"How LONG *could* it live?" an earnest woman holding a redwood burl in one of her gardening-looking hands and a five-dollar bill in the other turned to ask of the man who stood next in line at the counter.

"*Could?*—oh a thousand years or more, I suppose it *could*, provided you gave it everything it needed." He inspected the knobby burl—a good one, pimply with buds. "Forever, maybe. They say the redwood has potential immortality."

"It would look like that one at first, I suppose," she pointed to the growing green of the exhibited burl, standing in a shallow dish of water. "I would thin those many shoots way down—just pinch them off I suppose, to a single one, and then plant it out in a good place in

ANTIQUES

my garden, and give it plenty of water. But look! It says here to lift the burl out of the water and wipe the bottom clean every once in a while to keep molds and fungi from growing. Well! How can roots grow if I do that? They can't, of course. Those green sprouts will live only so long as the nourishment in that piece of burl lasts. They would need to be attached to great old wide-spreading roots of the tree.

"Oh well, it will make a good conversation piece on my antique coffee table, for a while."

And so it would, or could—conversations about potential immortality, about the dangers of too much peace, about antiques, and about the ethics of a sanctuary.

We went out from the merchandising display of snippets and chips of reality into the redwood forest with its unreal reality.

As we walked or rode or stood silenced among redwoods of parklands and forestry lands and campuses and croplands and treated ourselves to the "Hallelujah Chorus" of the Avenue of the Giants, the "potential immortality" phrase spoken by the man in the shop was constantly under consideration, together with his "provided you gave it everything it needed."

Those needs, after consideration, seem to be four major ones.

THE FIRST NEED:
The antique redwood forest must have the antique climate which gave it birth.

The redwood, which seems to be of the very essence of California, turns out, in the scale of geologic time, to be a veritable newcomer. It is a part of Yellowstone's fossil forest of 50 million years ago. In the Sierra Nevadas, fossil foliage and cones record its presence there 20 million years ago. A forest of redwoods was buried under the ash of a volcano in the Cascades, five million years ago. A mere two million years ago the last redwoods were driven out of Japan and the Himalayas and western Europe by the advancing ice-sheets. At last, driven out of all its ancient haunts, by cold or drought, it survived only on the west coast of our continent. There it has thrived in the antique climate of winter rains and daily fog baths.

It arrived, not suddenly like an advancing army, but gradually, as redwood seeds found sunny openings where a palm, or an avocado, or a mahogany tree had died before the cold creeping down from the north. Slowly the tropical forest retreated south before the redwood forest which was itself in retreat.

While this single surviving species of one branch of a line that had been on earth long enough to have known the dinosaur was being driven into its fortunate sanctuary, a single surviving species of another branch had made its retreat into the Sierra Nevadas, where it became reduced to 70 small scattered groves. Now it is surviving a continuing battle between botanists, who have changed its name from *Sequoia gigantea* to *Sequoia wellingtonia* (with British botanists holding out for *Wellingtonia gigantea*, and an American patriot trying for *Americus giganteum*) and recently, after a counting of chromosomes, to *Sequoiadendron giganteum*, a name so new that it may have to bow to the protocol of botanical nomenclature and give way to the seniority of *Wellingtonia gigantea*.

These two trees, coast redwood, *Sequoia sempervirens* along the Pacific slopes, and the big tree, *Sequoiadendron giganteum*, were considered sole survivors of a mighty line, until a long-lost relative turned up growing unsung along a stream in China. This relative, last surviving member of a third branch, was known to paleobotanists as a fossil only, until in 1944 a Chinese forester noticed it and brought back a specimen to Nanking University. Ralph W. Chaney, paleobotanist of the University of California, flew out to see it and its associates. He found the trees growing in their river valley in association with the same trees that were preserved around it in American fossil beds: chestnut, oak, maple, and katsura trees. The Arnold Arboretum gathered seeds, in a hurry, just before the "bamboo curtain" closed down. Trees from these seeds are now growing around the earth in arboretums and botanical gardens. They stand apart, often carefully unlabeled as "Dawn Redwood, *Metasequoia glyptostroboides*," lest collectors of fossils, rarities, or antiques be tempted to overprune them.

In the far past the dawn redwood had a wide range across Asia, Alaska, and the western parts of America. Part of its range was so far north that only arctic tundra can survive there today. It retreated, as climates changed, to a place of summer rains and occasional freezes, which it may have been able to tolerate possibly because of its deciduous habit.

Of the three survivors, coast redwood, big tree, and dawn redwood, the one with the greatest number of surviving members and the widest range is the coast redwood.

I stood one afternoon in a high clearing north of the mouth of the Navarro River, and watched the fog rolling in. It seemed to be roughly sketching the outline of a typical redwood sanctuary as it rolled, turning with each turn of the Navarro River, and resembling a giant roll of fluffy cotton bandage, unraveling into the side valleys as it went, and fraying up the slopes. Later, inland, up the river, I stood in the drip of the drenched redwoods. Up and down the coast, from Monterey to southern Oregon, similar reminiscences of antique weather were refreshing the antique forests.

THE SECOND NEED:
Disturbance by occasional floods was a part of the redwoods'
life, long before man saw them.

True there are fine redwoods growing, or being grown, on slopes without the chance of floods and heavy silting. But the imposing ancients that stretch our spirits—those are growing in alluvial flats receiving the wash from many steep heights. Now and then a massive flood is bound to swell a stream until the waters crash around the redwoods, carrying logs and branches and mud. The bumping and bruising by logs and other debris stimulates the redwoods into the formation of a sort of scar tissue called burls, and stimulates the burls into forming buds. The accumulating debris smashes and smothers the seedlings and young saplings of Douglas fir, and hemlock, and grand fir. If permitted to grow, those shade-tolerant trees would inevitably rise above any redwood replacements, whether seedlings or rootsprouts. Then, when the mature giants died, Douglas fir, hemlock, and grand fir would take over the forest. And, in the deep shade on the forest foor, hemlock and grand fir would be succeeding best. A self-replacing, quite different forest would have supplanted the redwoods.

The flood-borne silt that smothers seedlings also raises the soil level around the redwoods, but they are peculiarly capable of adjusting to that. They put out fine roots that (contrary to the nature of roots) grow straight up, and even show emergent tips at the surface of the silt. After two or three years the redwood puts out new horizontal roots near the surface.

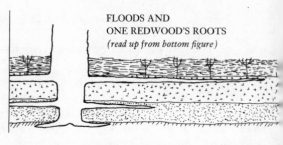

**FLOODS AND
ONE REDWOOD'S ROOTS**
(read up from bottom figure)

6. A new layer of fallen debris accumulates. The root sends up vertical rootlets to the surface—and so on.

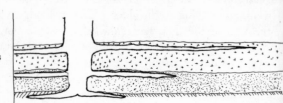

5. A new horizontal root grows. The vertical rootlets die off. The deeper roots cease to function.

4. A flood washes away the fallen debris and deposits a layer of silt, killing off seedlings. The deeply buried roots send up vertical rootlets to the surface of the silt.

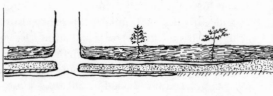

3. Fallen debris accumulates. Seedlings start growing.

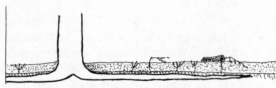

2. A flood washes away the debris and kills the seedlings, as it deposits a layer of silt. The root sends up vertical rootlets to the surface.

1. A thick layer of debris of fallen plant parts accumulates. Seedlings of Douglas fir, tan oak, and others are starting.

Long before man ever saw the redwood forests they had established a sort of rough rhythm with floods, with stretches of peace interrupted by periods of violence and mud. But we are here now, and we make dams and bigger dams, and admire each other for doing it, or scorn each other, according to our lights. And we "harvest" forests where rain, broken by layered branches, once sank silently into the humus; and we leave stripped earth where rains rush off into the streams, and gather into devastating might, until they scour out whole valley bottoms, taking even sand and small gravel and leaving only boulders and bare rock in a giant flume. After such a flood as the one of December 1964, when uprooted redwoods, and logs, and lumber, and sawmills, and parts of farms were washed away, there were people who talked about the hills laid bare by the "harvesting"; but there were many, many more people who begged for more and bigger dams.

If those dams are built, and if they are successful in preventing even the less-violent floods that the redwoods knew before man came among them, then we newcomers are going to have to take steps to assure the future of the redwoods. We are going to have to halt the advance of the shade-tolerant trees—unless we are convinced that the world has no need for antique giants with their heads in the clouds.

The Third Need:
Disturbance by occasional fires helps maintain the redwood forest.

Actually the number of seedlings necessary to the maintenance of a redwood forest is miniscule. Root sprouts alone are capable of maintaining it.

A few pots of seedlings, grown in the mineral soil, and in the sunlight that they require, and set out by hand wherever an unoccupied chimney of sunlight can be found will suffice for the sake of the race.

Unfortunately, the setting out of sturdy seedlings, or the broadcasting of seeds by tanned young men in a sunny place where deer and rabbits frolic and birds wing across the blue sky, makes attractive full-page advertisements for lumber companies. Certainly seedlings can thrive in such croplands; they have mineral earth which bulldozers and rain have exposed, and they have plenty of sunshine. (Wheat could be grown on the land if Chartres Cathedral were razed; corn could be grown where Mayan temples are permitted to stand.) We only have to wait a thousand years or so for a mature redwood forest to return to its former place. But that maturity would not be permitted. The crop will be harvested long before that—as soon as the trees have finished the swift growth of their youth.

A California resident wrote me:

> I just witnessed the kind of mayhem wrought by bulldozers on the land next to ours. There were some trees worth harvesting there, so they took them out 1973 fashion. That means that they made a road for their goddam bulldozers about every 50 feet or so—because no respectable lumberjack would ever walk into the woods to chop down a tree. He *rides* into the woods atop a machine, wearing a battle helmet. And if the machine he must use to get around from tree to tree, and to pull the minor fraction of the forest which is marketable out of there, destroys the whole surface of the earth which was there before, that won't bother our lumberjack nor his employers.
>
> It's only a matter of a few short years before the population/resource pressure is great enough to justify intelligent management and husbandry of the forests instead of the current practices which amount to rape. If you could see what is left by those bastards in their bulldozers you'd think of it in those terms. It is ugly.

Foresters are discussing alternate means of getting the mature logs out by means of long steel cables stretched from ridge to ridge across a valley. The logs are hauled into the sky and over to a central point. No roads need be cut. In a short while this kind of logging may be even profitable.

The redwood is at the mercy of those who admire it most. On the one hand are those who admire it as merchandise, and are aware of government tests that rate it for fire resistance, durability, insulating qualities, termite resistance, and dimension stability. On the other hand are those who treasure it as an experience, and would like to build a fence around its sanctuary. In between these two classes of admirers are those who are armed with chain saws, herbicides, axes, and fire and rakes. They are trying to substitute for fires and floods, and are bearing up under the distrust of some conservationists.

One tall tree ("palo alto") of Palo Alto, stands alone, five miles away from a redwood forest. It may have arrived as a seed traveling in a creek now at the tree's feet. For almost 500 years it throve with the help of the creek; but then came a university and a town, and a series of flood-control dams. The town saw its favorite tree slowly developing the "spike top" which is considered the beginning of the end. The city fathers spared no expense. They consulted experts, and installed a microclimate—a fog sprayed out through the top of the tree from an inconspicuous 100-foot-long pipe. The tree is healthy again, wrapped in its own private fog.

BIBLIOGRAPHICAL NOTES

"Preservation of Coast Redwoods on Alluvial Flats" by Edward C. Stone and Richard Vasey. *Science*, **159** (January 12, 1968), Number 3811, 157–161.

The Redwoods by Kramer Adams. Popular Library, New York.

Redwoods of the Past by Ralph W. Chaney. An eight-page pamphlet published by Save-the-Redwoods-League, San Francisco, California.

Story Told by a Fallen Redwood by Emanuel Fritz. An eight-page pamphlet, published by Save-the-Redwoods-League, San Francisco, California.

The Coast Redwoods, Water and Watershed by Peter E. Black. A study for the National Park Service Washington, D.C.

The Coast Redwood and its Ecology Agricultural Extension Service, University of California (1965).

"Objectivity, Values, and the Redwoods" by Thomas R. Vale. *Landscape*, **19** (Winter, 1970).

19

A Pygmy Forest

OR

TERRACES OF THE PACIFIC SLOPE

"A PYGMY forest?—Did you say a *pygmy* forest?"

People tend to repeat it slowly, carefully lest their hopes show—hopes of plump dwarfs, and deep green shade on mossy banks, and ancient gray-beards weaving strange tales, and magic. Then they pull themselves together and suppose,

"Oh, something new in Disneyland, probably."

But the pygmy forest is in Mendocino County, near Fort Bragg. It has no green shade. Its dwarfs are scrawny, its beards are ragged lichens, and its mosses look threadbare. Nevertheless, magic is there, in the tales told by the scrawny dwarfs and by the earth under them; and in the ways in which men have learned to read those tales.

Because I was unaware of the work of those men, my first view of a pygmy forest was a distasteful shock, interrupting as it did the impressive procession of giant trees down the slope toward the Pacific. It was as if one had been admiring the displays on Michigan Boulevard and then had found oneself, after a false turn, in a ghetto alley, scuffing ashes and being stared at by starvelings.

"There must have been many fires here." We shrugged it off, and continued on our way past tall trees, hearing the sea ahead.

We leaned on the wind as we crossed a prairie-like expanse of grasses and brown seedpods to the brink of a cliff rising a hundred feet above the beach. We watched a wave smash, and then waited for the next big one, and the next. We were back with California bigness: the Pacific, the tall waves, the wide terrace, the high cliff, and the giant trees on the slope. It was enough—for the moment.

But not enough, when everything was reconsidered, on the drive back to Berkeley. Questions began to rise, not about the beautiful and impressive sights (those are ever hard to discuss), but about the freaks, the ugliness (these are ever easy to discuss).

"Those dwarf trees, if they were actually trees, why were they different in kind as well as size from the tall trees all around them?"

"Why were the scrawny dwarfs standing in puddles, or in ground half-covered with lichens?"

"Why did the situation repeat itself so exactly at a second place?" (passed on our way home).

"Why did the tall forest stop so far back from the edge of the cliff?"

"Why was the top of the cliff sandy like a beach?"

Before we went back for another look at the pygmy forest and its setting, we paid a rewarding visit to the Forest Service of the United States Department of Agriculture in Berkeley, and were given explanations, and copies of articles in journals, and some references which we pursued through the Forestry Library. We came back to what we had called a "slope," aware now that it was in fact a series of terraces, or steps—indeed, a famous series, shaped by the waxing and waning rhythm of the periods of continental glaciation, though the continental glaciers themselves never advanced as far south as this area.

Back to the edge of the cliff we went, and looked again at the wave's might gnawing the face of the hard graywacke sandstone and the beach formed of the sandstone's weathered bits, seeing it now as a part of the story.

The story started (if it is being read correctly) on a beach like the one below the cliff there. The beach grew broader, until it was a mile or more wide. The ocean was shrinking because vast quantities of water were being impounded into a great continental ice sheet.

Years passed, thousands of years. Then the ocean level rose again, swollen with meltwater, and chewed its way into the beach which was steadily being uplifted by forces within the earth. The beach became a terrace. The wind brought fine sand up onto the terrace, and molded the sand into dunes. The wind brought fogs, too, in which redwoods thrive; but it brought salt spray as well, which redwoods cannot tolerate, nor can their companion trees. So the grasses got to take over the new terrace, grasses, and some perennials, especially lupine, and two kinds of pine trees. One of these pines is noteworthy because of its enormously wide range and its ability to tolerate practically any condition, except shade. This is the lodge pole pine, *Pinus contorta*. The other one is the bishop pine, *Pinus muricata*, noted for its narrow range along part of the coast of California, where it is restricted to places that other trees cannot tolerate, sandy, salt-sprayed places like the dunes on the terrace.

More years passed, more thousands of years. Again the shrinking sea withdrew from its beach as ocean waters were locked into the ice cap. Again, after the passing of more thousands of years, the swelling ocean returned to cut a second cliff into the second terrace topped with uplifted beach. Again the dunes were formed; and again the grasses and the pine trees came.

But now the first terrace to be formed was a step above the new one—a high step, about one hundred feet. And now the salt spray was no longer a deterrent, and the redwoods and Douglas firs together with some western hemlocks and noble firs took over and shaded out the pine trees. Other changes were taking place: the dunes were changing from gray to a rich brown of iron oxide; and some clay was forming. The always-heavy winter rains soaked down through a layer of humus, mildly acid enough to be favorable for a forest, and through the sand of former dunes, and the beach deposit of a former beach. Where clay had puddled and water tended to stand without draining off, the tall forest trees gave place to smaller ones.

Again, a glacial period started another re-enactment of the same series of events: shrinking sea, beach deposit, swelling sea, cliff cutting, dune formation, grass and pine trees.

Three terraces had been formed, and more thousands of years had passed.

FOUR TERRACES ON THE COAST IN MENDOCINO COUNTY

profiles of the supposed manner of development of

terraces
dunes
hardpan

STAGE 1—shrinking preglacial sea deposits beach sand

STAGE 2—swelling postglacial sea erodes cliff
in rising graywacke sandstone

wind blows sand up to terrace
and molds dune

STAGE 3—repeats stages 1 and 2; hardpan
forming on upper terrace

STAGE 4—repeats stage 3
hardpan forming

STAGE 5—repeats stage 4

THE PLANT COVER
(adapted from *The Pygmy Forest Ecosystem and Its Dune Associates of the Mendocino Coast* by Jenny, Arkley and Schutz in *Madroño* vol. 20)

grass

pines

redwood–
Douglas fir
forest

wax myrtle–
chinquapin

pygmy cypress

And again, yet another glacial period with the same sequence. Four terraces had been formed.

But at this point there was a change in the sequence. Up there where the oldest terrace was now far away from its original position at the edge of the sea, the redwood forest had given back its holdings to the original settler, the bishop pine.

Another glacial period made yet another terrace. The original terrace where our story started had been uplifted to become the fifth step above the ocean. The bishop pine, with wax myrtle, *Myrica californica*, and chinkapin, *Castanopsis chrysophylla*, maintained its grip on both the fourth and the fifth terraces, with an occasional lonely redwood. While the old pine dominated the old dune, now bleached white, another dynasty was taking over more and more of the old terraces. The flat areas, where the cold heavy winter rains stood long in puddles in the ashen soil, were being populated by pygmy forests.

We went back to the pygmy forest that had first claimed our attention and prowled around, scrunching layers of lichens and thin patches of moss and gritty dirty-white sand and splashing through standing rainwater, while the rigid unyielding gray trees tore at our sweaters with dead branches, crusted with lichens.

The gray trees were Mendocino cypress, *Cupressus pymaea*. This is one of the four ancient California native cypresses, each of them restricted to sites that other trees find intolerable.

Usually it is easy to see the various hardships that the other cypresses face. The much-photographed Monterey cypress faces the salt spray and wild wind on a few exposed remnants of its former domain. This cypress demonstrates no need for the conditions of its salt-sprayed headland when it is transplanted for a landscape project, but simply grows fat and prospers, and no one takes its picture any more. A second cypress, the macnab, *Cupressus macnabiana*, has a tenuous grip on a few arid mountain slopes and dry gulches. A third cypress, the gowen, *Cupressus goveniana*, gets certain dry slopes exposed to frequent fires.

But there was no obvious explanation for the takeover of a redwood forest by a pygmy forest, composed largely of Mendocino cypress, with a few lodge pole pines, and a few glossy-leaved manzanita shrubs, *Arctostaphylos nummularia*, all of them quite capable of making normal-sized growth elsewhere. The explanation was buried in the ground. It had to be dug for, by men with soil augers, microscopes, laboratories, chemicals, rain gauges, and knowledge of plants and soils and rocks and glacial periods.

W. A. Gardner investigated a still-forming dune on the first terrace, where bishop pine and lodge pole and lupines and grass were beginning to stabilize the accumulating sand. Under the dune sand he found that the beach sand had already, before the dune began to blow in, had time to be covered with vegetation, and to have the rains begin to bleach the color out of its top layer; and had begun to form, beneath the top layer, a forerunner of a hardpan, rusty-colored, weakly cemented.

This same man investigated the ancient great dune resting on the fourth terrace. He found, under its much-weathered mantle, that the ancient dune still showed its characteristic dune slopes, oriented as very young dunes are, to the direction of the wind. Twenty feet down the dune sand rested on beach sand, slightly bleached, resting on a rusty, partly formed hardpan. The whole situation was much like the one investigated on the most recently formed terrace. But on the part of the terrace not covered by dune, there was real hardpan, cemented and thick, impermeable to rains and roots. On the basis of the weathering of the original rock, Gardner worked out a mathematical scheme for estimating the age of the soil on the highest terrace. The estimate: about a million years.

The hardpan, in its development from its first prophetic appearance on the newest terrace to the final full development on the highest terrace, has turned out to resemble an oversized clay flowerpot, hardbaked, and without a drainage hole in the bottom, and ever-watered. Its former occupants having drowned in the brown, acid, boggy water, the pot now holds a lot of meager plants that can never amount to much.

In attempting to find the consistency and thickness of the layers of soil under a pygmy forest, two men with a soil auger found that it took them two or three hours to reach the underlying bedrock. The uppermost layer was four inches thick, dark gray, and extremely acid. The second layer was bleached almost white, sandy, fourteen inches thick. The third layer was the hardpan, like concrete, from eighteen to

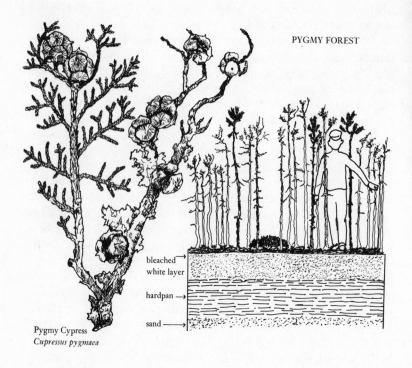

bleached
white layer

hardpan →

sand →

Pygmy Cypress
Cupressus pygmaea

thirty inches thick. Below the hardpan there was sand again, rusty, and then at about seven feet down the sand was the original beach material, as deposited long ago by a shrinking sea. It rested, unchanged, about fifteen feet below the surface of the soil, on the surface of the graywacke sandstone.

We cut an eight-inch piece from the top of a six-foot high lodge-pole pine growing in the pygmy forest, and counted its rings. There were nine of them. Then we cut an equal length from a slightly taller pine growing in a ditch that had been cut beside the road at the edge of the pygmy forest, and counted its rings. There were two of them. The ditch diggers must have broken through the hardpan.

A similar case was discovered when a bishop pine that had grown tall in the midst of crowded pygmys was investigated. Hard layers were chiseled away, and an amazing root was exposed, a tap root that had somehow made its way through the hardpan and into the deep, porous layers beneath it. Perhaps it had found a crack in the hardpan.

A larger-scale release came to a pygmy forest of great age when the canyon of Jug Handle Creek bit into the hardpan of the fourth terrace and started its disintegration.

A casual visitor may go down the slope to the sea without ever noticing that the slope is terraced. That is easy (we did it) because time, in its time-honored way with right angles on the land, has masked the

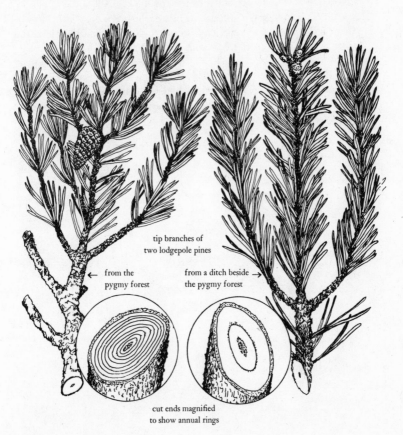

tip branches of
two lodgepole pines

← from the
pygmy forest

from a ditch beside →
the pygmy forest

cut ends magnified
to show annual rings

meeting place of each horizontal beach with a vertical cliff, using humus and sliding sand for changing an angle to a curve.

The figures above show this masking, as well as the angles, and the vegetation, and the growing hardpan. The profiles on the upper part of that page show the physical changes only, stripped of plants.

The glaciers are not shown. They were too far away.

BIBLIOGRAPHICAL NOTES

"The Pygmy Forest-Podsol Ecosystem and Its Dune Associates of the Mendocino Coast" by H. Jenny, R. J. Arkley, and A. M. Schultz. *Madrone,* **20**, 60–74.

"Characteristics and Vegetation Relationships of some Podzolic Soils Near the Coast of Northern California" by Robert A. Gardner and Kenneth Bradshaw. *Soil Science Society Proceedings,* **18** (1954), 320–325.

Forest Trees of the Pacific Slope by G. B. Sudworth. U.S.D.A. Forest Service 1908.

Foundations of Plant Geography by Stanley A. Cain. Harper, New York, 1944. Chapter 9, "Certain Aspects of the History of Cenezoic Vegetation of Western America."

20

Standing Alone in the Sun

OR

INDIVIDUALS OF THE SOUTHWEST DESERT

WHEN we saw that each plant cut a black hole of a shadow, and that no shadow reached another across the naked grit, then we knew that we were truly in the desert.

But when we came to an area where the shadows and the grit were veiled and gentled by a tender tissue of color, we stopped the car and stepped out on the roadside.

And looked down. Instantly we shifted our monstrous-looking feet from the uplifted faces of delicate flowers topping inch-high plants. A bee landed on a flower. The plant had barely enough substance to support the weight of his fat body.

I pulled up three of the plants, and measured their stature, root and all—one to two inches. (Those three plants, pressed, are before

297

me now, mounted in a notebook on a page marked March, 1961.)
Slightly taller plants grew at the very edge of the road. They got an additional bit of moisture from the rainfall or dew collected by the pavement.

What I held in my hand was a minimum mechanism for making seeds and thus ensuring a tomorrow for its kind. But each plant in its brief season had to do more than make a seed—it had to equip that seed for waiting, and waiting not only for enough rain to enter the seed and cause the embryo to burst its skin and put out root and shoot. That is common. A desert plant cannot afford to be merely common. Its seed must be able to wait—to wait until there is enough water to supply the plant until it makes a flower with some attraction for an in-

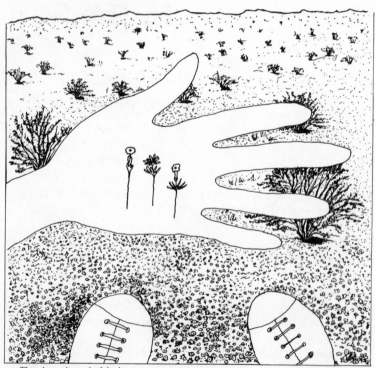

The ephemeral annuals of the desert

sect who will fertilize the embryo; and enough leaf surface to package enough of one spring's sun energy to start next year's plant. Fritz Went, in the laboratory of the California Institute of Technology, spread desert soil containing seeds of desert annuals on top of sand, and sprinkled it.

He found that the seeds germinated only if an inch of "rain" had fallen on them. In another experiment he made all conditions as in the first one, except that the water soaked up from below instead of falling from above. Those seeds never germinated. Fritz Went concluded that the seed coats were equipped with a water-soluble inhibitor, which prevented germination unless it was washed away. Washing away is not accomplished by water that soaks up through the soil, but a good rainfall can wash seeds clean.

Not all desert annuals are tiny; and they have various ways with rain. Some seeds wait until they have had a series of rains; some have other requirements. The timing of rain is important. To make a memorable spring requires over an inch of rain, falling in November or December. No other timing will do it. Some seeds wait in the earth, not germinating. That is well. It ensures the survival of the kind even if there should be two years, or several years, without the required rainfall.

Time and stress have selected these ephemerals of the desert to complete their lives in a minimum of time, with a minimum expenditure on the factory itself, and with a minimum of water; also (and this impressed me most) with a minimum expenditure on competition. The expanse of working flowers was composed of plants of equal stature, each one standing alone, upright, and surrounded by as much of a bit of naked earth as was necessary to its brief economy.

Such a display of the ephemerals I have not seen again, though I have returned often to the desert. My timing or the winter rains must not have been right.

Around us the desert rolled away in every direction, with plants that were stiffer, less vulnerable, longer-lived, much taller than the ones in the flower carpet at our feet. But the basic character of the larger-scaled desert and the miniature assemblage of ephemerals was the same: no elbowing, no overshadowing, just spare economy.

The desert, dry as it is, is basically refreshing—especially if one comes to it sick of committees, clubs, associations, brotherhoods, togetherness. Here stand individuals, leaning on nothing, well-developed on all sides, not needing to conform to the shapes or habits of neighbors. Upright, unmolded by passing winds. Enduring. For some reason they reminded me of a line spoken by President Kennedy at a dinner honoring Nobel Prize winners.

"I think that this is the most extraordinary collection of talent, of human knowledge, that has ever been gathered together at the White House—with the possible exception of when Thomas Jefferson dined alone."

Probably the upright and spaced individuals were especially impressive on that March morning because we had just come south from the high semi-desert of the Great Basin. There the sagebrush humps off in every direction, looking dull gray at some times, but violet and silver at others. Because altitude favors the Great Basin with more rain than falls on the lower deserts, the sagebrush can afford more leaves; but the leaves face the hot sun from under the protection of a downy silver coating, and of oils. The tingling aroma of those oils bore memories of sunbeaten plants of other places; rosemary and thyme along the Mediterranean, and sayberry beside the Atlantic. When the sun relents for a season, then the sagebrush must be able to tolerate occasional frosts, and to bear the weight of snow.

This tough plant comprises the world to a sage grouse. Not only is the sagebrush its chief, almost its only, food; but the eight to twelve down-covered chicks are hatched there from greenish-tan, brown-flecked eggs. They hatch ready to run around at once and to follow the female into a more grassy area and find more tender tidbits of green—if the cattle have not found it first. When winter comes, the grouse shelters under the gray thatch, stretching up to feed on its leaves. They can walk on the snow because they have feathered pants, and comb-like scales on their toes.

Out of sagebrush, chiefly, the male grouse builds up an impressive self, of six pounds or more. The female is only an unimpressive three or four pounds.

When late February stirs the male he advances, before daylight, to the ancestral courting grounds, where others are arriving. His six pounds start to swell, as he prepares to show off how superior are his splendors. His white surplice fluffs out into a feather boa. His two neck pouches expand to the size of two oranges. He holds his wings

Sage grouse and sagebrush

stiffly, and extends his tail feathers to form a spike-tipped fan. While he struts and jerks and booms and creaks, the females wait, pecking.

The grouse might have joined the passenger pigeons and others into oblivion. Hunters, and poison bait for grasshoppers, and overgrazing, were writing the end of the sage grouse story, when biologists studied their ways and started working toward changes in hunting laws and management. They were saved.

We left the realms of the sagebrush and the sage grouse (they are much the same) and headed south and downhill. As the rainfall decreased (to less than 7 inches) and the temperature rose, a mealy-white shrub called shadscale that had been a minor ingredient of the sagebrush desert began to take over. Spaces between plants widened. Whiteness and spininess became noticeable features. These features

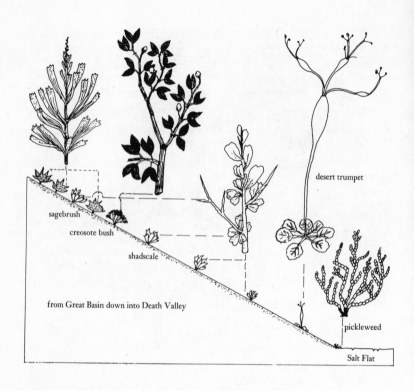

desert trumpet

sagebrush

creosote bush

shadscale

from Great Basin down into Death Valley

pickleweed

Salt Flat

appear in the species names of two plants that joined the shadscale: hopsage, *Grayia spinosa*; and winter fat, *Eurotia lanata*. The dark green of creosote bush also became a part of the scene.

Near that scene was the roadside described at the beginning of this chapter—the roadside with the inch-high annuals.

As we continued on our way toward Death Valley, plants stood further and further apart, and wore more and more spines and whitish coverings, and smaller and smaller leaves.

Death Valley had once been much like the other long trough-like valleys between its neighboring mountain ranges, until its bottom dropped down, way down, to 280 feet below sea level. Stress and strain within the earth had cracked two long parallel faults, or rifts, in the mountains, and caused the long block between the cracks to slip downward. Lake Superior lies in such a rift valley, as does Loch Ness, the Rhine, the Red Sea. The Dead Sea fills the deepest one of all, and lies 1,292 feet below sea level.

As the plants were spaced ever more widely we found ourselves often standing on a hard surface, coarse-textured, and shiny. This "desert pavement" has been formed in places where the wind has blown away all lighter stuff. The shine or "desert varnish" on some larger bits of rock comes after they have lain undisturbed for a long, long time in the desert sun.

We approached a white-crusted flat where not even a white-crusted shadscale could grow, nor anything else, surely. But there at the very edge of the crust was something that could possibly be a plant. It was green, and shaped like a string of tiny pickles, and tasted salty. It was pickleweed, scraggly, half-sprawling on the hot grit, most salt-tolerant of all. The swollen fleshy joints are its stems; small inconspicuous leaves like ridges grow at the bases of the joints.

The pickleweed was growing at the edge of a lake bed, of sorts. The white flat, though crusty underfoot and bitter on the tongue, was, nevertheless, left by water—water that had a long trip. First it hurried down the faces of the surrounding mountains; then it trickled as evaporation took its toll; then it disappeared into the hot sands; then it was lifted by capillarity, and was finally evaporated from the surface. But the salts accumulated on the trip down the mountainside were left behind. More salts were brought down, and more, and the alkali flat grew.

Not many steps away from the salt flat stood another plant, not quite so strange as the pickleweed, but strange. Its broad leaves were plastered tightly against the sand, and from their flatness rose a stalk, smooth, swollen, inflated, dividing into smaller swollen stems. This was the desert trumpet, or inflated-stem buckwheat, *Eriogonum inflatum*. It was no surprise that it tasted bitter.

This is one of a group of plants that starts its growth in the winter (after fall rains) and attains greater stature than the spring annuals.

The only animal we saw near the pickleweed and the desert trumpet (except for a red-tailed hawk that circled above) was stolidly withdrawn into a sort of sand cape, and didn't care to move. When I nudged him gingerly, he stirred so languidly that it seemed as if he preferred our shadow to our absence. He was a desert horned lizard, often called "horned toad." He let us photograph him, blinking only a little. Perhaps he was going to be a mere lump in the grit, until the ants in the nearby anthill emerged in the afternoon coolness from their deep cool galleries, in search of food. Seeds are the ants' food, and they themselves are the chief food of the horned lizard, who is only one item in the food and water supply of that circling hawk.

In the cool of that evening we walked on the desert at Stovepipe Wells, hoping to see creatures emerge from the many holes in the ground and go about their business. When the stars had grown bigger and come closer, we decided to "freeze" for a while beside a black hole and wait. We had hardly breathed for many still minutes when a jackrabbit suddenly exploded almost at our feet and was gone. Bats darted past the stars, but nothing came out of our hole. In the morning we located the same hole by its position halfway on a line between two creosote bushes. We saw many marks of tiny feet going into the hole, and of tails, evidently narrow tails; and hoped that, down under our feet, the long tails were wrapped around creatures sleeping with full stomachs—full enough to last through a burning day and supply energy for another busy night.

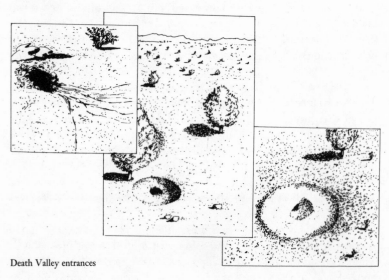

Death Valley entrances

On our next day we thought about the many creatures sleeping it out in cool darkness, and wished we were following their example. We had left the lowest parts of Death Valley, with its two to three inches of annual rainfall, or less, but were crossing long stretches where creosote bushes stood widely separated by areas of barren grit. And then a dust storm started blowing the desert around. We drove through miles of it, not realizing how it was sand-blasting our windows.

The dust storm was subsiding when we came to the Joshua tree National Monument, and to a wildly gesturing, unkempt individual that was the first of the Joshua trees. The Mormons gave it this name, perhaps because it was bearded, or because its arms seemed raised in blessing, or because it gestured to point out the way to them; but what a messy beard, what a threatening blessing, and what a confused direction!

Among the trees were shrubs of several kinds: The creosote bush, of course, but also the dark green of Mormon tea with its twigs like erect pine needles, and its leaves reduced to scales; and brittle bush forming its compact hemisphere of leaf-bearing stalks, looking like a pincushion stuck full of the long flower stalks; and the short bulk of barrel cactus; and the flat-jointed stems of beavertail cactus. Each individual had a shape so unique that it could be identified by its silhouette alone.

Joshua tree desert is high, from 2,500 to 5,000 feet, and usually on gravelly slopes of the mountains. Because of the altitude this desert does not face the severe drought and heat of lower deserts. But the drought and heat that it faces is bad enough, especially since it must endure occasional frost and occasional snowfall as well, and is limited to having winter rainfall only.

The Joshua tree cannot afford to expose more than a small amount of leaf surface to the thirsty sun and wind of the desert summer. Each year it encircles each branch tip with a ring of new leaves, spiky, bayonet-like, but vulnerable. Meanwhile the leaves of the last year are gradually softening and slowly turning back along the branch to form a green thatch that slowly turns brown like the older thatch, and eventually drops off of the old trunk, showing the rough bark.

The Joshua trees were not yet in bloom on that day in late March; but we came back, in April of another year, and walked among the

Mormon tea

Joshua tree

Mojave yucca

beaver-tail cactus

barrel cactus

trees in the moonlight. The flowers were open. On some trees there was only a spike or two; but on others there were many great spikes of flowers, a foot or more long, gleaming white. We had not to wait long to witness one of the most unique of all pollination procedures.

I watched the chalky-white yucca moths perform on these yucca blossoms, that happened to be on a yucca tree, exactly in the way I have seen them perform on a 3-foot-high yucca plant in a midwestern garden.

The female moth collects the sticky pollen from several flowers, rolling it into a ball as she goes. Then she thrusts her sharp ovipositor into the ovary of a flower, in among the ovules which must be fertilized if they are to become seeds. Then she proceeds to push the mass of pollen into the pistil. The pollen fertilizes the seeds. The eggs hatch into larvae which eat some of the seeds, and eat their way out of the seed pod, eventually becoming yucca moths, pollinating other yucca flowers in the moonlight. The seeds that were not eaten, if not eaten by something else or otherwise interfered with, eventually become Joshua tree seedlings. What series of accidents started this relationship between a moth and a yucca flower? We speculate, and argue.

Like any individual standing alone and successful, and inevitably gathering a following, the Joshua tree has its coterie. The Scott's oriole flashes in and out of the thatch of leaves, weaving its pouch of a nest out of yucca fibers, as the Indians have long woven quivers and loin cloths and baskets and sandals.

The thatch of dead leaves is a hiding place for the desert night lizard. He feeds on the tree's insect population, which is large because the pulp of the trunk and old branches rots easily and harbors many termites, and larvae of the yucca boring weevil, and others. This insect-rich pulp invites birds—the ladderback woodpecker, and others.

The Joshua trees and their company were left behind as we headed southward and downhill. We missed its vague mad gestures at first. But then, after an expanse of spaced desert scrub, we were stopped by a tall prickly exclamation point, the best known individual of the Sonoran Desert, the saguaro, or giant cactus.

The ranks of the saguaros thickened across the gravelly foothills. But they kept their distance from each other. We had a chance to see the structure of the spaces between the uprights. A bulldozer widening a small road had sliced off almost half of the circle of one saguaro's rootspread. We could stand on the new part of the road and examine the fine roots of the thin disk that spread out like a wheel around the tall column that rose from its hub. We teased out the dusty rootlets at the extreme edge of the wheel and saw how they lay just below the surface of the earth, in a position to capture any rain as soon as it fell. Those final rootlets were thirty feet out from the base of the column.

That thin disk of intake equipment does not always work. It is inefficient at absorbing the cold rains of the Sonoran desert's winter rainy season. But when the summer rains come the roots will garner every available drop as it falls. Then the column of the saguaro will swell with water storage. The accordion pleats of its green surface will be further and further apart; but they move closer together again as the tree gets thin during a drought.

It is the two rainy periods that have made possible the saguaro's survival as well as that of the many other succulents, and the varied

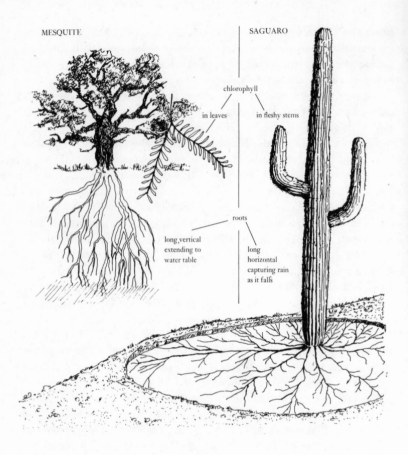

MESQUITE   SAGUARO

chlorophyll

in leaves   in fleshy stems

roots

long, vertical
extending to
water table

long
horizontal
capturing rain
as it falls

assortment of living things that attract so many people to the Sonoran desert, above all the other deserts—and also bring bulldozers to widen the roads for those many people's cars. Bulldozers sometimes slice off half of the intake equipment of a probably eighty-year-old storage tank, such as the one whose root spread we had examined.

That saguaro was over thirty feet high. The many others that ranged as far as we could see along that gentle slope were, some of them, a few feet taller, or a little smaller. There seemed to be no smaller, younger ones; not even a twenty-year-old, which would have stood about ten feet high. Knowing that the seedling usually gets its start in the light shade of a small tree, most often a palo verde, we searched under some of those trees for a small beginning, and found none.

Our failure was no disgrace. Back in 1910 Forrest Shreve of the Desert Laboratory of the Carnegie Foundation wrote:

> Young plants less than 1 cm. in height are so rare, or inconspicuous, that nine botanists who have had excellent opportunities to find them have never done so. . . .

Shreve suggests that, since it is evidently not maintaining itself in certain areas, the germination and behavior of seedlings should be studied, as well as climatic change in the area.

Other botanists have found that the saguaro is maintaining itself in the wetter pockets in the foothills; and still others have suggested that saguaro seedlings are failing to survive because they are losing the shelter of the shade of the palo verdes, and of other small trees which are dying out as a result of a drying climate. Others put the blame on man because he has reduced the predator population, which formerly reduced the population of the rodents which relish saguaro seedlings.

Certainly there is abundant production of seeds on the saguaro—the red fruits that circle the tip of each saguaro and its branches in the burning days of summer have plenty of seeds in their pink pulp. But the white-winged dove of the desert relishes them, and many other birds, and ants, and even coyotes eat them, and they are so important to the Indians that the Papagos have their new year at the time when the fruits are ripe; and the Pimas have named July "the Saguaro Harvest Moon."

In addition to the foodseekers, the saguaro has many other satellites seeking other benefits. The Gila woodpecker pecks out a hollow high in the column, long before the nesting season. Then, after the soggy pulp has had time to line the hole with scar tissue, the eggs are laid in the dry pocket. The elf owl may take over the nest later. I saw the fluffy small face of one blinking at the light in the entrance to one such high hole. We had watched an elf owl for a long time on the previous evening. He was on the ground up in the foothills near Tucson, where we were waiting with our headlights on, to see if we could catch a glimpse of a bit of wild night life. The owl stayed a while, perhaps he was making an owl pellet. I hoped he would cough it up right there so that we could see what he had pounced on in the desert night. He left but others came: a white-footed deermouse, a skunk, and a jackrabbit.

Not far from the saguaro hole where the elf owl was spending its day was another saguaro where a jackrabbit was finding shade. He was lying up close against the base of the trunk and moving as the shade moved.

The saguaro with its green trunk does not afford green leaves with their water loss. But other green-trunked neighbors put on short-lasting leaves after the spring rains. And one unique individual puts out a fresh batch of leaves after each rain, and sheds them during a drought. That is the ocotillo. When it sheds the leaves it keeps their stout center veins, and proceeds to stiffen each of those veins into a sharp thorn.

The ocotillo, like the other outstanding individuals of the desert, has its following. Hummingbirds drink from the deep red tubes of its flowers borne at the tips of its long thorny stems in April and May. The desert mule deer relish the flowers and manage somehow to stamp the long stems down until they can reach their sweetmeat. The Indians make a sort of barbed-wire palisade out of the branches. I happened on a small burial plot tightly barricaded by such a fence. Many of the stems had rooted and were green with leaves.

The Sonoran Desert has another outstanding individual that is like barbed wire, a tangled roll of it in an awful no-man's-land war scene. This is the cholla. The earth around it may be covered with its broken-off joints, all splintery with erect spines. There are several chollas. The biggest of them is *Opuntia bigelovii*, called the jumping cholla because its joints seem to jump off at a touch. It covers hillsides in southern Arizona, and when a hillside is seen against a low sun in the spring each cholla looks as if wrapped in silvery gauze, because the joints have new, shining, close-packed spines. This is sometimes called the "teddy-bear cactus" though it is far from being cuddly. Each joint is capable of becoming a new teddy bear.

The cactus wren has somehow come to terms with this bristly individual and actually builds its nest within the entanglement, working out a sort of front porch outside the entrance to the flask-shaped inte-

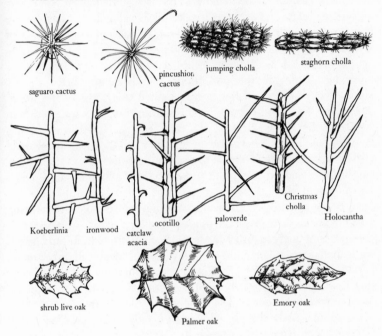

saguaro cactus

pincushion cactus

jumping cholla

staghorn cholla

Koeberlinia

ironwood

catclaw acacia

ocotillo

paloverde

Christmas cholla

Holocantha

shrub live oak

Palmer oak

Emory oak

rior. Rats, hawks, and coyotes are discouraged, but a snake may manage to reach the eggs or nestlings. While the female sits on her eggs in a silken lining of feathers and grasses, the male watches his territory from a higher vantage point.

Another creature that can cope with the bristly cholla is the pack rat, or wood rat. In other deserts he uses other building materials, but among chollas he actually manages to build with their joints. His nest looks like a swept-together heap of rubbish. Besides the cholla joints we could see stones, grass, bark, and a bit of aluminum foil. We chose not to investigate further, but investigators who have pulled the heaps apart have reported that they are evidently cemented together with urine and feces. A camper tells that a pack rat took his watch and left a stone in payment. Because of such "payments" he is often called the trade rat. Probably he had seen the face of the watch shining in the night, and had simply preferred it to the dull stone that he was carrying home. Some day the watch may prove valuable for establishing time to some anthropologist or botanist, as the contents of pack rat structures have done in caves in Texas.

There Philip V. Wells investigated ancient pack rat deposits. He found bits of pinyon pine, and juniper, and oaks, and seeds of many kinds. By radiocarbon dating it was learned that some of the woodland plants had lived there 11,560 years ago; and that some of them had lived there more than 36,600 years ago. But that area is now a desert. Woodland has evidently come and gone, twice, as recorded in the pack rat's collections. What an honor, sometime in the far-distant future, to contribute to the knowledge of the human race by having one's gold filling shine out of antique pack rats' accumulations. I'd prefer to be dated by the tree rings of thousand-year-old tree growing over my grave, or by bog pollen.

It was not easy to turn away from the Sonoran Desert, but one day we started eastward and upward, leaving the desert of two rainfall periods with its saguaros behind, and climbing onto the high plateau that holds the biggest of the southwestern deserts, the Chihuahuan. Most of it is in Mexico. The rains come in the summer, mostly.

Rolling grassland stretched before us, most of the grass low and in bunches, with bare earth between the bunches. Punctuating the grass stood the palmilla, or soapweed, *Yucca elata.*

The soapweed was conspicuous, raising its long cluster of white flowers high on a long bare stalk rising from clustered stiff leaves from a trunk thatched with old brown leaves. The Indians are said to eat the pulp of the stems and to make a drink from it. Cattlemen sometimes chop off the leaves so that their cattle can get at the pulp. Another plant with clustered leaves and a narrower, unbranched tall spike of flowers was the sotol, growing in the higher and drier places.

Much of this high Chihuahuan desert was covered with woody, spiny shrubs, and small spreading spiny trees—many more of them than one expects to see in "desert grassland," and many more than the cattlemen or the cattle can tolerate on their ranges.

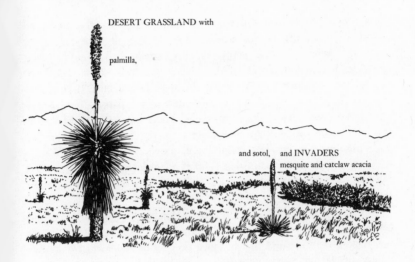

DESERT GRASSLAND with

palmilla,

and sotol, and INVADERS
mesquite and catclaw acacia

For this invasion blame is usually placed firmly on the cattlemen. Before Americans settled on the desert grassland, there were fires, occasional fires running through the grassland (Indians and Spanish cattlemen must have seen the fires, and possibly set some of them). Such occasional fires killed off the woody seedlings while they were still tender. But fire is prevented now, as much as possible, and the woody seedlings grow into redoubtable tough thickets and spread rapidly.

To the spread of mesquite, most prominent of the invaders, the cattle themselves may have contributed. They relish the sweet mesquite beans, and some of the seeds pass intact through the cow's digestive system and are left behind in the cow dung—all ready to go, with a rich supply of fertilizer.

The mesquite and the varnish-leaf acacia are advancing into the edges of the open oak woodland that extends higher up the mountains.

Other creatures beside cattle play a part in weakening the hold of the grassland. Poison bait may have killed off so many predators that the rodents have been left to nibble and litter in peace, thinning the land cover and exposing the land to erosion.

Certainly, whatever the cause, arroyos with their flat bottoms and perpendicular sides have bitten further and further into the land, and widened. According to observation, the coming of barren arroyos, some of them replacing gently sloping, green-clad stream banks, began to be observed about 1890.

While the thinning landcover, the spreading shrubs, the advancing arroyos all seem to point to cattlemen as the cause, there is evidence of a cause that is not man-made. There are accounts of fires in the area, accounts written by travelers around 1850. And there are early photographs. An 1891 photograph shows grassland without mesquite, but with many palmillas. Those palmillas are single-stemmed; but fire, burning the tops and leaving the roots, would have caused multiple-stemmed plants.

The University of Arizona has published (1965) a book, *The Changing Mile* by Hastings and Turner, that makes the changes in the desert graphic and dates them. For a given area there are two photographs on facing pages, with their dates, and with interpretations of the changes. After giving the various theories for the changing desert grassland, the authors conclude "that climate and cattle have united to produce it."

From the desert grasslands, with their changes, we continued eastward through landscape that varied with the slope and with the nature of the bedrock, with the creosote bush dominating large areas. Suddenly we faced the barren whiteness of gypsum dunes, molded and rippled by the wind. As we went down into the Tularosa Basin to the White Sands National Monument, we were once more, as we had been at Death Valley, on a rift valley that dropped down between long faults in the mountains. A thick layer of gypsum lying far beneath the valley floor was formerly continuous with the gypsum layer that can be seen up in the side of the mountain. The White Sands are made of gypsum from the mountains. Rains bring it down and spread it; the heat dries out the surface; and then the wind lifts it and tumbles it and heaps it and shifts the heaps.

One fragrant sumac bush stood high on the crest of a gleaming dune. It couldn't have started life there—no plant can do that. The seedling must have put out its first growth down in a flat between dunes. Then, as sand collected around it and started to bury it, the plant must have been able to elongate its main root and to put out many side roots just below the surface of the dune, and to keep its leaves above that ever rising surface. In its position at the crest, it was hit by many gypsum grains as the wind lifted them up the westward side of the dune and left them to roll down the eastward slope. Eventually the dune was going to move away and leave the shrub behind, standing on top of a pedestal of gypsum that would be held for a time by the many roots.

We saw plants that had been left behind like that, each on its pedestal of root-bound gypsum. Not all the pedestals were topped by fragrant sumac. Others that are able to hold a place on a growing dune are Mormon tea, and palmilla, and the Rio Grande cottonwood.

A swale between dunes attracted us down there by it greenness. Plants of many kinds throve in that moist place that was not yet bombarded by advancing sand. The plants grew close together, but we could pick out and salute the few that would be able to survive when a dune started building in that place, and would end up topping a gypsum pedestal when the dune had passed by.

From the White Sands we turned back west. Soon we were among widely spaced creosote bushes, as we had been so often on every day of our desert journey. A few buzzards had been a part of most scenes, and often there was a lonely soaring hawk, and many a lone roadrunner had stalked across our way, and gambel quails had bustled in the stream beds, but always there had been creosote bushes, the smell of the near ones and the polka-dot patterning of the far ones across the outwash fans at the bases of the mountains.

Of all the individuals standing alone in the desert, this is the lonest one, and it engineers its own separateness, adjusting to the water supply. Its expanse of wide-reaching roots are ready to catch rain as soon as it falls. But these bushes do more than catch rain; they control spacing by exuding a toxic substance that will kill a seedling that might start too near the parent in a place where rainfall is not enough to supply both parent and seedlings. In places where rainfall is greater, enough of the toxic poisons are leached away so that the seedlings can grow closer to the parent.

The creosote bush builds tissue throughout the year, and must not only get but also hold on to every possible bit of moisture. The resin coating on the leaves helps to reduce evaporation, as do the special guard cells on the stomata, and the tight compactness of the inside of the leaf.

But creosote bushes sometimes die anyway. In the severest droughts whole mountainsides of them have died. First, the green leaves drop off. Smaller brown leaves last for a while longer. When, finally, these brown leaves drop, the whole plant usually dies. But their dying does not mean that the place of the creosote bush in that excessively dry area is taken over by some opportunist. Nothing comes to replace the dead bushes; nothing else is able to endure what they can endure. In time the creosote bushes return, as seedlings, and form an even-aged group. In time the individuals will stand just as far apart from each other as individuals in the former group stood.

Day after day in our trip from desert to desert, we had been in the presence of this redoubtable creosote bush. It had been the accepted,

Looking down at desert from the tops of mesas

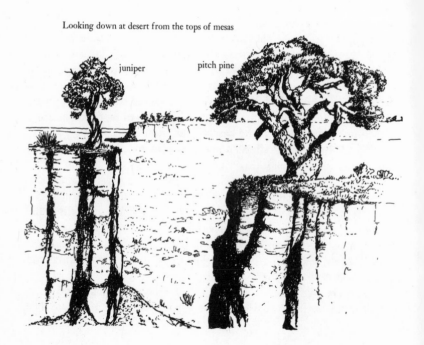

juniper   pitch pine

often ignored background. But, in most days, there had been interludes when we turned our backs on the broad face of the desert, to enjoy the interludes in its sternness: the rain-catching high places and the stream-catching low places.

Those high flat plateaus, called mesas, jutted green-topped and khaki-cliffed out of the desert. We went to them, partly because the Indians had so often elected to build their towns there. We went to Acoma; and to the First Mesa, and the Second Mesa, and the Third Mesa of the Hopi; and to the wide, high "Painted Desert," and the Mesa Verde. Two individuals dominated the scene, both of them trees, both compact, both evergreen, both supplying food to the Indians: juniper, and pinyon pine.

The lowest places lured us even as oases have ever lured the traveler, whether the place was a canyon in the Mohave desert with that most impressive individual, the Washington palm; or the Canyon de Chelly, with its most unwillow-like yew-leaved willow; or the Sabino Canyon with its most photogenic individual, the Arizona sycamore; or any stream with its cottonwoods, willows, box-elder, and walnuts.

It was time to go home, almost time. But first it was time to see that dynamic part of any landscape (or civilization)—the edge, where one way of life meets another. It was time, as well, to see more microclimates, those conditions that cause bits of one landscape to be framed within another, holding their place by grace of a hump or a hollow, or a stream, or a slope, or a quality of the soil, or a neighbor.

It was time to see edges and microclimates; but we had not the time to search them out. We settled for a telescoped, uptilted assemblage. We returned to the Tucson area and climbed Mount Lemmon.

The following page diagrams that climb.

We mounted through these changes:

1. from plants with no leaves or small ephemeral leaves, to plants with many leaves, mostly evergreen
2. from spininess to lack of spininess
3. from dwarfness to tallness
4. from shallow, wide-spreading roots to deep roots (notice that the microclimate of water available either in a stream or underground is indicated by a down-curve at the base of a tree)

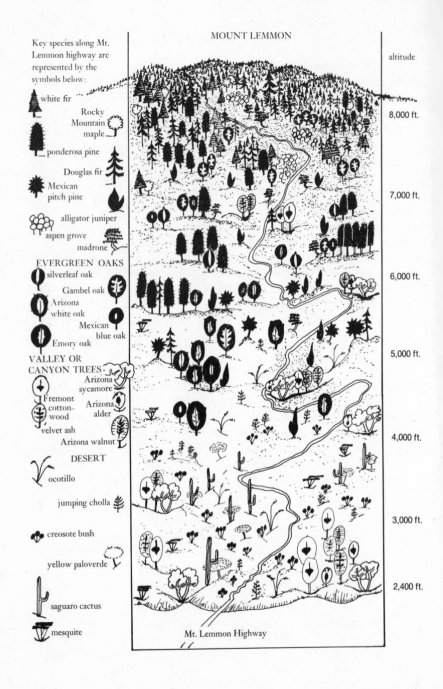

MOUNT LEMMON

Key species along Mt. Lemmon highway are represented by the symbols below:

white fir

Rocky Mountain maple

ponderosa pine

Douglas fir

Mexican pitch pine

alligator juniper

aspen grove

madrone

EVERGREEN OAKS

silverleaf oak

Gambel oak

Arizona white oak

Mexican blue oak

Emory oak

VALLEY OR CANYON TREES

Arizona sycamore

Fremont cotton- wood

Arizona alder

velvet ash

Arizona walnut

DESERT

ocotillo

jumping cholla

creosote bush

yellow paloverde

saguaro cactus

mesquite

altitude

8,000 ft.

7,000 ft.

6,000 ft.

5,000 ft.

4,000 ft.

3,000 ft.

2,400 ft.

Mt. Lemmon Highway

5. from representatives of southern latitudes to representatives of northern latitudes

6. from widely spaced individuals to crowded communities.

The time had come for us to return to our own niches in crowded communities in a more northerly latitude, where an individual's shadow is rarely sharp, or intact.

BIBLIOGRAPHICAL NOTES

Vegetation and Flora of the Sonoran Desert by Forrest Shreve and Ira L. Wiggins. Two volumes. Stanford University Press, Stanford California, 1964.

"The Desert Vegetation of North America" by Forrest Shreve. *The Botanical Review*, **VIII**, 1942.

"Ecology of Desert Plants, II" by Fritz W. Went. *Ecology* **30** (1949), 1–13.

The North American Deserts by Edmund C. Jaeger. Standford University Press, Stanford, Calif., 1957.

The Trees and Shrubs of the Southwestern Deserts, by Lyman Benson and Robert A. Darrow. University of Arizona Press, Tucson, 1954.

Southwestern Trees, A Guide to the Native Species of New Mexico and Arizona by Elbert L. Little, Jr. Agriculture Handbook, No. 9, United States Department of Agriculture, 1950.

An Island Called California, by Elna S. Bakker. University of California Press, Berkeley, Calif., 1971.

The Desert World by David F. Costello. Crowell, New York, 1972.

The Changing Mile, an Ecological Study of Vegetational Change with Time in the Lower Mile of an Arid and Semiarid Region by James Rodney Hastings and Raymond M. Turner. University of Arizona Press, Tucson.

The Land of Little Rain by Mary Austin. Houghton Mifflin, Boston and New York, 1903.

The Desert Year by Joseph Wood Krutch. William Sloane Associates, 1951.

21

The Stylish House

OR

FASHIONS AS AN ECOLOGICAL FACTOR

THIS is going to be an account of a certain old house, and the plants in its life.

There has been a definite succession of these plants, and the major ecological force in determining this succession has been *style*.

This old house has always belonged to stylish people. Always stylish, never queer. (No doubt the present owners would, with a shudder, substitute "smart" for "stylish," and "unadjusted" for "queer," and that is in character.)

Everyone knows this house, or its counterpart—everyone who knows midwestern towns, at any rate.

It is two blocks uphill from the bank corner, on the "good" side of the tracks, on the street with the tallest elms.

Jonathan and Patience were the dignified names of the first owners, and their dog was a collie named Rover.

The first thing that Jonathan planted was a white pine tree, on the southwest corner of the lot. That was in 1856. He bought the pine from a traveling nurseryman, who put a nose bag on his horse and stayed to lunch himself; and he had a beard, as Jonathan did, too. He was inclined to be skeptical about the virtues of used tea leaves as a stimulant for plants. But that was what Patience used just the same, and it certainly seemed to agree with the pine tree.

The first things that Patience planted were the Harison's yellow rose in the front yard and the cabbage rose against the board fence. She had brought slips of those along from Ohio. They did well out in the full sun. The lilies of the valley, that she planted against the east side of the stone basement, throve, too, and spread so that she was able to give roots to newcomers in the Ladies' Aid at church, just as they had been given to her.

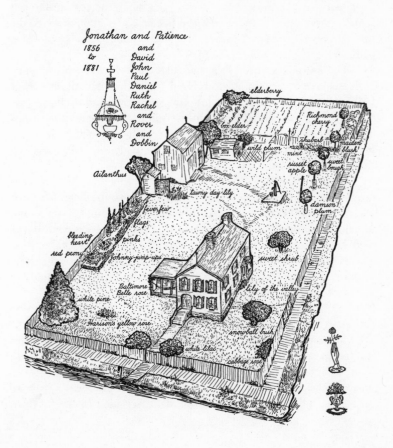

The ostrich fern and the lady fern were brought back from the Sunday School picnic out at Sugar Grove, and planted against the basement on the north side.

There was a russet apple tree, a sweet bough, a maiden blush, a damson plum, a Richmond cherry, raspberries and grapes. Jonathan had bought those along with the white pine, and the elms beside the hitching post.

The box-elder out behind the barn came of its own accord. So did the ailanthus tree back of the outhouse, and the wild plum inside the chicken yard, and the big elderberry in the back fence corner.

Patience planted the gourds on the trellis in front of the outhouse door, and the two rows of tawny day-lilies along the path to the outhouse. "Privy lilies," her friend down the street called them as she dug up the roots for Patience, from among those beside her own outhouse path.

The flower bed was a long straight stretch along the board fence. Hollyhocks bloomed in it, and a red fern-leaved peony, and sweet Williams, pinks, feverfew, Johnny-jump-ups, and yellow irises ("flags," Patience called them). In the spring there were blue squills. The children always used a few of those with the lily of the valley, and some hepaticas from the woods, when they made their May baskets to hang on doorknobs.

Jonathan kept up the bed of mint, the rhubarb, the asparagus, raspberries, and the big vegetable garden down back of the barn, where he was considering experimenting with some of those new tomatoes, having read of the success that plant breeders were having with increasing the size of the fruit and taking out the wrinkles.

Plants prospered. There was plenty of horse manure, and chicken manure, and wood ashes. When Jonathan went fishing, he could find plenty of plump earthworms in the garden.

The grass was scythed, and the horse was tethered out on it occasionally.

There were no massed shrubs for privacy. Jonathan and Patience wanted to see who was passing when they heard horses on the dirt road. But there were two white lilacs beside the front gate, and two great shrubs set in the middle of the side lawn. One was a snowball bush. The other was a sweet shrub. Patience used to tie one of its mahogany-colored flowers in the corner of her little daughter's hand-kerchief on Sunday, to help her through the sermon by letting her smell its fragrance of crushed strawberries.

The yard was quiet, except for the sound of horses passing, and an occasional rooster, or church bell, or a boy holding a stick against a picket fence as he ran by.

Inside the house, the sound of the grandfather clock was loud, and there was the smell of baking bread, wood smoke, and kerosene lamps.

Red geraniums bloomed between the lace curtains of the front windows, and in the dining-room bay window, and in the kitchen, too, where the air was rich and steamy, with no gas. A huge Boston fern backed up the geraniums in the dining room, and near it Patience was coddling a cutting from her neighbor's Christmas cactus.

In the front parlor wax flowers stood stiffly under a glass dome, on a marble-topped table, under the picture of "Pharaoh's Horses" and between the big family Bible and the stereoscope.

Flowers lay flat within the Bible, too—pressed ones, representing memorable moments: lily of the valley from a wedding bouquet, Queen Anne's lace from a moonlit surrey ride, a pansy from a chris-tening, and a four-leaf clover or two.

On the corner of the melodeon, beside the hymn book, under the "Stag at Bay" by Sir Edwin Landseer, a pink luster vase sometimes held a tight little nosegay known as a tussy-mussy. Rose geranium leaves encircled the tussy-mussy, and it usually contained mignonette and pinks, and a little lemon-verbena.

Roses in several forms graced the front parlor. A red rose was embroidered in gleaming silk on the round black cushion that stood upright on the horsehair sofa under the picture of "Breaking Home Ties," and a big pink rose flowered on the hooked welcome mat. And on the white marble mantel in the back parlor there was a rose jar filled with a potpourri from the cabbage roses in the yard.

There were roses in the dining room, too, mixed with daisies and forget-me-nots, on the cross-stitch sampler with "God Bless Our Home."

Sometimes Patience would put a rose into one of the pieces from her collection of china hands—the one with the two slender hands upheld to form a vase. But if she put it on the table, the menfolks seemed to find it in the way of the caster and the spoonholder, the accepted occupants of the center of the table.

More roses were on the shade of the hanging lamp with the crystal pendants.

There was a rose on the sampler over the spool bed in the bedroom. But the doily under the pitcher and washbowl on the commode was embroidered with silken violets.

Jonathan and Patience had six children, named David, John, Paul, Daniel, Ruth, and Rachel, after Biblical characters:

When the eldest son, David, brought his bride, Mary, home to live, some changes were made. That was in 1881.

The board fence was taken down, since there was no longer much danger of a stray wandering cow. A stout wooden fence topped with big wooden balls was substituted.

One day David had to cut down the big old snowball bush. In its place he made a circular bed.

On Sunday afternoons, when David and Mary went for their walk around town after dinner, to work up an appetite for an early supper—early so that they could wash the dishes before evening service, and get to bed extra early because Monday was washday—they looked at other people's circular flower beds. So they planted red cannas in the center, encircled by nasturtiums, with a final edging of dwarf blue lobelias.

With the snowball bush gone, the sweet shrub looked wrong, standing there in the center of the lawn, so they took it out, and made another circular bed. In this one they planted castor beans, encircled by red geraniums and outlined with sweet alyssum.

These gay beds were so much admired that David and Mary decided to outdo themselves for the ice-cream sociable, which was to be held in their yard under strings of Japanese lanterns.

First they planted a weeping mulberry in the side yard. Then they formed a big star-shaped bed around it. The center was massed with red cockscombs. Each point of the star was filled with golden-foliaged coleus, and outlined with variegated-leaved coleus. Then the whole was outlined with hen and chickens.

Then they put in the fountain—the one with the little girl and boy under the iron umbrella, with water shooting out of the tip of the umbrella and dripping down the sides into a little circular pool. The pool was surrounded by green-and-white-leaved plantain lily, encircled by abalone shells side by side, with one edge thrust into the ground so that they made an upright pearly scalloping.

The garden really looked like an embroidery piece under the Japanese lanterns, especially so since the lawn was clipped more closely now, with the new lawn mower.

Later, when the strawberry sociable was held on the lawn of another home, David and Mary admired the iron deer, and the iron dog standing guard over a sleeping iron child, but they really envied the new decorations on the house itself, the scroll-saw work made possible by new machinery.

They decided to have some, and before the house was painted (yellow), they had its edges embellished with wooden tatting, and the corners filled out with scallops and eyelet embroidery in wood.

They built a porch out over the front stoop. It covered the setback door with its side lights, but it made room for more scroll-saw work, and the two posts could hold porch boxes.

There was no question about what to plant in the center of each porch box, that was established—*Dracaena indivisa*, for a stiff upright element. There was no question, either, about the lower masses at the base of the stiff dracaena. They were pink geraniums (redness was having a tendency to leach out of the possessions of Mary and her friends). But there was some choice in the matter of the drooping material to drizzle over the edges. One might choose asparagus fern, or coleus, or variegated vinca. Mary mixed them.

Somehow, during the installation of the scroll-saw work, the crimson rambler on the side porch died. Mary planted a pink Dorothy Perkins instead.

David liked to build. He put up a grape arbor across the end of the vegetable garden, with a pleasant seat where Mary liked to shell peas or string beans. And he built a peaked roof over the pump, and put a wind vane on the barn, when they took the lightning rod down.

They had only half as many chickens as Jonathan and Patience had kept, but they used the extra space to make a paddock for the horse, now that the nearby field was no longer available for pasture. And there was a dog run, for the airedale, now that the garden was so trim, lest he blur the corner of some star or crescent.

When Mary brought her flowers into the house, she did not pack them so tightly into the vases and bowls as Patience had done, and she left more leaves on the stems. The flowers she favored were the globular, thoroughly double ones.

In the dining room she massed zinnias in a cut-glass bowl on the sideboard beside the chafing dish. The silver fern dish was usually in the center of the dining-room table on a crocheted doily.

In the parlor she put a vase of round red dahlias on the organ that had replaced the melodeon there against the wall where the crayon portraits of Jonathan and Patience had replaced the "Stag at Bay." (Later, when the children insisted on having the parlor organ replaced by a player piano, the crayon portraits were replaced by the "Song of the Lark," and presently "Pharaoh's Horses" was replaced by a tinted photograph of the Rheims Cathedral.

"Breaking Home Ties" had been the first of the old pictures to go. It went out with Patience's horsehair and walnut furniture, when the new three-piece golden-oak suite was bought from the mail-order catalogue, along with the Brussels carpet.

Geraniums no longer throve in the windows, after the gas was installed. But there was a rubber plant in one window and an umbrella plant in another. Even without the gas, the geraniums would probably not have thriven as they did in Patience's day, because the window hangings were now of heavy stuff with a fringe of red balls. They shut out the light, but they matched the heavy portieres, and the velvet cushions of the Morris chair in the cosy corner.

In the bedroom Mary sometimes put a bowl of pansies on the bamboo table where she kept the *Ben Hur* that she was going to read on top of the *East Lynn* that she was reading. Over the big double brass bed, with the spread embroidered in lazy-daisy stitch and French knots, hung several pictures of the Gibson Girl, upon whom Mary's appearance was patterned. David's was patterned on the Gibson Man, to such an extent that he finally shaved off his curving mustaches, and took to wearing those padded shoulders in his coats.

Out in the kitchen the geraniums had moved from the window sills to the curtains, where they were embroidered. The new gas range caused that change.

The dining-room geraniums had moved, too—onto the hand-painted china plates along the plate rail. A mother-in-law's tongue and ivy took the place of the geraniums in the bay window.

In spring, when Mary brought the first bunch of lilies of the valley into the house, their fragrance no longer mingled with the smell of kerosene lamps and wood smoke. The new furnace, one of the first in town, smoked only a little. But there was still the smell of new-baked bread and simmering soup.

When David sat in the Morris chair in his smoking jacket on winter evenings, and read seed catalogues, he saw the first pictures of the new sweet corn. Mary read about the regal lily that E. H. Wilson had brought home for gardens from the alpine meadows of Tibet, and the butterfly bush, and the beauty bush.

Mary and David had four children, named Theodore, Ethel, Victoria, and Charles. The names were taken from the Teddy Roosevelt family, the Queen of England, and Dickens.

When Theodore and his young wife, Elizabeth (named after Beth in *Little Women*), decided to take down the picket fence, they did it partly to be "neighborly." Everyone else was doing it, too. That was the influence of the realtors, who were subdividing big corner lots like this one into smaller plots for bungalows and who needed to have places look, at least until sold, more spacious than they actually were.

But after a few years of crisscross paths on the lawn showed that corner lots make a good short cut, Theodore and Elizabeth began to put back a barrier. Everyone else was doing that, too. The fences themselves were not put back, but small plantings that could be counted on to grow rapidly and insinuate themselves into the scene without being abruptly unneighborly.

A barberry hedge was the solution that Theodore and Elizabeth chose. Most people did, although a few chose privet.

At about that time, Elizabeth began to read gardening hints in the *Ladies' Home Journal*. She found out about foundation planting. Simultaneously she found out about bridal wreath, *Spiraea Van Houttei*. Soon the high house was set afloat in a billowing sea of bridal wreath. No slightest contact with the earth was visible, except at the steps of course, where a gap was necessary.

Then Theodore learned about the popular demand for Lombardy poplars that was making them hard to get. So he managed to get some, and planted a row along the fence.

With a house so abreast of the times as to be embowered in bridal wreath, ringed with barberry hedge, and edged with a row of Lombardy poplars, it was to be expected that Elizabeth would be invited to join the new garden club.

At her very first meeting she learned that David and Mary's round beds in the center of the lawn were "wrong." The centers must be kept open, to create a sweep of lawn, a "vista." She learned that straight lines and scallops were out. Flowing, "naturalistic" curves were in.

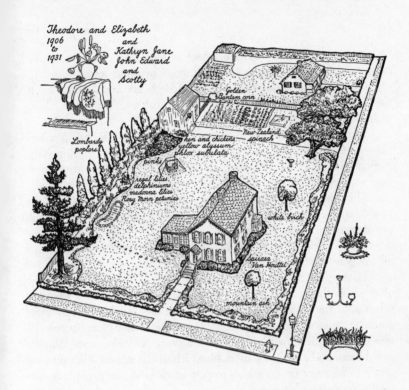

Theodore and Elizabeth
1906
to
1931

and
Kathryn Jane
John Edward
and
Scotty

Lombardy
poplars

pinks

regal lilies
delphiniums
madonna lilies
Rosy Morn petunias

hen and chickens
yellow alyssum
phlox subulata

Golden
Bantam corn

New Zealand
spinach

white birch

Spiraea
Van Houttei

mountain ash

There came a lady lecturer who told the garden club members to go home and get out their garden hoses, but not for sprinkling. They were to lay down the hoses to shape the edges of their borders, and then dig to follow those natural curves.

Elizabeth did it. So did her neighbors. She never spoke of her "garden" again. She spoke of her "borders."

Everything was wide open with flowing margins.

Presently the garden club had a lecture on rock gardens. The magazines were full of rock gardens, too.

The instructions said to bury two thirds of each rock in the soil. But by the time Theodore and Elizabeth had broken the springs on their Ford carrying home rocks from all over the country, they could not bear to conceal two thirds of that carefully selected mass.

They constructed a sort of pinnacle, with a suggestion of a grotto about it. On this pinnacle they planted a lot of *Alyssum saxatile*, basket of gold: *Phlox subulata*; maidenhair fern; thyme; winter aconite; pinks; and one *Daphne cneorum*, and one Christmas rose.

The yellow alyssum and the pink phlox lived, and so did a few of the hen-and-chicken plants that Elizabeth had saved from the edging of Mary's star-shaped bed.

In her flowing borders, Elizabeth specialized on big brilliant zinnias—at first. But later she heard so much about subtle coloring at the garden club, that she eschewed red flowers, regretfully because Theodore seemed to like them.

She was veering toward pastel shades. She had memorized the hint that one did not approve of magenta, but was not quite certain about what that color looked like.

She was planting in "drifts," instead of in rows or masses, and always planting three or five or seven of a kind.

Having an automobile instead of a horse brought about some changes in the yard. The ailanthus tree and the box-elder were cut down after they had dented fenders on the car. There was no longer abundant manure for the garden. Theodore missed that because he was growing the new Golden Bantam corn, and Kentucky Wonder pole beans, and a row of giant dahlias. Elizabeth missed it because she was turning away from annuals to perennials, and had decided to specialize on delphiniums.

When the chickens were finally given up, there was room for a sandbox and a lawn swing, and a basket for basketball practice was attached to the barn. There was a dog run, too, for the wire-haired fox terriers.

When Elizabeth picked flowers for the house, she planned them carefully for different rooms. On the round pedestal table in the dining room, she put a low loose mass in soft pastel tones. *Delphinium belladonna*, with baby's breath and Rosy Morn petunias, was a favorite; or love-in-a-mist with salmon-rose zinnias, in a green pottery bowl.

In the living room she arranged marigolds, or sunflowers, in a bean pot on the monk's cloth runner on the new black mission table that had replaced the golden oak. It stood beside the blue plush overstuffed chair under the Maxfield Parrish picture with the very-blue sky, that had replaced the Rheims Cathedral. ("The Song of the Lark" had been replaced by a picture of "Old Ironsides," and the crayon portraits by Whistler's "Mother.")

Elizabeth did not pick flowers for the new upright piano. She dusted the dried bouquet there, carefully, because she had spent a lot of time, first out in the fields looking for the big curled-up leaves of the prairie dock, and then painting them silver and bronze. It had taken time, too, to dip the milkweed pods in silver paint, and then tint the inside of each one a bright orange. They stood in a black vase, with three silvered Osage oranges lying casually at the base, on the random folds of a fringed and embroidered Oriental shawl that was draped across one corner of the piano.

In the bedroom, Elizabeth sometimes slipped a pansy or two under the plate-glass cover of the chiffonier, where stood the two big tinted photographs of their children, Kathryn Jane and John Edward, in silver frames, flanking the silver-backed comb and brush set. And she put one rose bud into the bud vase on the table between the twin beds with the blue silk spreads. The bud vase stood between the A *Girl of the Limberlost* that Elizabeth was reading, which was covered by the Carl Sandburg poems that she intended to read; and *The Call of the Wild* that Theodore was reading, which was covered by H. G. Wells's *Outline of History* that he intended to read.

Elizabeth did not have many house plants, except for Mary's Christmas cactus in the dining-room bay window, and a small-flowered pink begonia. But there was an abundance of flowers, thoroughly naturalistic, on the cretonne drapes at most of the windows. And the trailing bunch of bittersweet that was placed in the pottery wall pocket each fall had a way of lasting most of the year.

When Theodore and Elizabeth read seed catalogues in the winter evenings, they sat on the side porch, which was a glassed-in sun parlor now, with steam heat and wicker furniture. There were Boston ferns in the wicker fernery, and a little green plant of cabomba in the fish bowl. And on the cretonne drapes and table runners and slip covers and pillows were big magnolia blossoms and parrots. Elizabeth started her flats of seedlings out there in the spring.

The new vegetables in the catalogues interested Theodore—New Zealand spinach and Chinese celery cabbage; while Elizabeth read about the tall English delphiniums.

When John Edward and his young wife, Nancy Ann, took over the old house, one of their first purchases was a pair of pruning shears—which, unfortunately, then as now, could be purchased without a license. Then John Edward proceeded to give his shrubs prison haircuts.

It didn't matter whether their charm was in arching sprays or in rugged gesture—they all emerged from the pruning with identical globular, twiggy forms. Even the billows of the foundation bridal wreath were transformed into leggy knobs.

This was neat.

At first the neatness pleased John Edward and Nancy Ann, but gradually the appearance began to bother them. The bare high stone foundation of the old house showed plainly between the shorn, leggy shrubs. Nancy Ann and John Edward looked at the other high old houses around the town. They found out what was being done.

First they had a terrace built, to cover the foundation. But the house still looked a little naked to them.

Then they went to a neighboring nurseryman. He came and looked at the house, but really he knew, before he looked, just what the prescription would be—evergreens. At each side of the front door he set a dwarf Mugho pine. Behind that he set a Pfitzer juniper, backed up by a red cedar. Around the foundation he used the prevalent "dot and dash system"—one high, one low, one high, one low.

Nancy Ann, at the garden club, had been relieved of her fear of straight lines. The taboo had been lifted. So the borders had been straightened out somewhat.

She had decided to specialize in hybrid tea roses. A sunken rose garden was worked out. The extra dirt was used to build up the terrace. But the terrace operations had broken up a part of the cement walk. They took it all up, broke it into random chunks, and laid it down again, flagstone style.

Nancy Ann decided that the walk should have a wide curve in it. But after the new curved walk was already laid, and after she had sprinkled portulaca seeds between the flags, the garden club had a lecturer who was quite merry on the subject of walks that had a curve when no obstacle necessitated it.

It developed that a walk must not curve unless there was something for it to curve around, but that it was quite within the rules of the game to plant the obstacle first, and then detour around it, or to plant it afterwards even, in the hope that it would appear to have been there first.

For the obstacle that was seemingly to have necessitated Nancy's curve, the nurseryman suggested the very thing that John Edward and Nancy Ann had been planning to add to their plantings, in some conspicuous position—a Colorado spruce. They bought one of the exceptionally blue ones.

The Lombardy poplars had been winterkilled. The barberry hedge caught every passing bit of paper, and Nancy Ann wanted a white picket fence anyhow. The gate that they installed was a wagon wheel that Nancy Ann found at a second-hand dealer's.

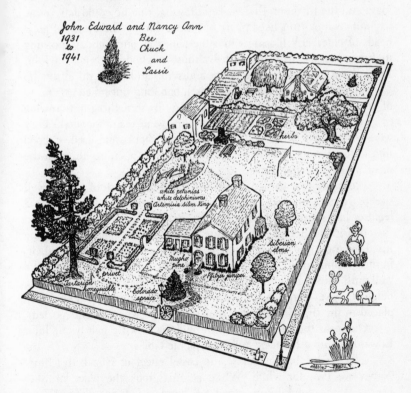

It all had a quaint look, especially after the old lamppost was installed in front of the blue spruce, and after they set up the humorous old hitching post, and the flamingo and a duck family.

John Edward was having a little trouble with his vegetables. There was no manure any more, except for a rare load when some farmer could be talked into delivering it. When John Edward tried to dig worms for the children's fishing, they proved scarce and rather lean. But he learned that other people were using chemical fertilizers freely on their gardens. So he tried them too. They seemed to work.

He had lost a part of the vegetable-garden area to Nancy's herb garden. Losing the space didn't bother him so much as eating the herbs. Parsley, mint, and chives, he was accustomed to. It was the basil in his lemonade; the bee balm in his tea; the marjoram in the pot roast; and the thyme in the chicken dressing, that he could have done without. Nancy Ann liked to try out these things. She even put great heads of elderberry blossoms into the pancakes one Sunday morning in June, but the pancakes tasted almost as good as usual, so John Edward put on a little more butter and syrup and didn't mind much.

The mountain ash and white birch had long since died as a result of borers. John Edward asked the nursery for something fast-growing to give shade on the lawn. Siberian elms were recommended. They were inexpensive so he bought six. Four of them were used, clipped into lollipop shape, one at each side of the two openings through the privet hedge into the sunken rose garden.

From the rose garden one could catch a glimpse of an old well sweep. Nancy Ann had bought that at an auction, and used it, as a lecturer had suggested, to disguise the incinerator.

But it did not stay there long. John Edward objected to being lured, by the suggestion of coolness and depth, to look down into half-burned orange peels. Nancy traded it to a neighbor, who filled the well curb with geraniums, and the bucket with balcony petunias. The neighbor gave Nancy two statues of elves, in exchange. They were placed in the shrubbery so that they peered out where least expected.

Out near the garage, where the old lawn swing had been, John Edward put up a fireplace and built picnic tables.

The garden began to lose the pastel effect of Elizabeth's time. Nancy went in for white. White petunias took the place of Rosy Morn. White delphiniums stood tall beside Madonna lilies. Silver-leaved plants were used freely. Agrostemma, dusty miller, artemisia, Russian olive, were favorites.

The flowers that Nancy brought into the house were usually white, now that the interior decorator had done the living room in silver and London fog.

The piano (it was a parlor grand, but seldom played because of interfering with radio programs) made a dramatic setting for a large mass of white peonies, or silver-poplar leaves. On the gray table, Nancy put Shasta daisies in a pewter tankard, below the ranks of etchings that had replaced Maxfield Parrish. Old Ironsides, and Whistler's Mother were gone, too, replaced by a Currier and Ives print, above the spinning wheel; and a page from Godey's Lady's Book, near the rush-bottomed spindle-backed chairs and the ship model.

Nancy Ann had a dried winter bouquet made of the silver moons of honesty, combined with Artemisia Silver King.

On the dining-room table Nancy arranged white roses, or white chrysanthemums, and five rhododendron leaves, asymmetrically in a low oyster-colored container, set on a mirror.

In the bedroom there was no room for flowers on the table between the spool beds with candlewick spreads, because the radio filled the place between *Gone With the Wind* under Robert Frost's poems, on Nancy's side, and *The Grapes of Wrath* under Toynbee, on John Edward's side. But there was a chaste flower print over each bed.

Nancy Ann favored miniature house plants. At one time she had a Japanese dish garden with tiny figures of ladies and herons and bridges, but she gave that up in favor of a cactus collection, which she arranged on glass shelves against the window pane. The cactus plants and other succulents were planted in quaint, often humorous, containers—elephants, dachshunds, ducks, and penguins.

She had a terrarium, too, pear-shaped, with partridgeberries and selaginella in it. She decided against joining some of her friends in their hobby of making arrangements on buttons.

John Edward and Nancy Ann had a Doberman pinscher, and two children, called Bee and Chuck.

Their stay in the old house was a short one—people weren't staying so long anywhere any more. In 1941 they moved out of town. Kathryn Jane, John Edward's sister, and her husband, Don, took over.

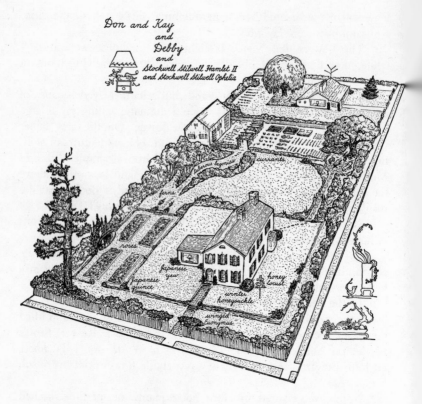

When Don and Kathryn Jane (she was called "Kay") looked over the grounds, they decided to enlarge the terrace to fit the height of the house. Then they took up the walk of broken concrete. They laid down a new straight walk of brick, in a herringbone pattern. Before they could get rid of Nancy Ann's curve, they had to move the blue spruce. It went over into the side lines, where it was presently joined by other displaced specimens.

The first plants to join the spruce did so as a result of a session of the new garden club, composed of men and women both, and meeting in the evening.

Don and Kay both attended that meeting, and learned with surprise that now, after the years of struggle to cover foundations stylishly, it was smart to reveal the fact that a house rested on the ground. They learned that corners were being planted, and entrances, but that the rest of the ground line was being left naked.

After a decent period of adjustment, they began moving the surviving units of the "dot and dash" period, over to join the blue spruce.

To replace the Mugho-Pfitzer-cedar combination at the front door, they planted two Hicks yews. They covered the ground at the base of the yews with Baltic ivy and planted white tulips in the ivy. For the corners of the house they chose spreading yews.

Arborvitae from the former foundation planting came in handy when Don and Kay learned about having a main axis in the garden, terminating at a focal point. They decided to feature the path from the house through the rose garden. At the end of this path they placed an oval pool, backed by a clump of arborvitae. Against this dark background they placed a statue of "St. Francis Feeding the Birds."

Soon afterward there was a hard winter that left the old privet hedge around the rose garden marred with dead patches. Don and Kay learned that there were other hedge materials besides privet and barberry. They replaced the privet with a low trimmed hedge of Japanese quince, knowing that its ribbon of color would be past its blooming before the roses brought uncongenial shades. An ice storm that winter broke up the Siberian elms. Don planted a thornless honey locust.

At the garden fair where they bought St. Francis, Kay saw a display of white iron furniture and a glass-topped table. She began at once to plan for a place that would do justice to such equipment.

So they paved an area under the old apple tree, using blue slate. There they set out the iron furniture, and also a chaise longue with a pale-green waterproof cushion.

Presently they decided to take out, or at least, to interrupt, the long line of Tartarian honeysuckle. There were two reasons for this decision. The first reason was that they wanted their backgrounds to have interest of varied combinations of texture, color, and irregular profile. The second reason was that word was going around that some of our native plants have more to offer in the way of both grace and hardihood than some of the European plants that had dominated gardens for so long a time.

Don and Kay added wild plum, wild crab, hawthorn, shadbush, witch-hazel, nannyberry, aronia, prairie rose, and New Jersey tea to their plantings. They developed a natural-looking bit of thicket out of these native shrubs and small trees, and wove a tanbark path through the thicket. In spring the path was bordered with mertensia, wild ginger, and wild phlox. In the summer there were lady fern, leather wood fern, and jewelweed.

Don and Kay used considerable peat moss on this and other plantings. And then, one evening, they had a lecturer at the garden club who talked about compost piles. In fact he practically divided humanity into two classes—those who have compost piles and those who do not. Don and Kay decided to join the new compost-pile aristocracy.

The compost pile gave Don and Kay the same feeling of respectability that Jonathan and Patience had obtained from their white pine tree.

Kay was all ready to send away for a package of earthworms, when Don happened to discover that their own compost was practically teeming with them.

Don gave compost offerings to the old white pine, the old apple tree, the bleeding heart, and the fern-leaved peony—the same plants that had been fed tea leaves by Patience, fresh manure by David, nothing by Theodore, and commercial fertilizer by Nancy Ann. They continued to thrive.

Kay used a lot of the compost for her new venture—tuberous begonias, out on the shady side of the barn.

The end of the barn had been converted into a garden house, but the garden-house end was gradually changing into a studio, now that Don had taken up painting.

Don was experimenting with roses, too. He owned an expensive array of sprays and fertilizers. He was hearing rumors of the wisdom of dispensing with these through the use of organic fertilizers only. But that far he was not ready to go.

In her flower garden Kay did not favor white flowers so much as Nancy Ann had, nor did she lean to the pastel shades as Elizabeth had. She planned her garden with a color chart, and chose analogous colors, rather than the complementary colors so long in favor. She liked such combinations as deep purple and clear blue.

When she picked flowers to bring into the house, she struck poses that fascinated Don. She would rear up, tilt her head back, squint her eyes, and sketch Hogarth's curve of beauty in the air with her clippers. Then she would ignore the lush, fulsome flower cluster that would have delighted Patience, and choose a tortured asymmetrical spray. From this, she proceeded to remove any leaves that interfered with the gesture, or movement, or flow of line, or mood. Sometimes all of them interfered.

She plunged her trophies deep in pails of water and took them down to the basement. The ritual of arrangement would come after they were thoroughly soaked, "hardened."

She had picked every specimen with a definite container, position, and background in mind. Since the woman's garden club had become practically an arrangement society, she knew all the latest rules—all that had been formulated up until the time of the last club meeting, at any rate.

First she made an arrangement for the marble-topped table in the living room. She had discovered that table in an antique shoppe. (It was an exact counterpart of the carved walnut table that Patience had had in the same position, and that Mary had sold off when her golden-oak suite arrived. It may have been the same table.)

Kay selected a low off-white bowl. At one end she arranged three sprays of weeping willow. She was careful to see that they soared to carry the motion rhythmically up and around, and then back to the bowl. She never failed to check the tips of the twigs to see whether an imaginary drip from them would fall back into the container. The flower-arrangement lecturers seemed to stress that point. At the base of the willow a little green Buddha squatted, and a few petals of a pale salmon poppy floated. Kay placed the arrangement toward one end of the table, to balance a Japanese print above the other end.

On the mantel Kay had her dried arrangement. The dominant gesture was created by a twisted piece of driftwood. It writhed upward from among five pine cones and three stalks of bayberry. The container was gray-green and low.

Now that the dining room had been done over, in chartreuse and muted eggplant, Kay used a pewter bowl on the buffet, with "wooden roses" and rhododendron leaves. On the table she had a large wooden leaf bearing a pineapple, three artichokes, and five red onions. These were everyday arrangements; on the day when the club met with her,

Kay used more exotic material, such as dead-men's-fingers (sponges), and unborn palm.

The scarcity of flowers in Kay's arrangements was compensated for by an abundance of flowers in pictures on the walls. There were great Van Gogh sunflowers in the living room, and flowers in the "Blue Vase" of Cezanne, and flowers in the glass paperweight collection that caught the light there on the glass shelves in the dining-room bay window, between various succulent-leaved and spiny-leaved foliage plants.

The dimmed light resulting from the Venetian blinds was just right for Kay's specialty, African violets. But the Venetian blinds had to go, in favor of draw drapes. The new picture window cut into the wing would have given a good sunny spot for house plants, but there had to be a lamp in the window, and besides, when the sun shone, the room became unbearable if the drapes were not drawn.

There was an abundance of ivy and philodendron around, in the various objects that had been converted into "planters." The old sugar scoop on the wall had ivy in it, as did the lamp made out of an old coffee mill. There was no place for plants in the big lamp made out of a churn, or the one made out of a candle mold, or the pair that had been wallpaper rollers, or in the book ends made out of horseshoes and stirrups, but there was a foliage plant on the magazine table made out of a cobbler's bench, and there was a copper pot of ivy suspended from each end of the old oxbow yoke on one wall. There was ivy in the lamp on the bedside table, where *The Egg and I* was covered by *The Mature Mind* on Kay's side, and *Peace of Mind* covered *Five Acres and Independence* on Don's side.

Kay stopped bringing flowers into the bedroom after she had painted the furniture with Pennsylvania Dutch motifs full of tulips and birds and hex signs.

Kay and Don have only one child, named Sharon. But they have two boxer dogs named Stockwell Stillwater Hamlet and Stockwell Stillwater Ophelia.

Sharon is growing up. She will no doubt have several children, probably four. The style in size of family has changed just lately.

Only the white pine tree, the bleeding heart, the apple tree, the fern-leaved peony, and the Christmas cactus have seen all the ways in which the old house has been stylish.

The Stylish House—Reconsidered

Sharon did not, however, follow the trend of having several children. The trend changed. The advent of the pill changed it. She has no children; but she has had two husbands, and a very large dog. Her first husband, Craig, was a junior executive. He and Sharon still meet over a friendly drink at the country club, but not over a bridge table—that was the area of incompatibility which their marriage counsellor was unable to adjust. Her present husband, "J.B.," is also a junior executive—what else? He has a beard and sideburns, much like those of Jonathan, the first owner of the house.

Sharon and J.B. have become mobile. Indeed, mobility is the chief factor in shaping the sixth stage of the old house and its garden. Not much personal mobility is involved, but plenty of high-powered encapsulated mobility.

J.B. and Sharon take interest in keeping their house in step with the times—"hopefully relevant," is the way Sharon puts it, "not a part of the establishment." J.B. adds, "We want our digs to say, you know, 'Come right in and kick off your shoes, and let it all hang out,' sort of, you know."

A garden seemed anything but relevant (though factory-patched and factory-faded blue jeans were) and other circumstances dictated that the grounds be drastically changed. Sharon and J.B. were not alone in their mobility—the mobility of the entire town demanded a four-lane street in front of their house, and beside it. The widened street absorbed the parkway and the sidewalks. Few people walked, anyhow. Then the police asked them, courteously but firmly, to remove the massed shrubs at the street corner, because, "safety-wise," it seemed advisable.

The area of their grounds had been reduced further by the selling off of a lot between the house and the lot that had been cut off years ago. The old barn was part of that sale. The new owners gave it a fashionable roof that looked like a stocking cap pulled far down around its ears, so that the lower windows appeared to be peering out over the ground for a last look before sinking. It has become a house.

Two requirements were stressed when J.B. and Sharon conferred with their landscaper: "adequate parking" and "minimum maintenance."

The landscaper went to work. His bulldozer flattened what was left. Then he molded a "berm," a long low mound, looking much like a tumulus where a Viking was buried. The berm was snugly and firmly covered with black plastic. Then the landscaper set into place the most important elements of the new look—the big glacial boulders. Sharon explained that the boulders were placed "in a hopefully meaningful relationship." (Sharon and J.B. had faith in their landscaper—they had used him some years earlier to landscape their bomb shelter—now erased.)

The plant materials were inserted around the boulders, in holes made in the plastic. Japanese yew, much pruned, and prostrate juniper, a red barberry with especially small leaves, yucca, and Colorado juniper already shaped by the nurseryman into five trunks each topped by a ball—and whatever else makes no mess that takes cleaning up.

A second, smaller berm was shaped and planted near the back corner of the property, to conceal the dog run for the big dog. He was a Great Dane, and looked impressive in the back seat of J.B.'s convertible. His name is Porno. The dog and his name make good "conversation pieces" for the "conversation pit."

Then the adequate parking was paved, enough room for their three cars: J.B.'s convertible, Sharon's sedan, and the camper for expeditions taken in long lines of similar campers to many parts of this country and others; and for their guests' cars.

The broad driveway that swooped up from the street, to pass between the berm and the front door, and swooped back again, permitted additional parking.

After a few groups of evergreens were added in black plastic here and there, the plastic was covered deeply with pebbles, egg-shaped and white. Any dropped needles or small leaves can sift down between their whiteness. And weeds cannot come up through the plastic.

After a Japanese stone lantern was placed on the main berm, and wires were installed for flood-lighting, the landscaper unrolled the sod to cover whatever surface was not covered by white pebbles on black plastic. On the last day he turned on the floodlights, and looked at his work and found it good.

When Sharon and J.B. returned from their camper expedition they decided that flowers were needed. The florist brought them the next morning: two big pots packed with thriving pink geranium plants, and placed them at the sides of the two front steps. The florist agreed to replace these pots with thriving flowering potfuls of chrysanthemums in the fall, and with petunias in the spring.

The yardman agreed to water the pots when he mowed the lawn. He was able to mow for the entire block. The neighbors, too, had shaped their landscaping to fit his tractor mower.

The florist provides house plants, rented for the periods when Sharon and J.B. stay at home. Big plants, with heavy tropical foliage, make strong accents against plain white walls. Palms seem especially effective when a concealed light at the base spreads their shadows across the wall and ceiling. To find a plain uncluttered wall is becoming increasingly difficult as Sharon and J.B. travel more and more, accumulating massive pieces of macrame, a growing collection of wine labels, masks, restaurant menus, travel posters, big keys, a crayon rubbing from a knight's tomb, a carefully hung patchwork quilt that did service a hundred years ago, and abstract prints, many and big.

Sharon uses the old bottles that J.B. collected on trips, in a cluster on the dining-room table. One tall bottle might hold a rose, or a stalk of asparagus, a smaller bottle might hold a gull's feather or a trailing bit of a grape vine. The idea was a casual look—as casual as the numerous pillows strewn around or heaped up, ready to be reclined against when you kicked your shoes off, and maybe put your feet up on one of the Parsons tables.

On the bedside tables two old bottles made lavendar by the desert sun hold dried flowers bought in the Alps. The book on Sharon's table is *Jonathan Livingston Seagull*. It covers a television guide. On J.B.'s table the book is *I'm O.K. You're O.K.* on top of another television guide. The set is just beyond the feet of the beds.

A rake, much like the one formerly used for leaves and grass, but smaller, stands in a closet. It is used for the wall-to-wall shag carpeting that is so comfortable to bare feet.

On the coffee table, beside a book about Marilyn Monroe, are a brass spittoon filled with marbles; and two giant jacks, reminiscent of the day when boys and girls actually played on the ground or the sidewalk, without the direction of a fun counsellor.

There came a day when J.B., fingering a cruise folder, looked up at Sharon in her bentwood rocker bent over her needlepoint (the floral center had been done at the factory, she only filled in the background, with the Williamsburg green that had been provided), and expressed what they both had been thinking for some time,

"Porno has got to go. The trouble of taking care of him when we are at home, or paying someone to do it when we are away, besides paying the boy who walks him every day—it's too much!"

The one who really cared was the dog walker.

But the Great Dane may have contributed a narrow wedge of an entry into first-hand living. His dog run still remained, back there in the corner of the lot, a spot that was unmowed, and not covered by black plastic and white pebbles.

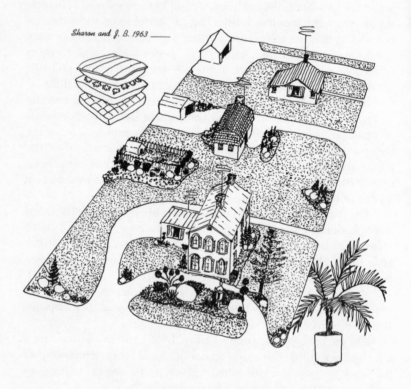

Sharon and J. B. 1963 ____

When Sharon and J.B. drove into their adequate parking space at the end of their most recent trip—a long one—they were a bit shaken. Their tank was full of gas, but they had waited in line four times to achieve that full tank. The ancient fern forests that stored ancient sunlight, the oil companies who were becoming aware that the barrels were not bottomless, and the governments that were finding that the barrels held political power as well as mechanical power—all were failing Sharon and J.B. It was irritating, especially because they had just met that congenial couple and were planning to drive to Alaska with them sometime; and because J.B. had invested in a new camera.

Next day, needing some tacks, J.B., to keep that tank full, walked down to the hardware store. In front of the store he met a friend and stopped to talk about the "energy crisis." But the friend was interested only in selecting packages of seeds: parsley, lettuce, radishes, green beans, and a bundle of onion sets.

"I'll get tomato plants and green peppers later," he explained.

J.B. walked home, but didn't go into the house. He went to take a look at the old dog run. The man with the mower couldn't object to what he did there—it was all fenced and screened.

Maybe, if the governments, and the oil companies, and the prehistoric fern forests all continue to cooperate, the old house will again be surrounded by a garden, fertilized, as Confucius considered best, "by the footsteps of the owner."

Whatever the outcome, it lies in the future. If we allot to the sixth stage in the story of the old house a span of years equal to the spans allotted to the five earlier stages, Sharon and J.B. have several years to go, and we must wait to see what happens.

BIBLIOGRAPHICAL NOTES

Our Times: The United States, 1900-1925 by Mark Sullivan. Scribner, New York, 1932.

A Treatise on the Theory and Practice of Landscape Gardening, Adapted to North America; with a View of the Improvement of Country Residences . . . with Remarks on Rural Architecture by Andrew Jackson Downing. A. O. Moore, New York, 1859.

Handbook of Practical Landscape Gardening Designed for City and Suburban

Residences, and Country Schoolhouses, Containing Designs for Lots and Grounds by Franklin Reuben Elliott. D. M. Dewey, Rochester, New York, 1877.

Old Time Gardens Newly Set Forth by Alice Morse Earle. Macmillan, New York, 1901.

Life in America by Marshall B. Davidson. Houghton Mifflin, Boston, 1951.

Here, Of All Places by Osbert Lancaster. Houghton Mifflin, Boston, 1958.

The Tastemakers by Russell Lynes. Grosset and Dunlap, New York, 1954.

Gardens and People by Fletcher Steele. Houghton Mifflin, Boston, 1964.

Index